POST-INDUSTRIAL
COMPLEX

A small sample of the diverse range of
brainpower that exists in metro Detroit

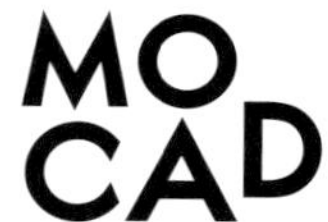

Museum of Contemporary Art Detroit | MOCAD
4454 Woodward Avenue | Detroit, MI 48201

ISBN 978-0-9823896-2-1

Museum of Contemporary Art Detroit | 2013
Book Design: Daniel Francis DeMaggio, a.k.a. Mister DeMaggio
Cover Photo: Corine Vermeulen
Print Buyer: Carl Smith
Printing and Binding: Team Detroit
Copy Editors: Michael Jackman and Greg Baise
Project Direction: Katie Grace McGowan

Major support for the *Post-Industrial Complex* catalog
provided by Team Detroit.

Funding for the exhibition and related programming
provided by the John S. and James L. Knight Foundation,
McGregor Fund, and Edith S. Briskin/Shirley K. Schlafer Foundation.

Post-Industrial Complex would not have been possible without all those who contributed to the project.

We'd like to thank Team Detroit for their generous support.

Additional thanks to the MOCAD staff, Kelli Kavanaugh, Kottie Gaydos, Jonathan Rajewski and Whitney Sage.

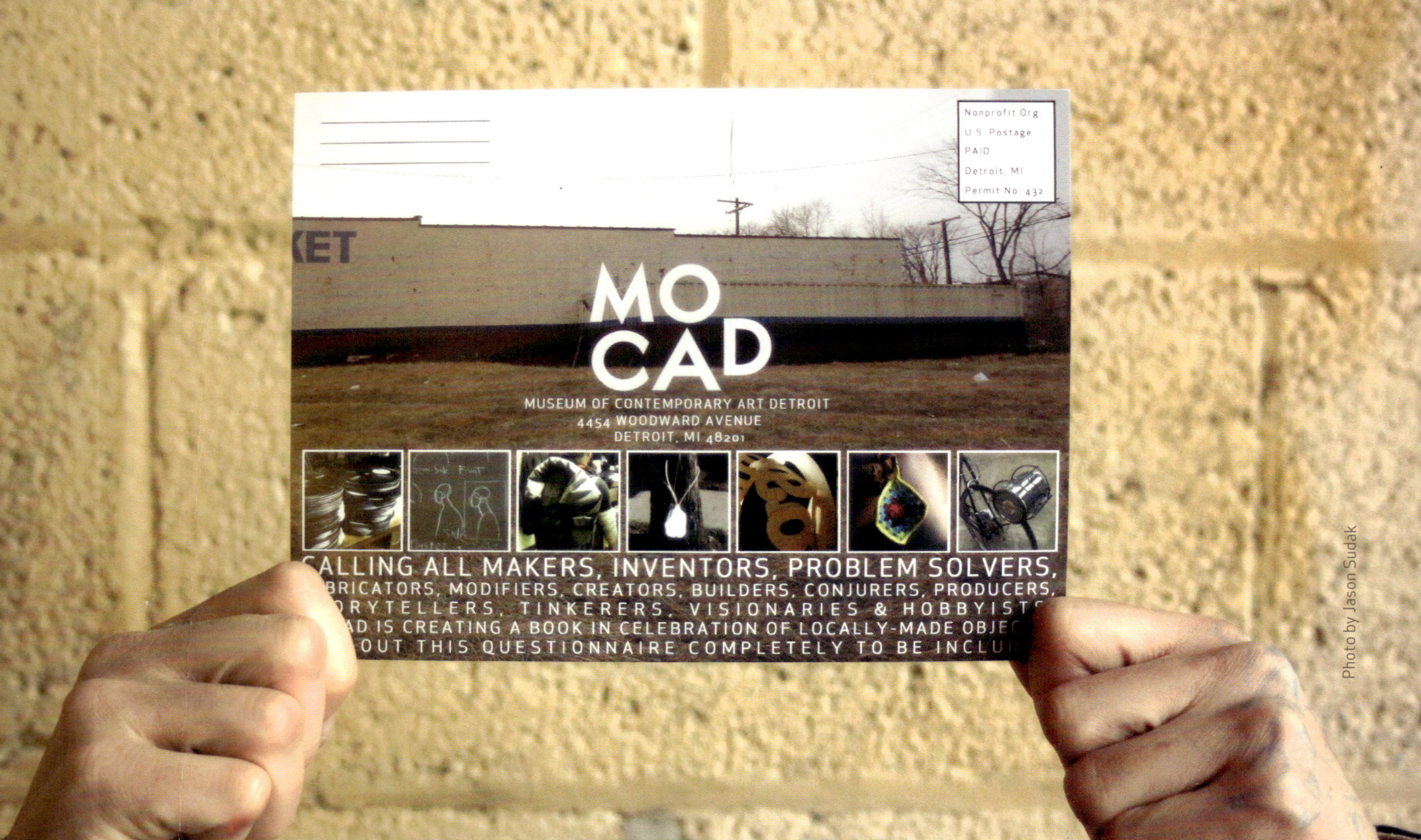
Nonprofit Org.
U.S. Postage
PAID
Detroit, MI
Permit No. 432
MO
CAD
MUSEUM OF CONTEMPORARY ART DETROIT
4454 WOODWARD AVENUE
DETROIT, MI 48201
CALLING ALL MAKERS, INVENTORS, PROBLEM SOLVERS,
FABRICATORS, MODIFIERS, CREATORS, BUILDERS, CONJURERS, PRODUCERS,
STORYTELLERS, TINKERERS, VISIONARIES & HOBBYISTS
MOCAD IS CREATING A BOOK IN CELEBRATION OF LOCALLY-MADE OBJECTS
FILL OUT THIS QUESTIONNAIRE COMPLETELY TO BE INCLUDED

CONTENTS

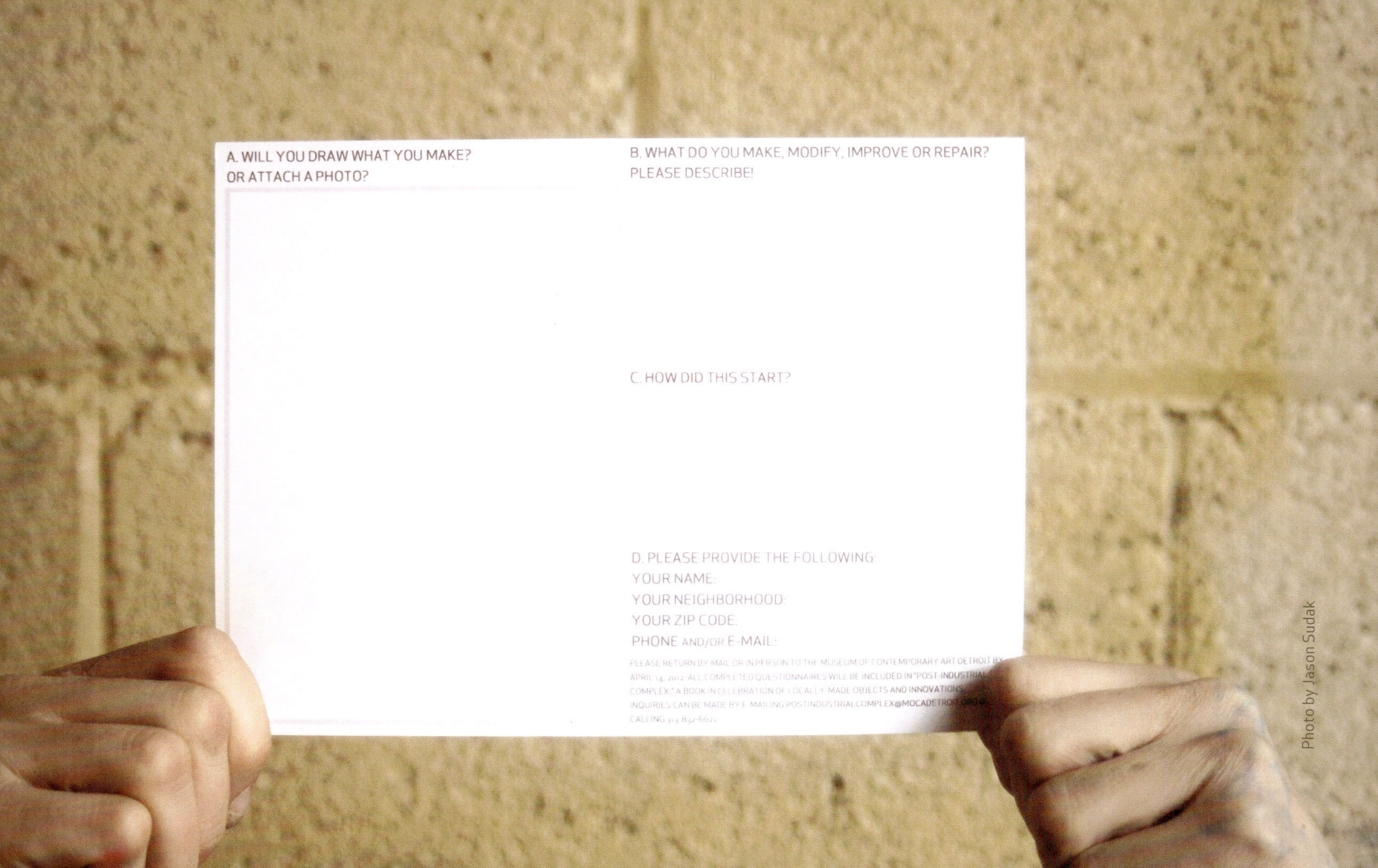

Photo by Jason Sudak

Post-Industrial Complex is a project that explores the ingenuity and adaptivity of human-scale production at the heart of Detroit.

From a prolific inventor to a collective working to keep an aboriginal language alive, the artists we included in the exhibition — all of whom responded to an open call for "makers, inventors, problem solvers, fabricators, modifiers, etc. ..." — were a small yet representative sample of the diverse range of brainpower that exists in a city often oversimplified by headlines. This book, on the other hand, includes all metro Detroit submissions received during the designated period. *Post-Industrial Complex* was the Museum of Contemporary Art Detroit's summer 2012 exhibition, on display from May 11 through July 29, 2012.

This project was fascinating to work on partially because of the different ways in which people understand the core idea. The project is political for me — a study of the ways in which humans innovate due to, or in spite of, the market, the art world or the economy. For me, *Post-Industrial Complex* is about labor. For my co-curator, Jon Brumit, the central idea felt more visceral. As a maker himself, Jon was drawn to the objects first and foremost; I was drawn to the people. We were both, however, pulled in further by the stories.

Detroit has been the star of many hyperbolic headlines in recent years. Discussions of the city — its death, the boom-bust cycle of the auto industry, or melodramatic narratives of Detroit as a phoenix rising from the ashes — have paid little attention to nuance.

Post-Industrial Complex aims to disrupt the notion that there is one story to the city. A true metropolis comprises multiple stories and multiple voices. Handmade jewelry, rockets, buckskin suits — and the stories surrounding them — weave together the textured yarns of Detroit and provide ingress into the art of the everyday.

During this contentious period for labor, cottage industry and personal labor provide vital counterpoints to the larger narratives of American industry. Here, we celebrate the proverbial little guy. As artists ourselves, Jon and I are interested in subverting tried conventions of exhibition-making. We love the idea of trying to make things fair for those quiet oddballs who make their art day in and day out without public recognition.

This collection of disparate entries reflects the creativity of individuals who make things just to make them. Their tenacity and command of resources make them worthy emissaries of the unvarnished Detroit. The book, we hope, will serve as a testament of our collective ability to make the world just a little more animated and fun by pursuing our passions.

Katie Grace McGowan is co-curator of *Post-Industrial Complex*, with Jon Brumit. She works as curator of education at the Museum of Contemporary Art Detroit.

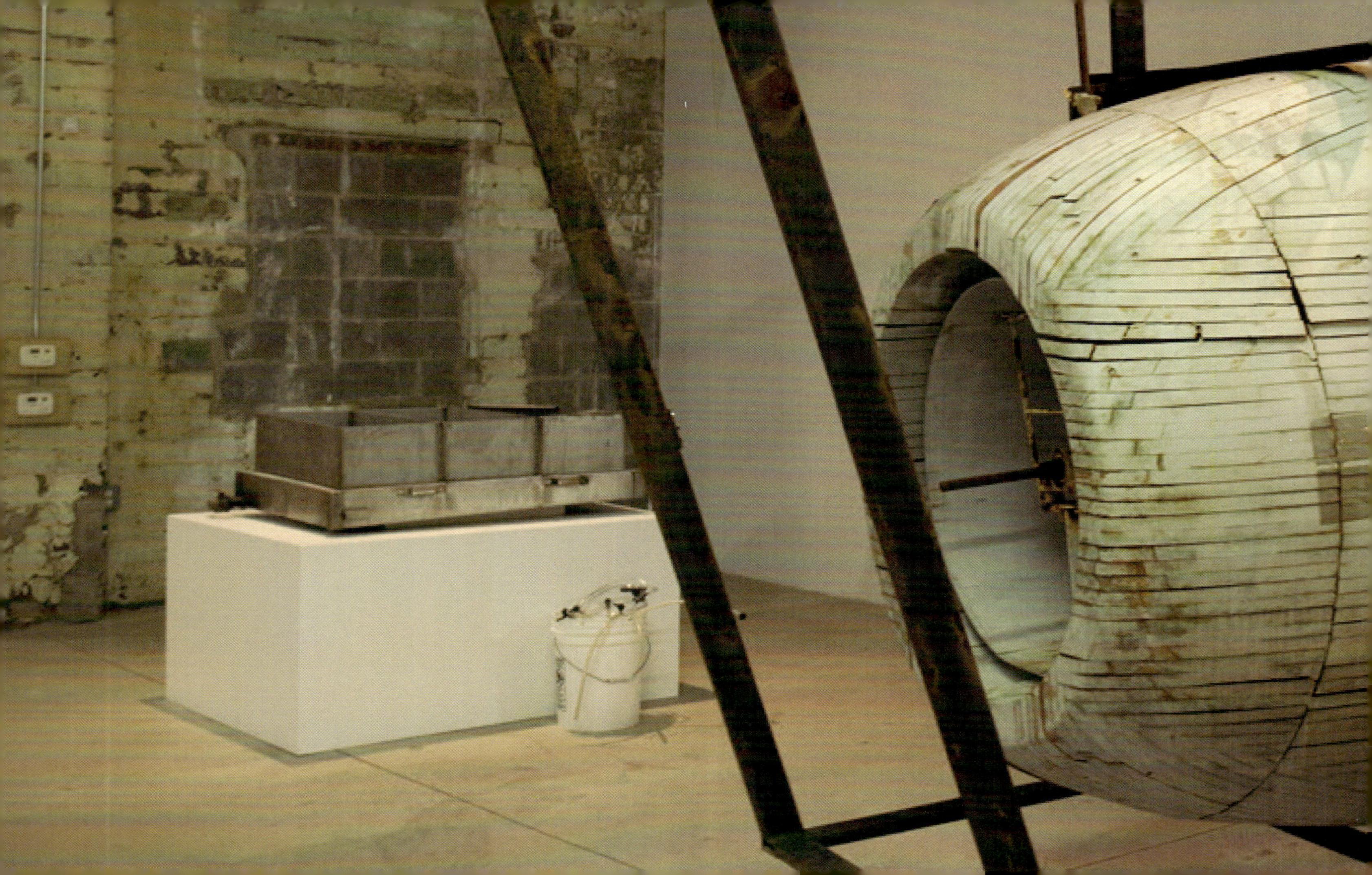

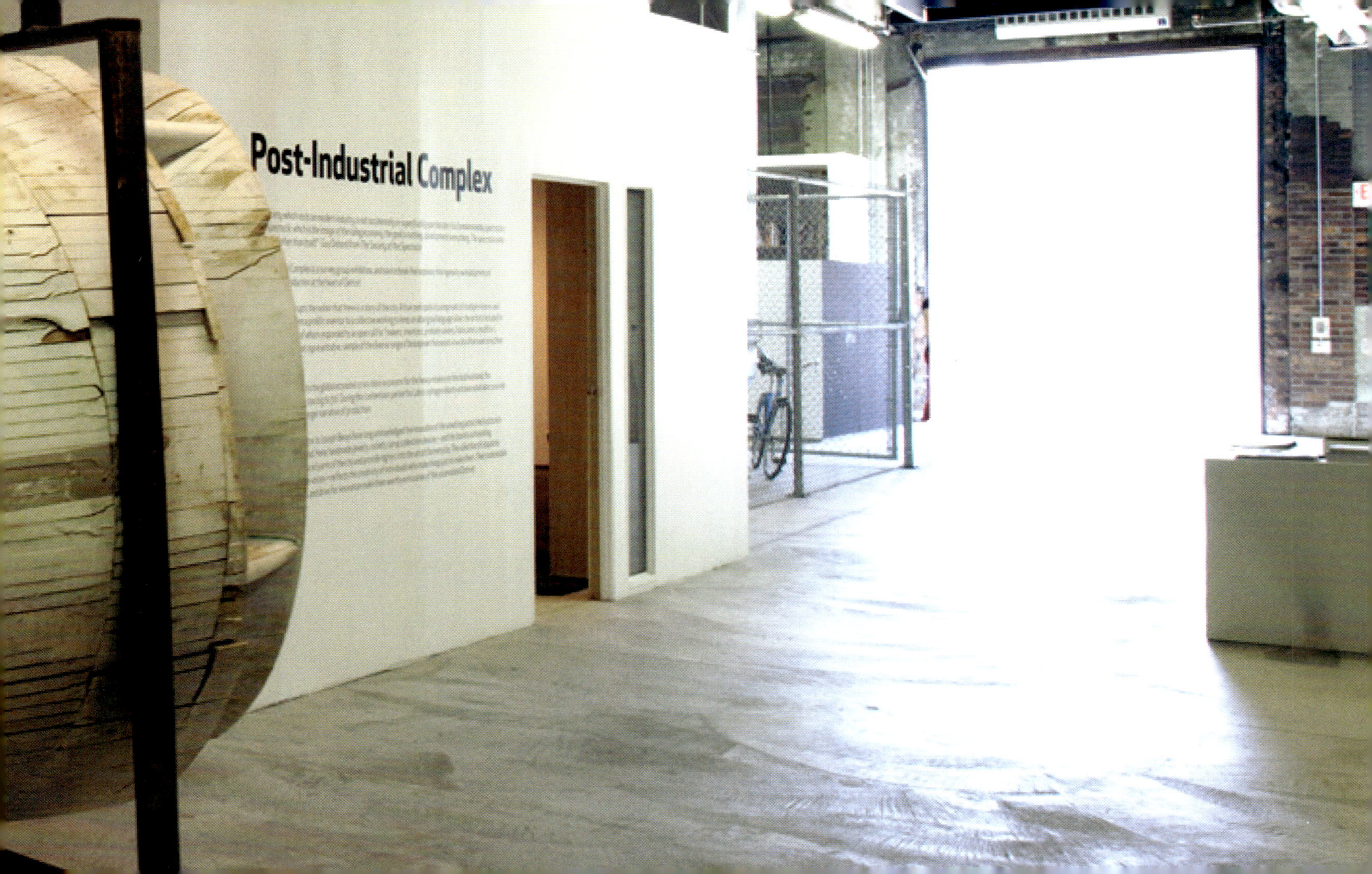

Post-Industrial Complex

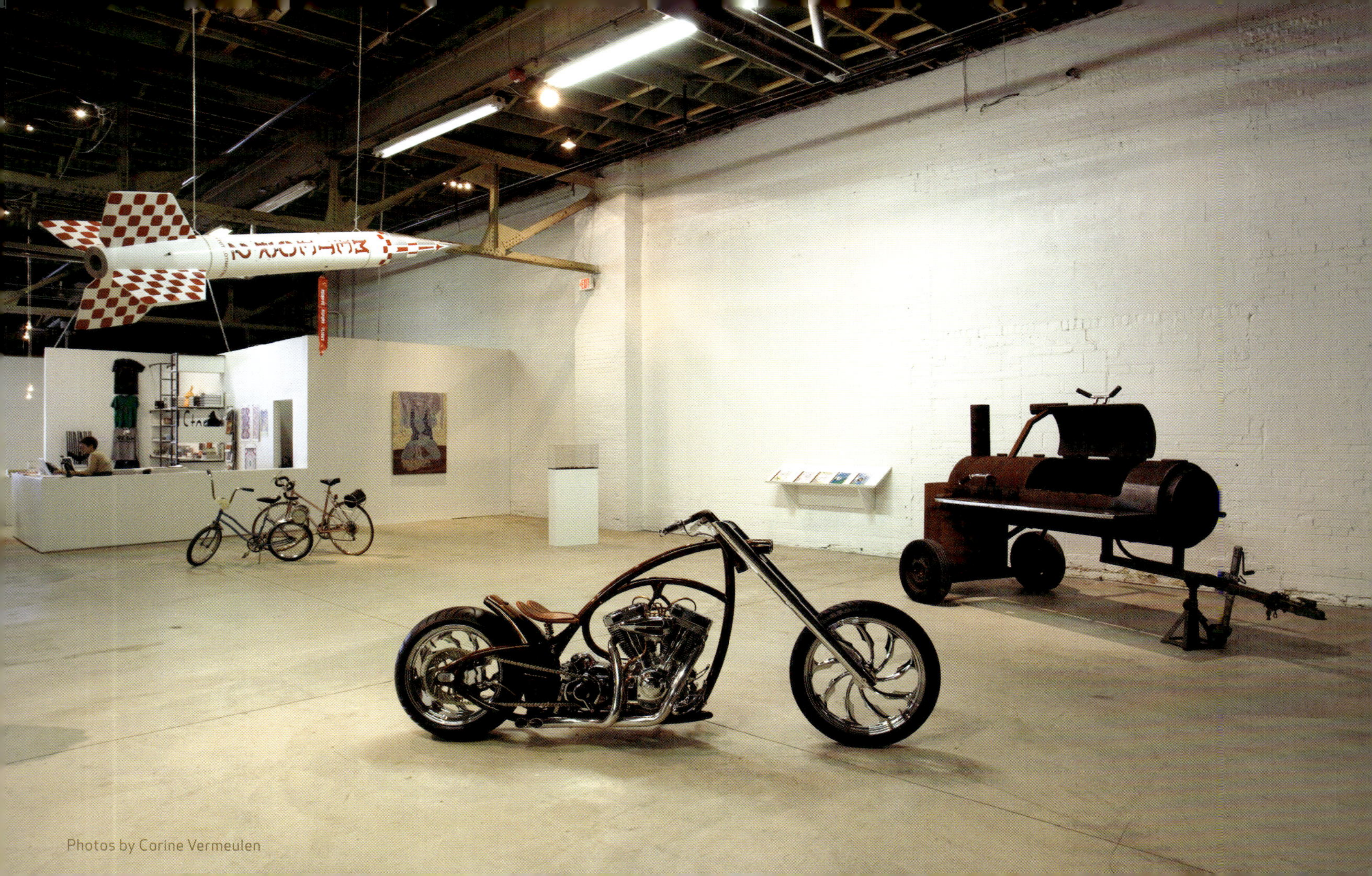
Photos by Corine Vermeulen

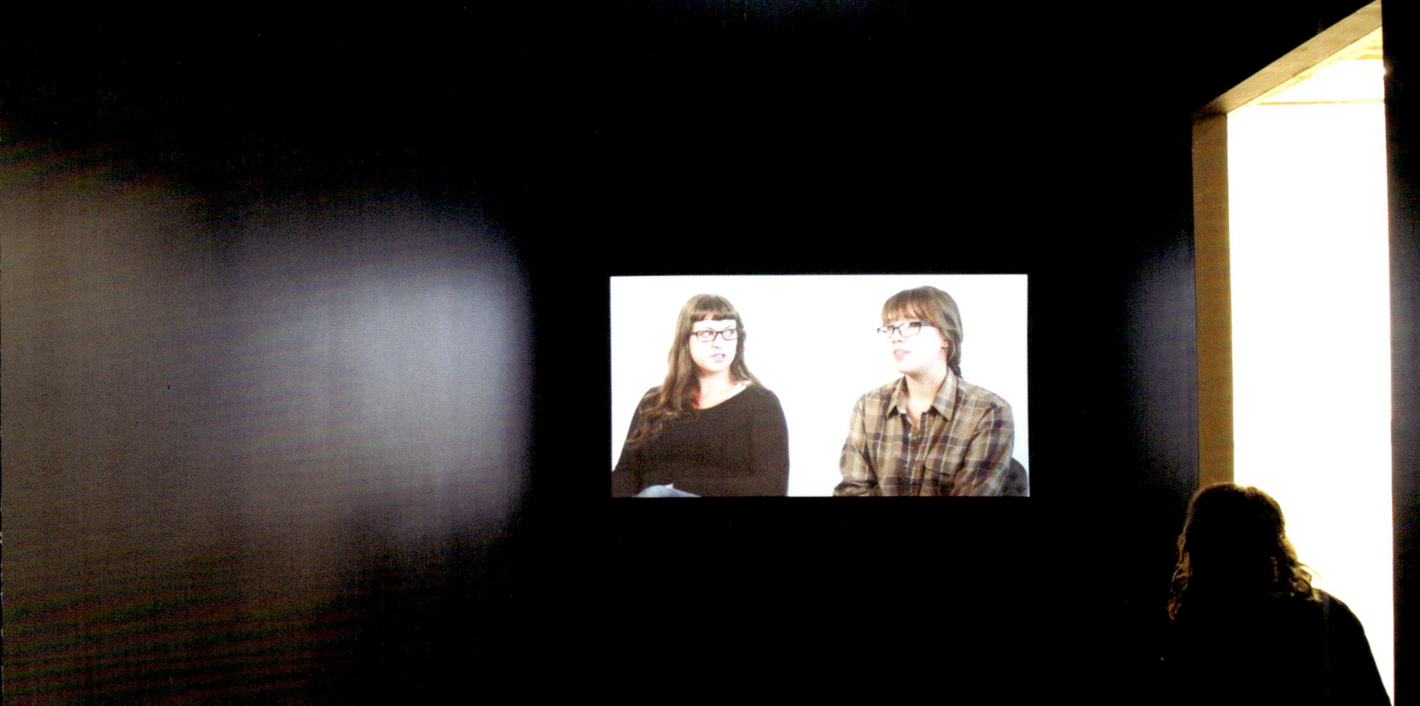

Julia Yezbick

Consider these satirical narratives: *Amid the smog of a struggling industry, a slowly dying behemoth — a victim of its own rampant growth — becomes the moribund post-apocalyptic playground for photographers with a penchant for decay.* Or the alternative image: *Despite high rates of unemployment, the resilient phoenix will rise from the ashes of industry and plant urban gardens with seeds of hope for the future.* Whether or not we agree with these common depictions of Detroit in the media, we can all recognize the inherent drama of these characterizations.

At the heart of the *Post-Industrial Complex* is an effort to show a wider breadth of production in Detroit, mitigating oversimplified narratives of the iconic city. The homemade and the handmade are displayed to blur the boundaries between art, craft, and industry, foregrounding ways of "making" in Detroit that tend to be excluded when the city's metonym ("Detroit") is invoked. Here, industry is not confined to the factory floor or to processes of mass production; it seeps and spills into the everyday. Indeed, as curators Katie McGowan and Jon Brumit demonstrate, the postindustrial is a rescaling of our efforts from the mass-produced to the "human-scale." With this, they present the gallery as an institution with a responsibility to its community. The exhibition and book celebrate the "art and industry of the everyday,"[1] reasserting the value of small-scale labor and innovation in our communities that serve both practical and aesthetic ends.

Although art, craft, and industry share a long and intertwined history in Detroit[2] the various modes of making, tinkering, and customizing highlighted here come at a particular moment in our city's and nation's history. The vexing uncertainty of what will become of our nation's manufacturing sector has not only cast an international spotlight on Detroit, but has also led many to wonder what happens when factories close and the economic core of a region shrinks to a fraction of its size. Today, in Detroit the diversity of human-scaled production subsumes and reorganizes industrial models through customization and appropriation of materials and methods, and in doing so it reclaims industriousness and craft to meet individual and local needs.

1. *Post-Industrial Complex* curatorial statement, MOCAD website: http://www.mocadetroit.org/picindex.html, accessed August, 2012.

2. In 1906, the Detroit Society of Arts and Crafts was founded to mitigate the increasing mechanization of labor and assert and support the power of handmade objects to transform the everyday. By 1918 the Detroit Society embraced the industrial arts and was the first gallery to recognize the automobile as an art form. The Society's scion institutions have continued this dedication to an amalgamated art/craft/industrial practice. (Detroit Institute of Arts. 1976. *Arts and Crafts in Detroit/1906-1976: The Movement, The Society, The School*. Detroit: Detroit Institute of Arts.)

At the height of modernist production, the sublime spectacle of industry was thought to reflect its power to bring about social progress. The *Post-Industrial Complex* points to the ways in which power resides in the hands of those who meet the daily challenges of our environment with artfulness and enterprise. Beyond the distancing gaze of spectacle, this project expands our sensory experience of (post)industry. The taste of Mr. Motin's maple syrup, the sound of John Marshall and Cezanne Charles' *ba-b&l (11111011100)*, the feel of the smooth chrome of Dozer's motorcycle or of potholes repaired by Aisling Arrington and Jill Bersche's *Human Powered Pothole Fixer-Upper* — these works beckon a more total engagement, one that emphasizes our common experience. Through barbecues, trading posts, and this publication, the *Post-Industrial Complex* extends beyond the gallery walls and invites us all to see works of art and ingenuity in shared experiences in our common environment.

The reimagining of Detroit is about changing our ways of thinking about neighborhood, community, and progress, about recuperating the *we* that was devastated by the myriad of forces responsible for Detroit's decline. Oftentimes, this we centers around our common love of producing things, of creatively solving problems, and enjoying the display of unique ways of making life a little easier or a little better for us all. It is a collective recognition of the part of the human spirit that cannot be abandoned or diminished by any amount of planned obsolescence.

Excavating the lesser-known modes of production in Detroit cultivates a shared history that is not bound to corporate definitions of production or growth, industry or art. To highlight and display human-scale production in a postindustrial city reminds us of our common bond as makers of the everyday — as collective craftspeople, making anew ourselves, our lives, our city.

Julia Yezbick is a filmmaker, Detroit resident, and PhD candidate in anthropology at Harvard University.

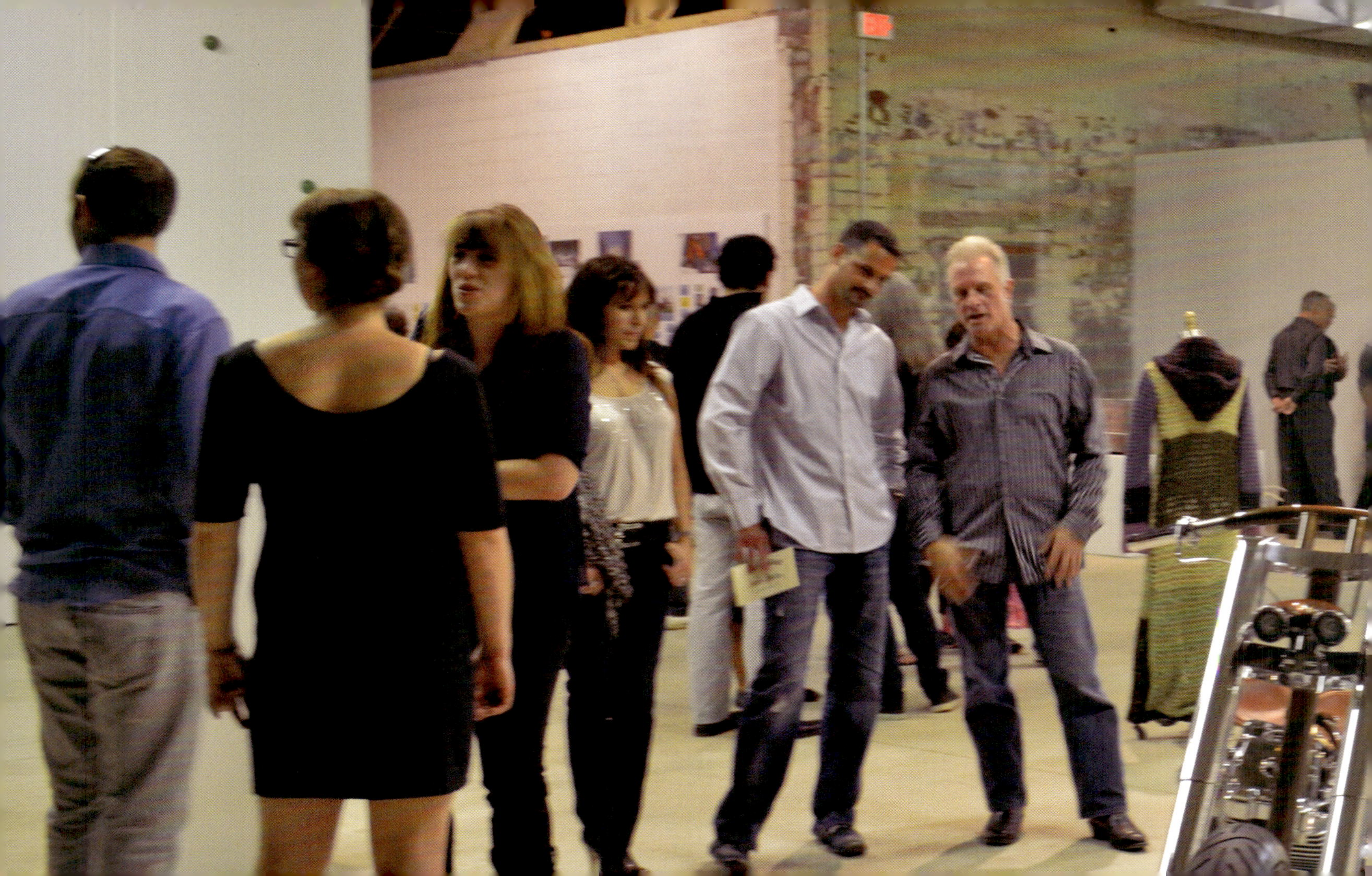

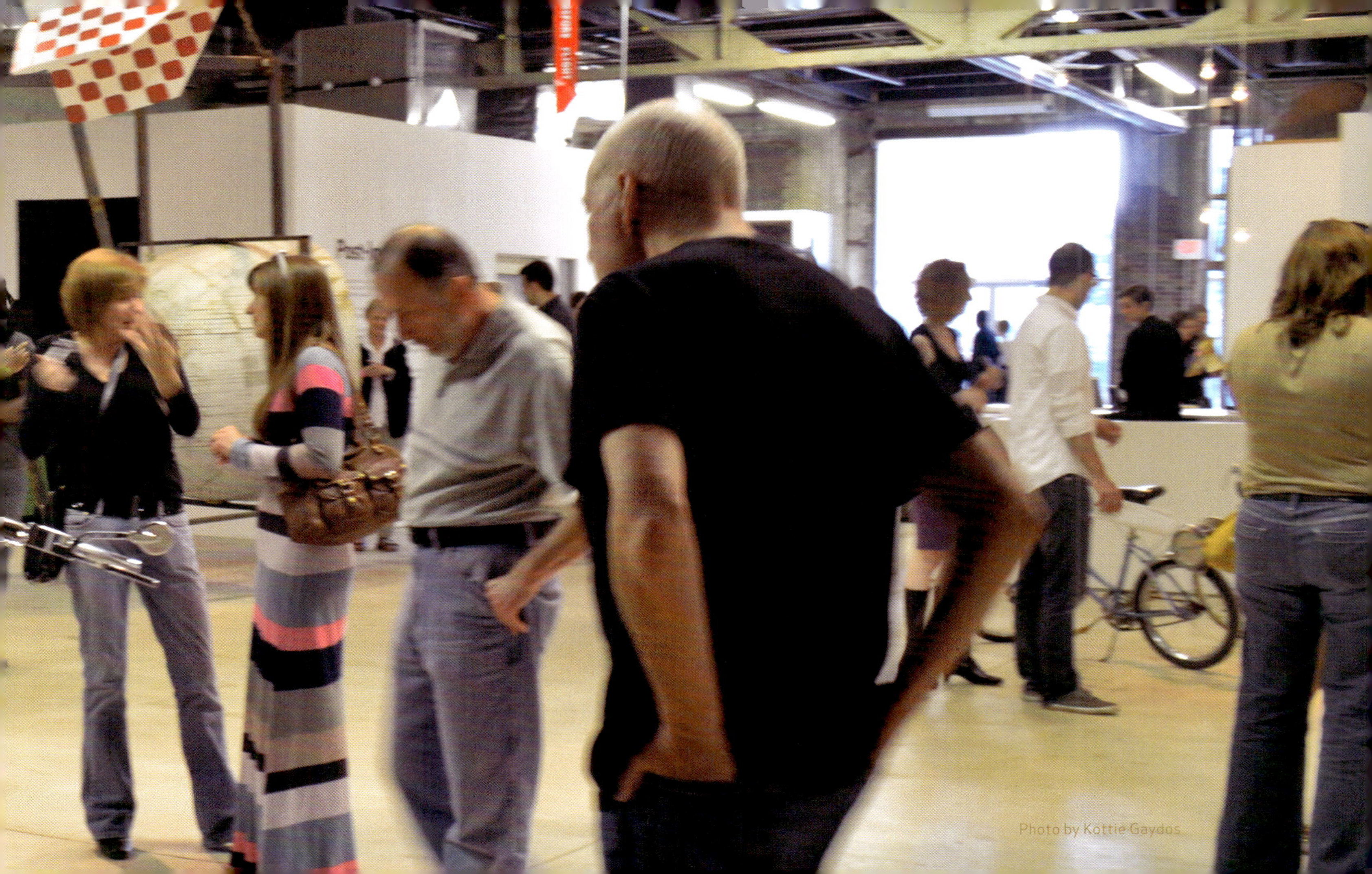
Photo by Kottie Gaydos

ART-I-FACT(ORY)

Francis Shor

When my family and I arrived in Detroit in 1974, we had just spent two years in Venice, Italy. On the surface, the contrast between the two cities could not be more stark: one, an unsightly metropolis once defined by its auto factories and now decimated by deindustrialization and deep racial polarization; the other, a sinking Rococo jewel, awash in architectural gems and besotted tourists. Knowing something about the radical history of Detroit and still inspired by its potential (as were other erstwhile leftists who referred to the city as a possible Petrograd of an American revolution), I had eagerly taken a faculty position in a new interdisciplinary program for working adults at Wayne State University. Little could I imagine the ways in which my students would challenge and expand my perceptions of the city and the surrounding metropolitan area, introducing me, in the process, to their sensibilities about its industrial environment and their own expressions of creativity.

One of the earliest confrontations between my expectations of what I could impart to my working-class students and the realities of their lives was a viewing of the magnificent Rivera mural "Detroit Industry" at the Detroit Institute of Arts. Most of my students were workers in several of the auto plants in the metro area. As soon as we faced the large north panel of the Rivera Mural with its engine block assembly line, one of the students remarked that the workers depicted by Rivera (representing mostly the faces of his assistants) were too close together, violating a clause in the contemporary contract about spacing on the line. The immediacy and concreteness of this comment demonstrated that our ways of seeing art were fundamentally shaped by our experiences.

Indeed, the experience of Detroit as a factory town has not only stamped its inhabitants with the markings of alienated labor, but also inscribed deep desires for creativity. For every Gertie Nevels, the tragic heroine of Harriett Arnow's classic novel *The Dollmaker*, there is a Fred Ellison. Gertie's "whittlin' foolishness" is transformed out of necessity into commodified assembly-line dolls, sold to sustain her family. On the other hand, Fred Ellison manages to use his time away from his groundskeeper job at Mt. Elliott Cemetery to create imaginative mosaics, given away as gifts to friends and family.

I once received a gift from one of my students, an assembly-line worker at a Ford plant that produced Mustangs. What this student did was "liberate" (as we used to say in the '60s) hood emblems of the Mustang and use them as buckles in leather belts that he artfully designed and fabricated. For him, the act of purloining company property that he, then, creatively used, was legitimate compensation for the heavy physical and psychic toll imposed on him by the corporate demands of factory life.

Other factory workers I came to know beyond the classroom found creative outlets in their hobbies. A whole group of my students from a west side Detroit plant were members of a motorcycle gang. They expressed their creativity, like Dozer and his cycle in the *Post-Industrial Complex* exhibition, in "souping up" their machines, even as the machines they came into contact with every workday subjected them to the tyranny and drudgery of factory life. Some of these same workers succumbed to anesthetizing themselves to their work through the amount of "Orange Plus" (OJ and vodka) they could consume on the job. For them, little about the industrial world inside the factory provided liberation, let alone rewarded sobriety.

Although not every artist has been inspired by Detroit (after numerous incidents of racial humiliation and prejudice, jazz great Billie Holiday called Detroit "a plantation with smokestacks), it is surprising how many creative people, both renowned and obscure, have found inspiration in the industrial environment of Detroit. Writing in 1932 to his friend Bertram Wolfe, Diego Rivera acknowledged the stimulating effect of the "industrial material of this place." More recently, Tyree Guyton has turned the artifacts and detritus of Detroit into a monumental and world-famous cityscape.

While having none of the fame of the aforementioned artists, the industrial artisans in the MOCAD exhibit and the workers in my teaching experiences manage to carve out their artistic creations in ways that attest to how the imagination can withstand even the most alienating and seemingly "ugly" environment.

Francis Shor is professor of history at Wayne State University.

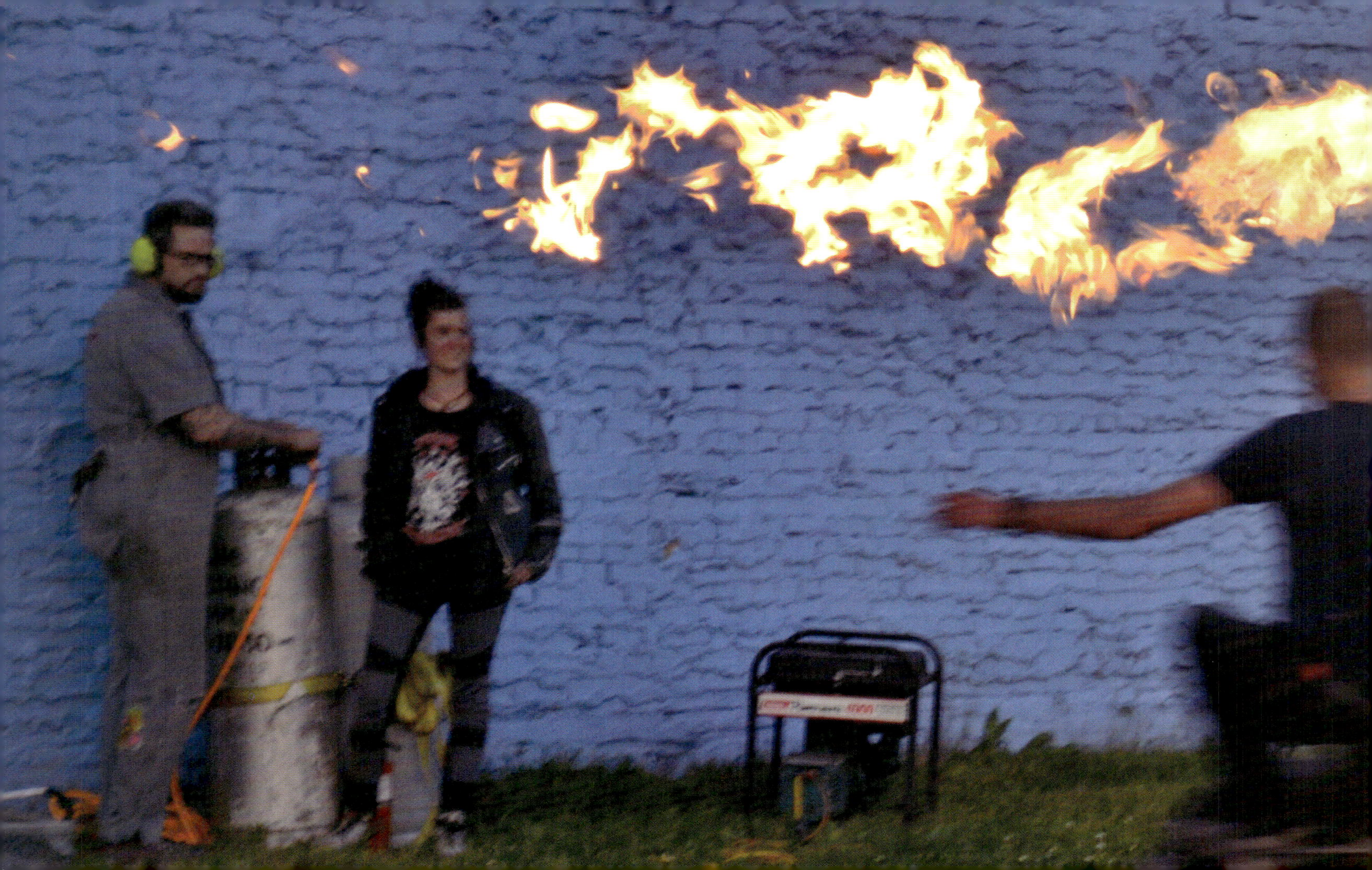

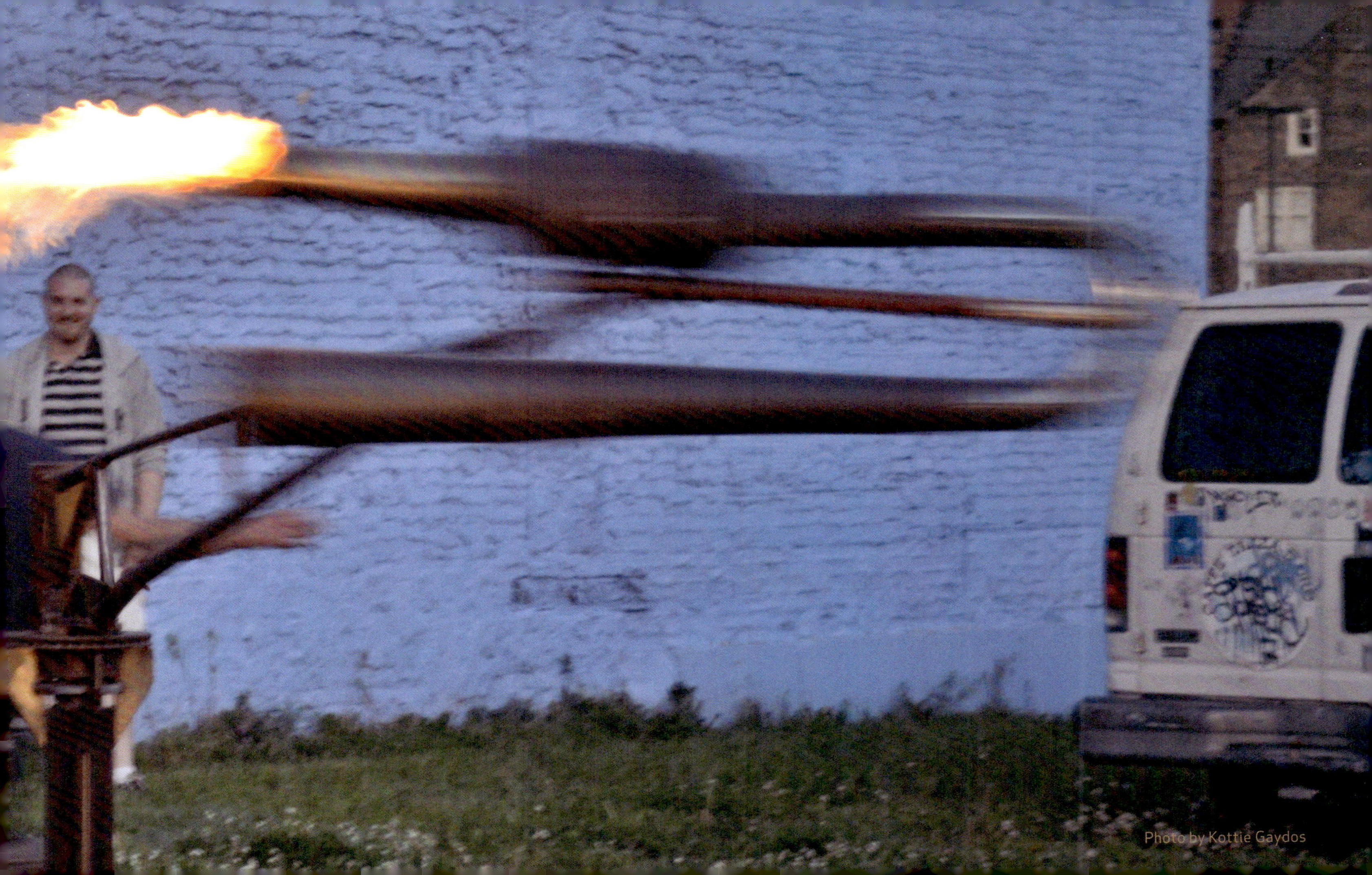

Photo by Kottie Gaydos

FLEXIBLE URBAN FACTORY / A SCALE SHIFT

Nina Rappaport

Daily, small boxes from around the world arrived at our New York City apartment. My husband would open them in his closet-garage, one by one. Emerging two months later was a complete bicycle assembled bit by physical bit in our own neo-cottage industry. Other tinkerers and inventors such as bakers, dressmakers, and flower arrangers can also produce goods and works of art for broader distribution from their urban spaces as long as they are plugged into a supply and distribution chain.

Often housed in what I call the *Vertical Urban Factory*, described in my traveling exhibition and project displayed at MOCAD in the spring/summer of 2012, this type of multi-story building either houses a complete factory or many different companies and manufacturers. *Vertical Urban Factory* explores the architectural origins of this building type, focusing on the modernist structures by engineers and architects, and contemporary examples, divided into the themes of "flexible," "spectacle," and "sustainable." A timeline of technology and industrial architecture, films, new architectural models, process diagrams, and numerous photographs highlights the need to maintain and reinvigorate the making of things — and thus the need for spaces in which to do so, in cities.

As large-scale manufacturing has been removed to sequestered sites on the periphery of cities, further from both consumers and the labor force, in what I call a "process removal," there is a simultaneous gravitation to the everyday pursuit of making things in smaller urban spaces. DIY (Do-It-Yourself) culture is blossoming not only because of those types of artisans and artists (who are part of the *Post-Industrial Complex* exhibition), but as small entrepreneurs who make things for the marketplace. These informal cottage industries could be recognized as part of the local economy, integrated into the city by eliminating the zoning restrictions that segregate building uses, and can allow people to live near their workplace.

Our culture values making things, not only for profit, but for satisfaction and achievement. Frustrated and bored by urban service industries, entrepreneurs are returning to small-scale and small-batch production in cities, similar to the small-scale pieceworker, or home worker, of the industrial revolution, and predicted in Alvin Toffler's 1980s "electronic cottage." However, just as factory workers were tied to their massive machines, now they are tied to their electronic machines as a kind of prosthetic device, pushing buttons rather than doing heavy lifting. With the scale-shift made possible via electronics comes a shift in the scale of urban manufacturing spaces.

When inventors need a community of workers for sharing expertise, tools and energy, large-scale vertical urban factories left abandoned by former corporations such as Russell Motor Car in Detroit, American Can in Brooklyn, and Standard Motors in Queens, N.Y., or former office buildings in the Little Addis area of Johannesburg, South Africa, offer new flexible spaces that different companies can lease and operate independently or collaborate with others.

In addition, larger manufacturers in New York such as Kerns, which makes engine parts for airplanes, or Smith Electric Cars, which makes delivery trucks for local companies, and, more recently, Fossil in Detroit, can also continue to make products, such as watches, in these same vertical urban factories.

Other urban companies have the potential to be networked together in neighborhoods to capitalize on the production expertise of skilled workers. For example, the Garment District in New York City could be reborn, modeled on its former life, just one step beyond the automation age in virtually linked factories. Expanding upon the current method, a designer in her office could complete a fashion concept, sending the drawing digitally to the pattern maker, who is linked to the sample fabricator, the designer checking it in feedback networks, and then finally sending it to the main factory for production controlled via electronic networks — with all participants clustered within blocks of one another.

With a growing interest in the locally made (as seen in the "locavore" movement), new industries, flexible and versatile, can supply goods to their communities, not just food products, lowering production costs and pollution with the elimination of long-distance shipping and warehousing. Clustering manufacturers of similar interests enhances new sustainability concepts of industrial symbiosis, rarely tried in cities, where each element in the production process is recycled into the next, and one factory's waste fuels another, or even an entire neighborhood. This clean manufacturing could be integrated into mixed-used areas to encourage working and living close together.

In the future neo-cottage factory the entrepreneur and local maker move beyond the modernist assembly line into the realm of integrated processing in a networked spatial economy rather than an isolated exurban space. This ubiquitous culture of making can co-exist with the everyday urban experience as part of the next urban economy to reinforce and reinvest in the cycles of making and consuming for more self-sufficient cities.

Nina Rappaport is a New York-based architecture critic and curator. Rappaport's exhibition, *Vertical Urban Factory*, was on display at the Museum of Contemporary Art Detroit [MOCAD] in the summer of 2012, alongside *Post-Industrial Complex*.

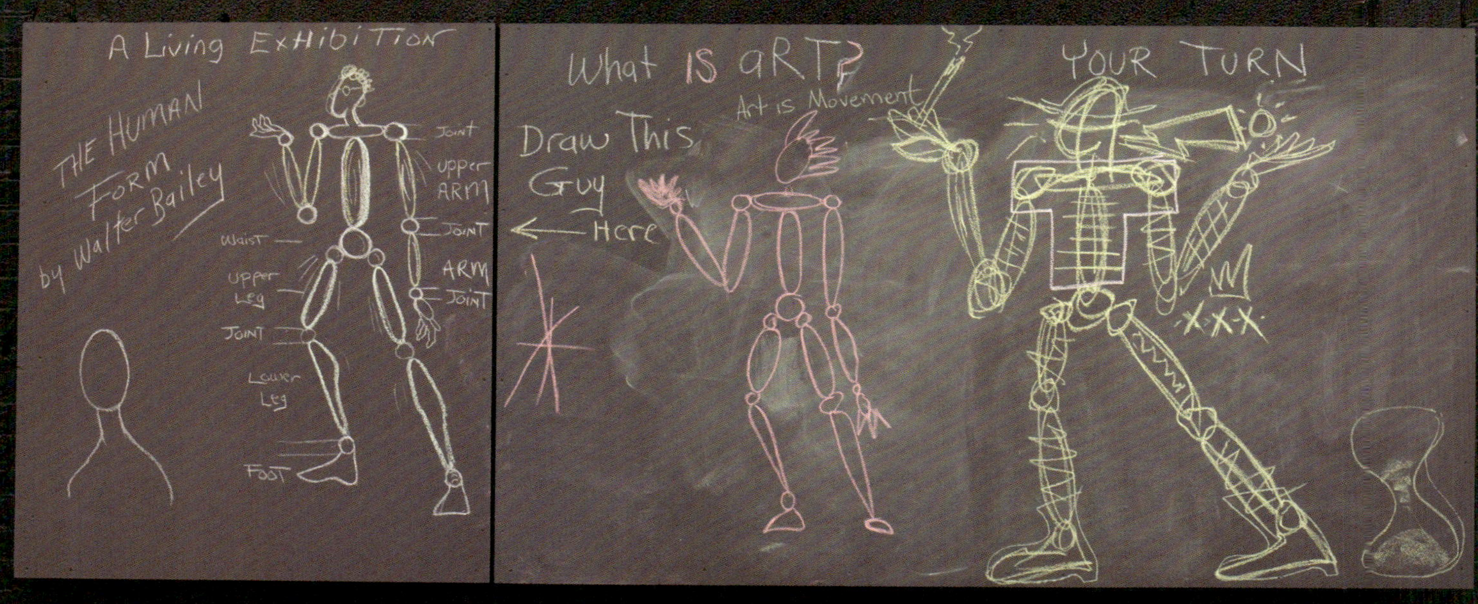
A Living Exhibition
THE HUMAN
Form
by Walter Bailey
Joint
Upper ARM
Joint
Waist
Upper Leg
ARM JOINT
Joint
Lower Leg
FOOT
What IS aRT?
Art is Movement
Draw This Guy
Here
YOUR TURN
X-X-X

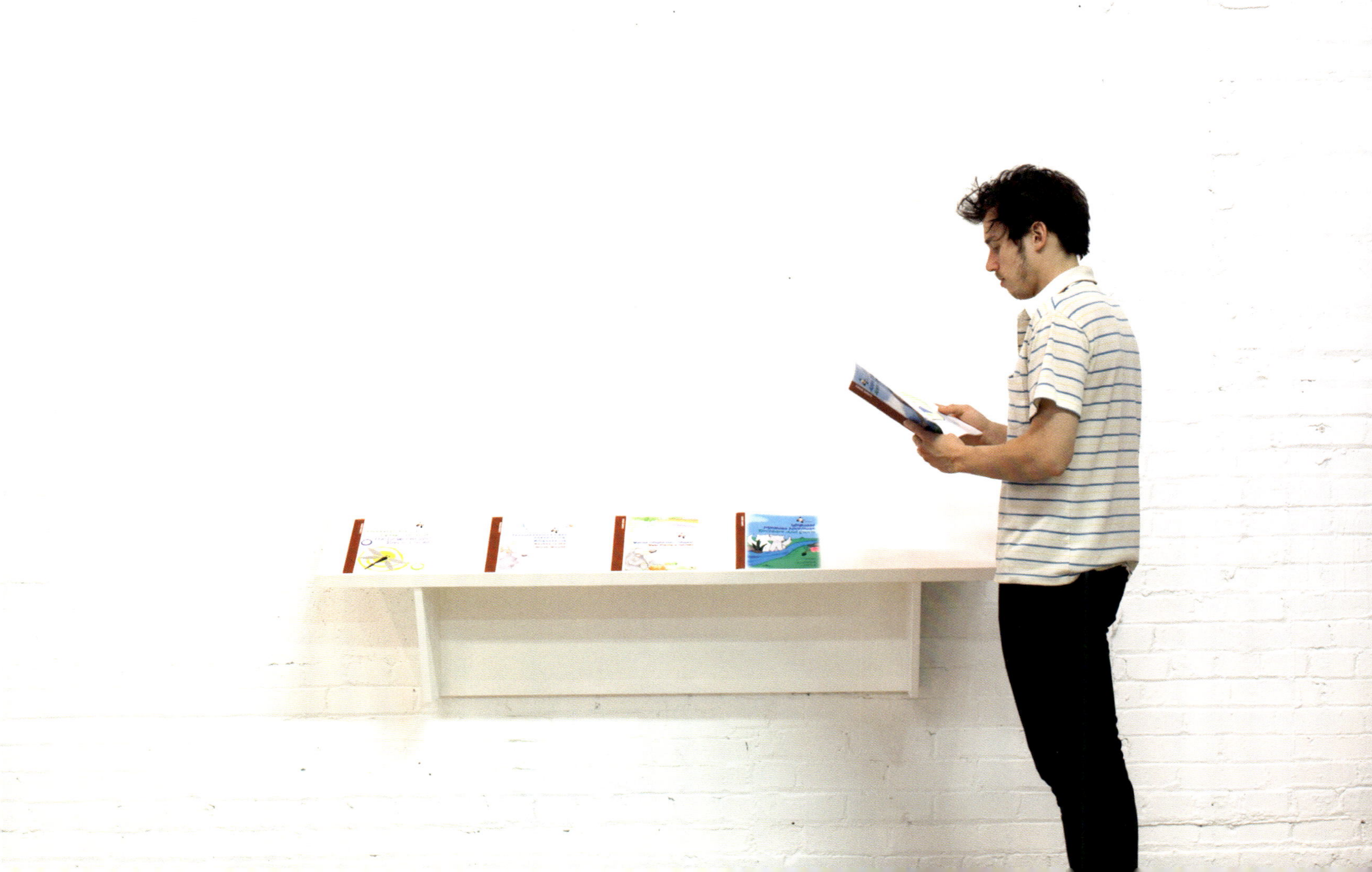

RYAN C DOYLE

What is it?

I make experiences for those who seek to view the world through my point of view. I apply my understanding of physical relationships and scientific laws to found objects, sound, light, and time. My intention is to provide the audience with a key to understanding their own subjective reality.

How did this start?

As a very young man I often found solace in the cathartic drawing and sketching of my thoughts as visual representations.

I draw upon my past experiences, concepts that have inspired, terrified, and ultimately rearrange my path of thought, and collection of materials to be attached and presented as a whole visual story.

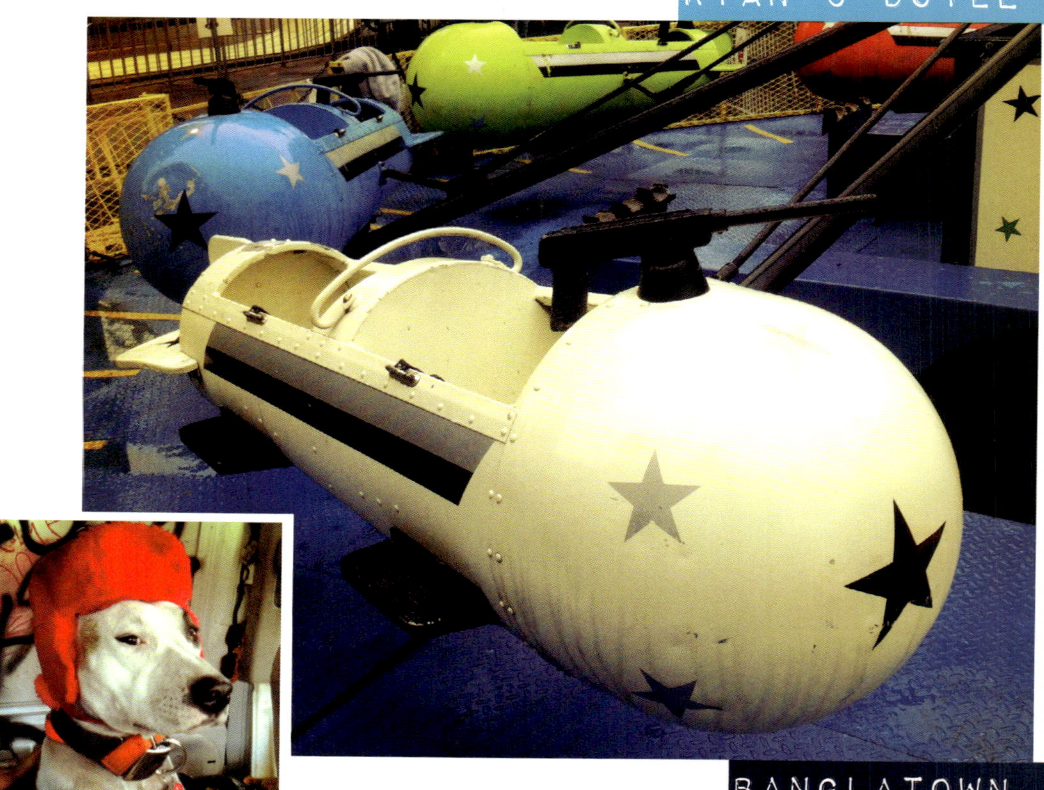

CLAUDIA WIGGER

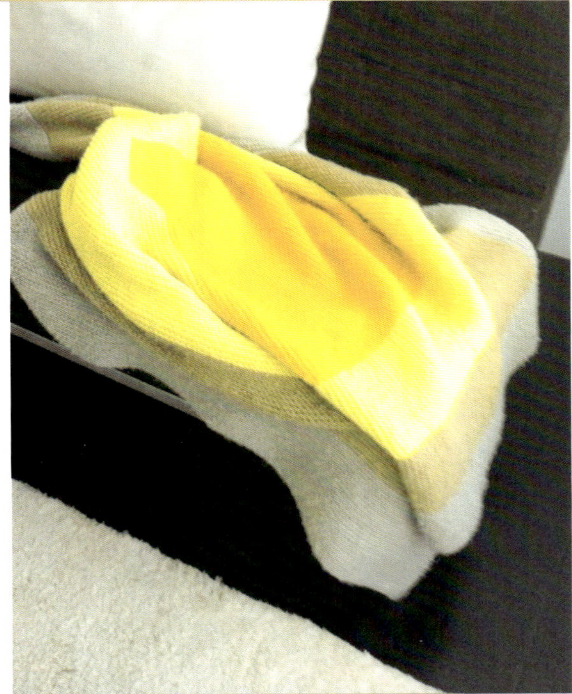

LAFAYETTE PARK
48207

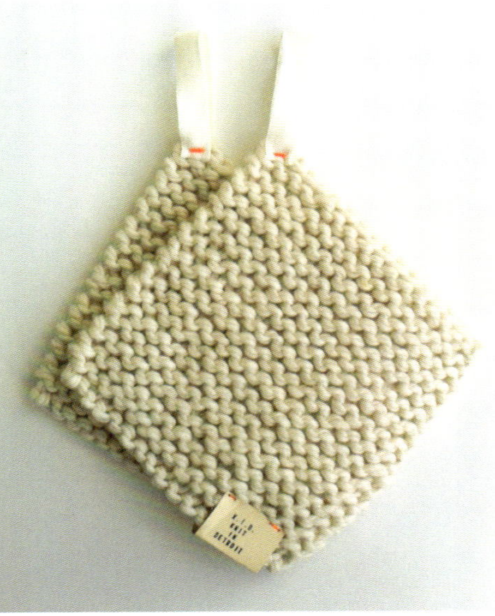

What is it?

I'm knitting all sorts of things

I'm mainly knitting graphical and color themed rectangular items, like blankets, potholders or cowls. I often use simple geometric shapes like triangles or rectangles in different shades of color.

How did this start?

It started with a knitting group I joined in my neighborhood when we moved here from Berlin, Germany one year ago. I restarted knitting mainly for social reasons, as I didn't do it for the last 20 years. Now I'm making blankets and potholders for a friend who is selling them at trade shows or in her B+B.

Recommendations?

All the great knitters of my Lafayette Park Knitting Group! I don't personally know these people but they all did different beautiful things for Honor + Folly: honorandfolly.com One of my neighbors, Andrew Kem, is making fantastic plywood furniture: kem3d.com

What is it?

ba-b&l (11111011100)

ba-b&l is a sound installation.

How did this start?

Originally created and shown simultaneously in Dayton, Ohio and Manchester, England in 2001. The original version used digital recordings of spoken texts about the development of language in ancient Mesopotamia. The texts we used were appropriated and reworked from Neal Stephenson's novel "Snow Crash", published in 1992. The texts were sliced into the most basic elements of language – the building blocks that are used to construct words. These phonemes were layered in order to create a real time mix between 5 sets of custom designed/built speakers.

For Post-Industrial Complex, we wanted to rework ba-b&l. The original 2001 work focused on the internal interactions between the audience's auditory and analytic processes, which were engaged in deciphering the babble to make meaning. This relies on the natural inclination of human beings to strive to make sense of any stimulus.

With the 2012 iteration we wanted to explore the capacity for the audience to now physically interact with the work in a way that triggers intact texts to be played by a text-to-speech engine.

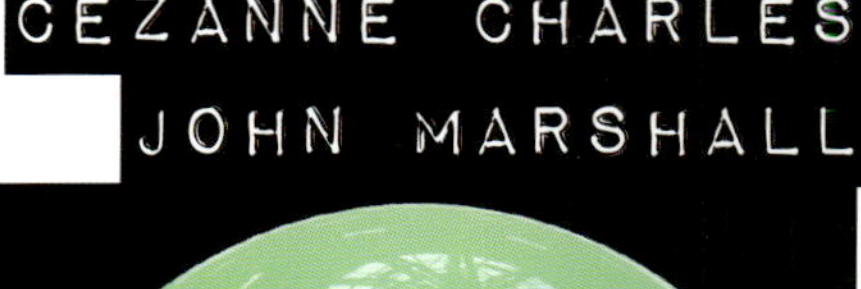

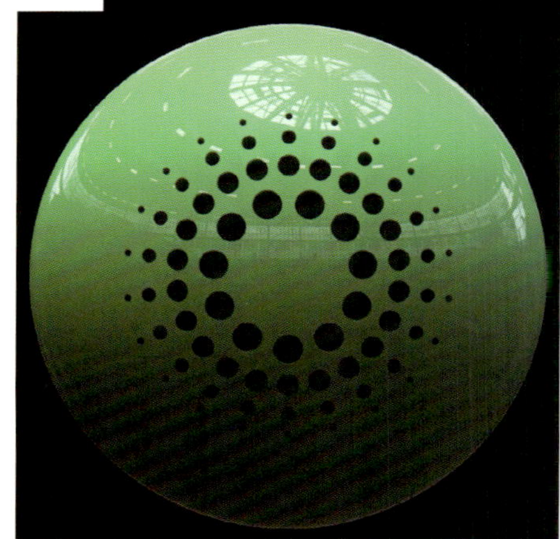

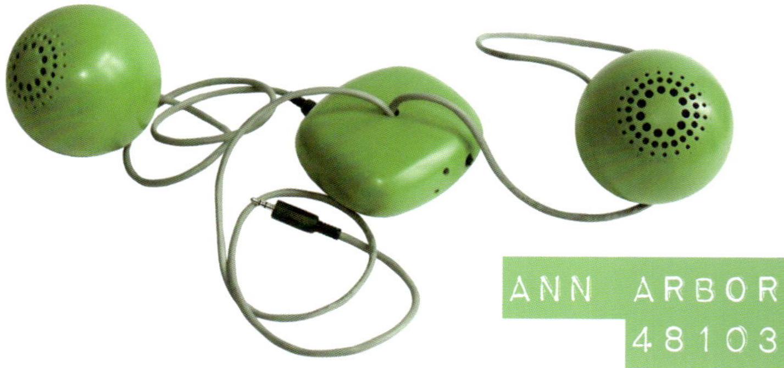

TOM HEADRICK

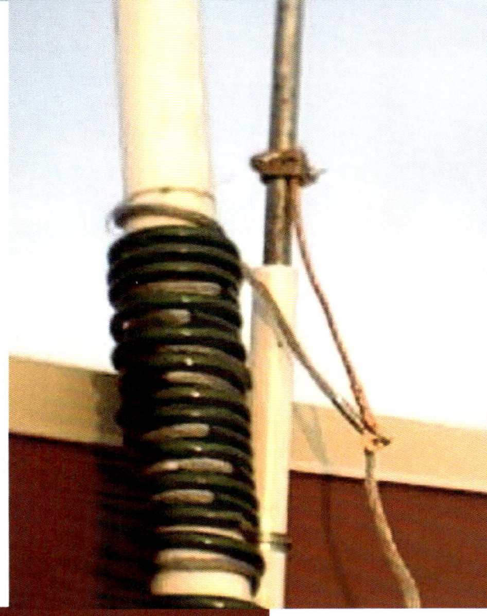

REDFORD

48239

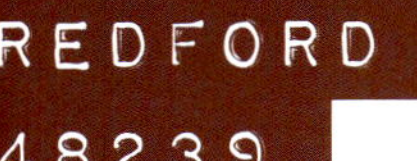

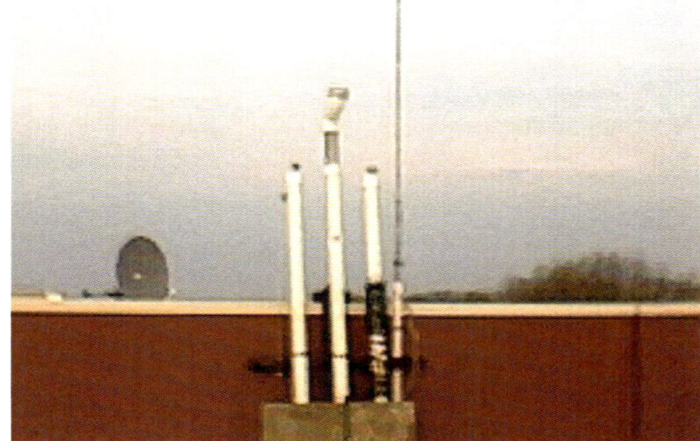

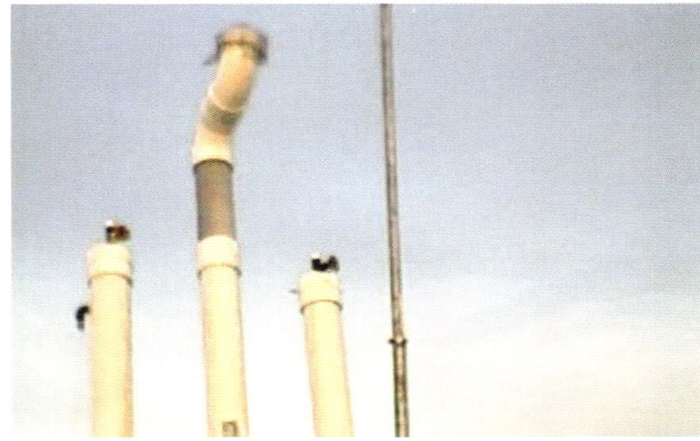

What is it?

Meta-Engineer.
Improve designs or concepts. Create new paths of developement for technology.

How did this start?

Playing with electronics and carpentry as a kid expanded into computers, mathematics, and physics.

Recommendations?

I only know his first name.
Todd.
Lives downriver.

sites.google.com/site/pchistorian

What is it?

Plaster and Lath Walls

Our work involves revisiting historic plaster and lath methods of constructing walls through the use of contemporary robotic fabrication. In a city where we commonly experience the nature of plaster and lath only through demolition, our work proposes to revitalize a dying trade through the use of advanced technology. The same technology invented to replace Detroit's auto workers is leveraged in our work to regenerate a lost trade and question the homogeneity of our modern drywall world.

How did this start?

After visiting Detroit's closed down US Gypsum drywall plant we decided to apply for a research grant to robotically revisit the craft of plaster at The University of Michigan.

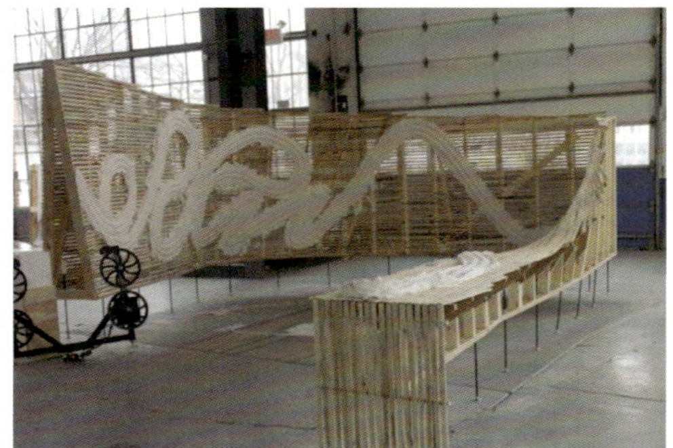

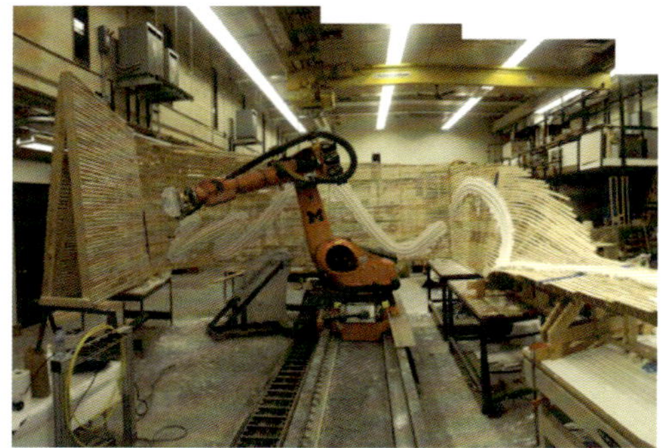

STEVEN MANKOUCHE

JOSH BARD

MATTHEW SCHULTE

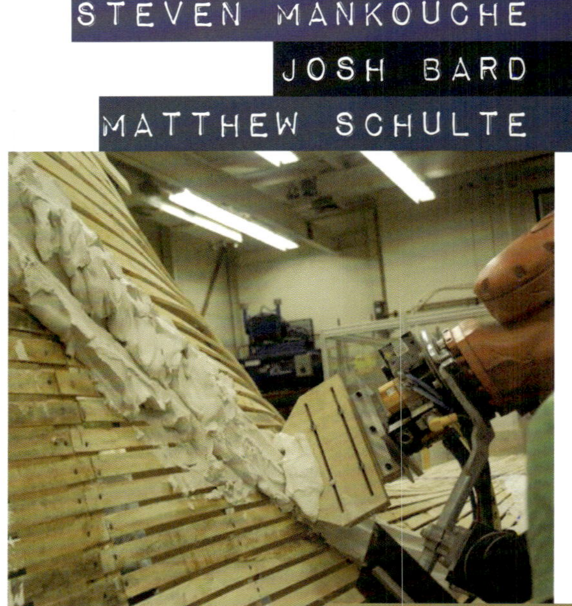

ANN ARBOR

48109

GLORIA J LOWE

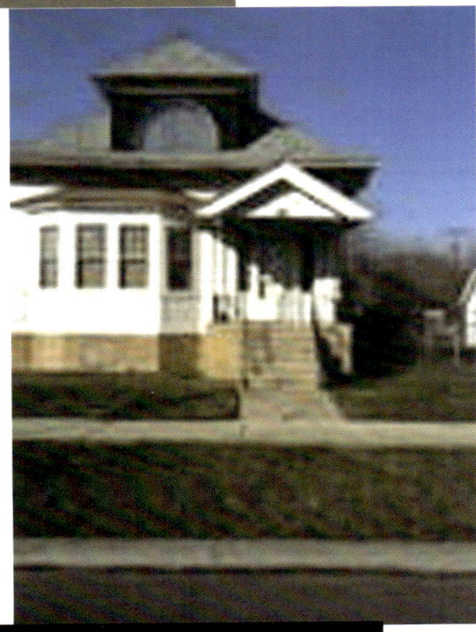

EAST SIDE, DETROIT
48214

What is it?

Sustainable Housing.
Homes

How did this start?

We train veterans, returning citizens, and youth in sustainable green building techniques: how to recreate housing and transform themselves.

We want green, too! Trains veterans, returning citizens in retrofitting, creating energy efficient homes. A conversation which led to a project in Jackson, MI and then a project on the East-Side and being presented to the East-Side community. (see http://www.yesmagazine.org/neweconomy/work-reimagined-detroit-gets-creative) Carlos Nielbock who takes recycled materials (metal) and builds wind turbines.

Recommendations?

Carl Nielbock, inventor and ornamental metal designer.

What is it?

Cyberoptix Tie Lab - I make "Ties That Don't Suck." We make hand screenprinted neckties, bow ties & scarves for guys who love (and hate) ties –simply, "Ties That Don't Suck." We've made hip guys, young and old, finally enjoy dressing up! We'll gussyup your gang of groomsmen.

How did this start?

Bethany Shorb is the founder of and designer at Cyberoptix Tie Lab. She's been working full-time in her Detroit studio for almost 7 years where she's hand-screenprinted over 80,000 neckties. Shorb founded The Cyberoptix Tie Lab in 2006. As a designer of witty hand printed neckwear, she has applied her experience as a sculptor, costume and graphic designer to transform a much maligned business necessity into a subversive object of desire.

Recommendations?

OmniCorp Detroit! omnicorpdetroit.com
Kristi Burgett: etsy.com/shop/EatDaRich

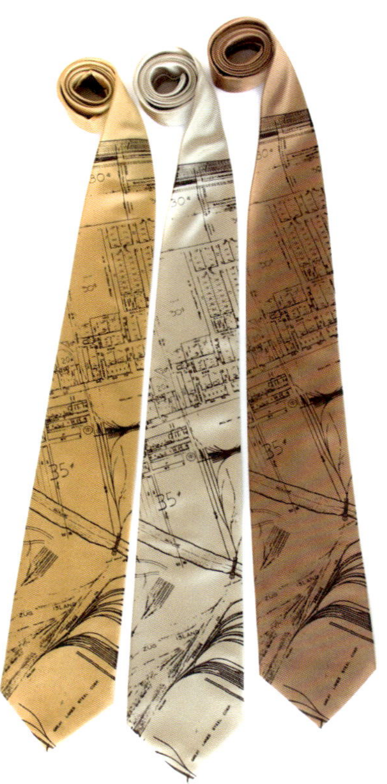

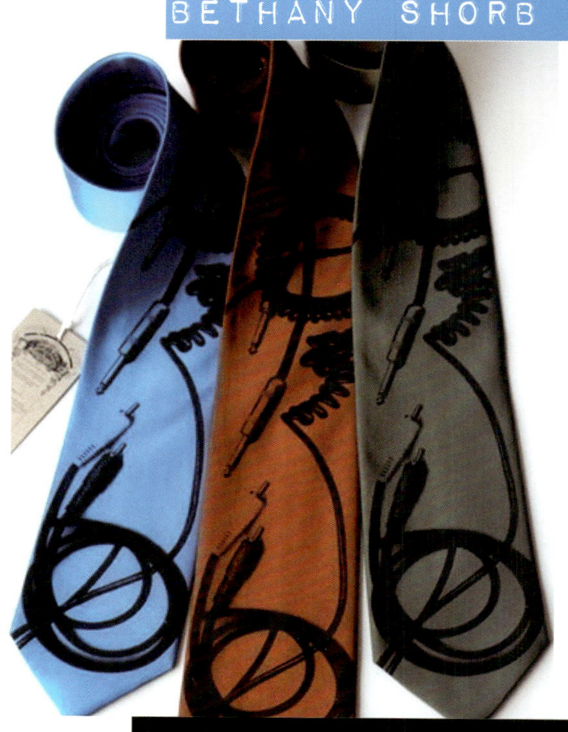

ERIKA HESS

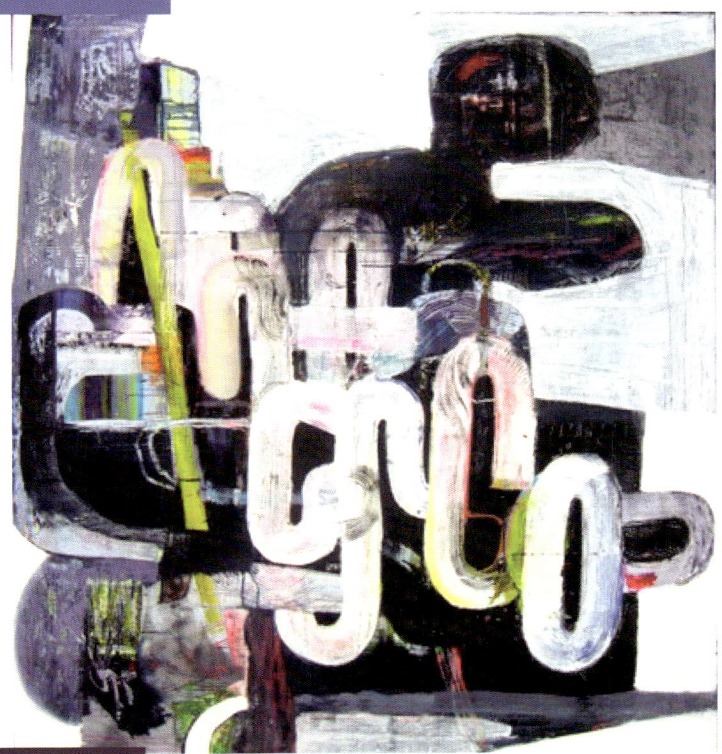

What is it?

Visual culture

I make paintings that include fluorescent colors from my youth. Lisa Frank pink, slime green. I call it "trapper-keeper aesthetics". Growing up in a middle-class midwestern town, this was the visual language I was raised with and embraced. I use old credit cards to swipe, move and detract paint from the canvas. If I want to modify the surface I allow the oil paint to dry and use a belt sander.

How did this start?

I began painting as a kid and developed my own work through playing, making, destroying, re-doing.

YPSILANTI

48197

OREN GOLDENBERG

What is it?

Films, Videos

I am a filmmaker who makes feature, short, and documentary films and videos about and for Detroit and its fine people.

How did this start?

I was in high school, upset that I couldn't draw, play music, or perform. My football career was ending. The most plausible art form for my ungifted self was video, and I haven't stopped since.

Recommendations?

Pat Dorn - head of Cass Corridor Neighborhood Developement Corporation. He makes and modifies section 8 housing in the Cass Corridor to maintain a diversity in population and demographics.

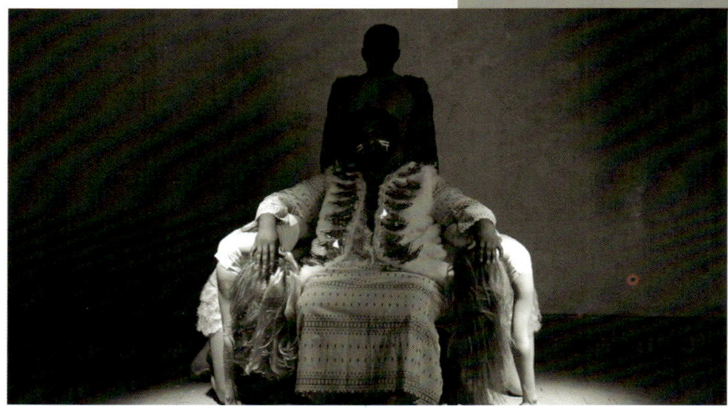

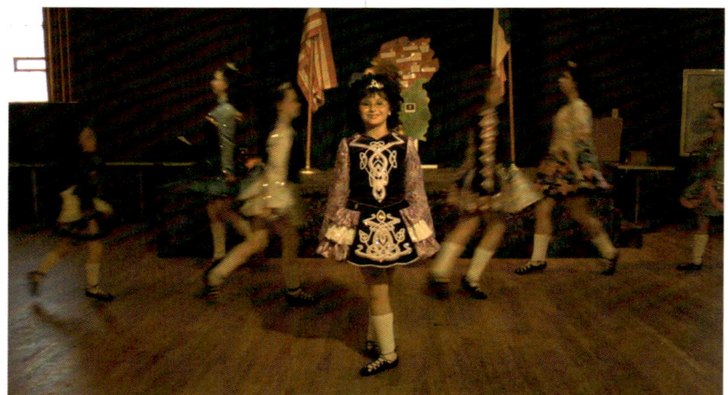

CASS CORRIDOR
48201

JEN DAVID

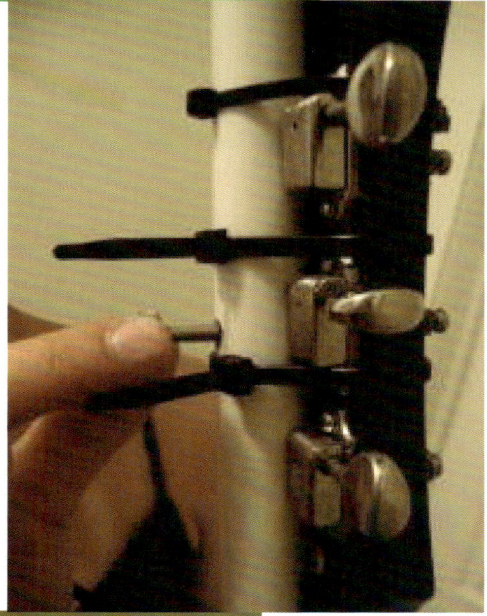

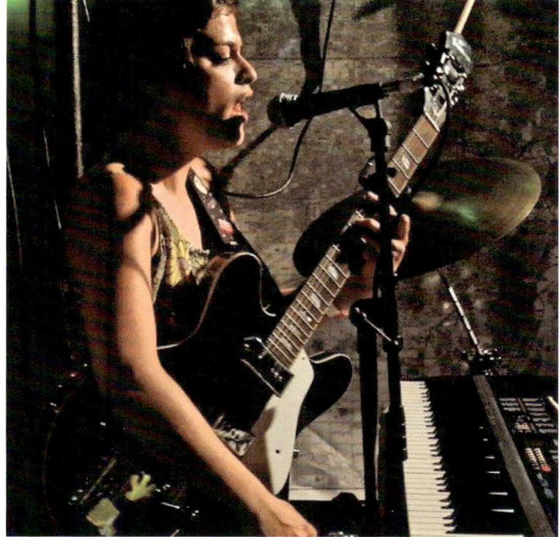

What is it?

Musical Instruments

A way for a two piece band to create as much noise as possible, without using any pre-programming. A guitar with a drum stick attachment to play cymbal. A drum with a kick pedal to be used by foot. A cymbal with a kick pedal to be used by foot.

How did this start?

A band member quit and we wanted to stay a two piece, but not sacrifice an instrument.

Recommendations?

Omnicorp

MIDTOWN

48201

CHRISTOPHER SAMUELS

What is it?

Fine art

Sculptures from found objects.

How did this start?

Birth

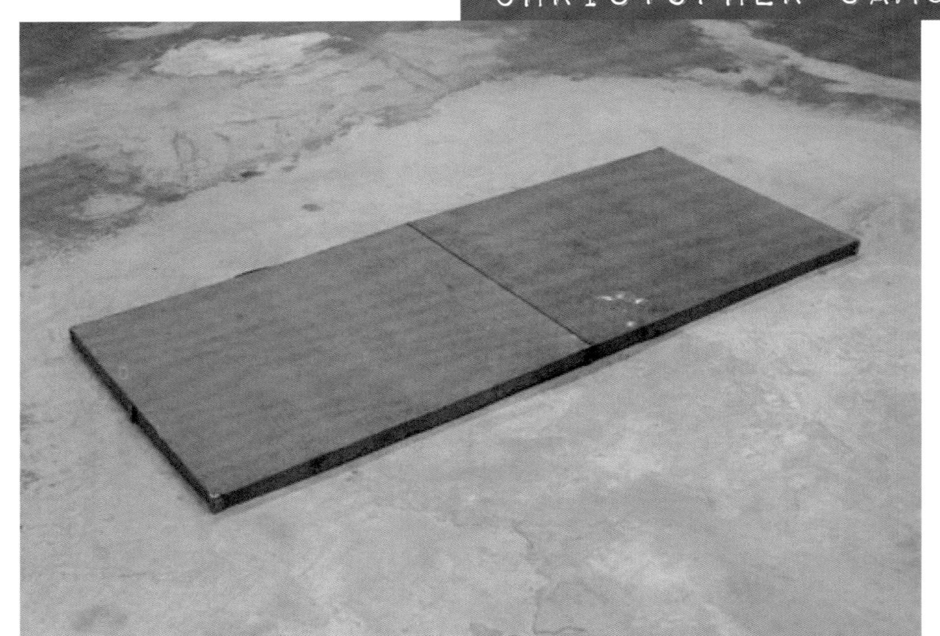

EASTERN MARKET
48207

KELLY SAGER

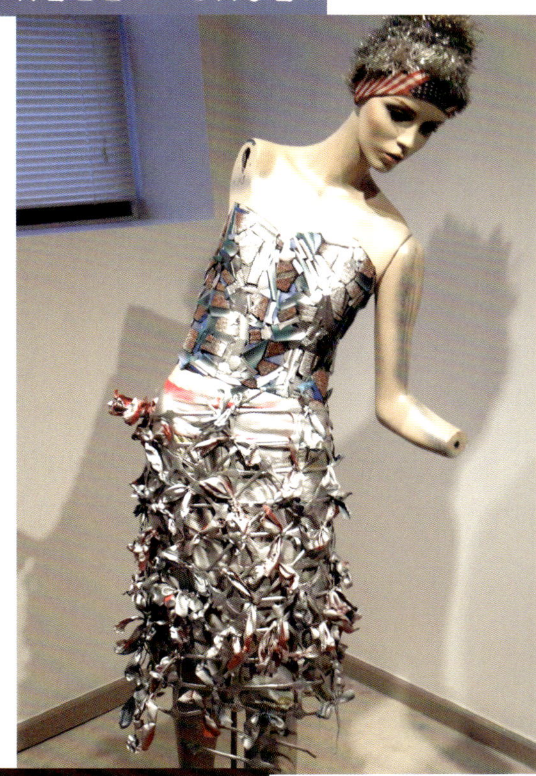

FERNDALE
48220

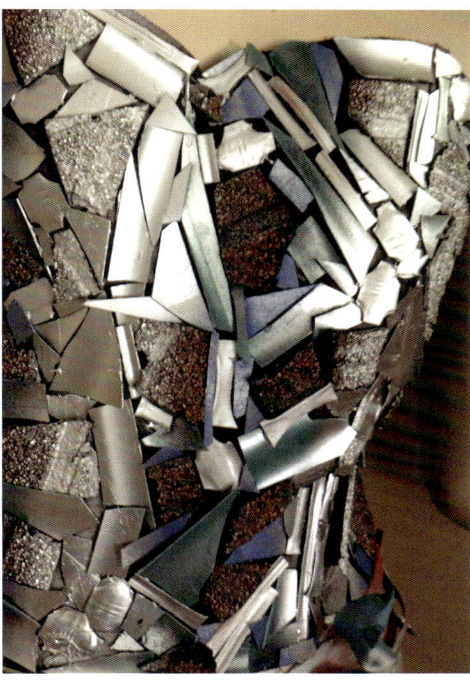

What is it?

Leather items

I collect old leather jackets, couches, other furniture, or any other leather good - cut it up and make wearable garments out of it.

How did this start?

I'm a fashion designer who loves working with leather, but since leather is so expensive and also an animal has to die for us to use its skin, I got the idea to use leather from discarded items no one wants anymore.

Recommendations?

zombiedgirls.com
modifies old porcelean dolls and turns them into zombies

What is it?

Old stuff

I make art from old stuff.

How did this start?

Being surrounded with crap, having talent
and going through a general malaise.

Recommendations?

Courtney Wilcox –Nests

MIKE BAKER

DETROIT
48221

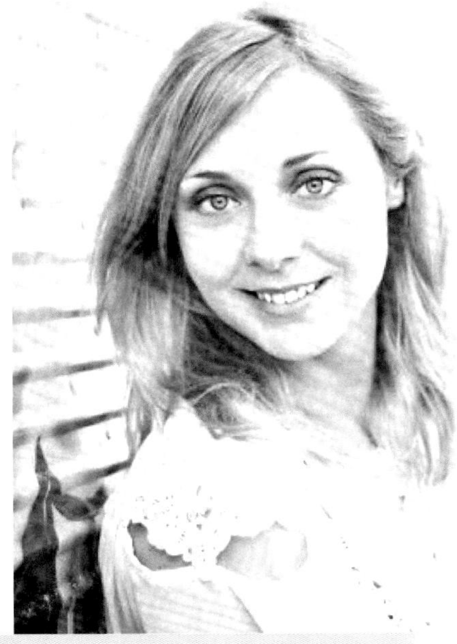

What is it?

Characters, Movies, Plays, Puppets

I create a fictional world, in a playing space or on digital video, reminiscent of real feelings and struggles, telling a given or imagined story. Speaking of acting in particular, creating a character for me is developing their inner and outer life, and through the art of performance (the physical manifestation of these minute details) I bring the audience to a closer understanding of and sympathy for people. In the greater picture of movie-making and directing or producing plays and puppet shows, I make scenery, puppets (2D or 3D sculpture), plan the movement on stage, or the look and movement on camera, the costumes, makeup, props, interactions of characters with one another, editing, and writing of the story, if it is original. Of course, this includes working in collaboration with other artistic individuals with these talents much of the time.

How did this start?

I was taught video production in high school, went on to study acting and performing theater in college (WSU, MXAT), and then began training and performing with Detroit PuppetART Theater, melded my acquired knowledge and wisdom, "et voila!"

Recommendations?

Yes, many. Carrie Elizabeth Morris, Emilia Javanica, Igor Gozman, Irina Baranovskaya, Luda Micheyenko, Aaron Timlin, Daniel Timlin, Rachel Timlin, Miles Rose, KT Andresky, Juan Martinez, Gary Schwartz, Inga Wilson, Stephen Dueweke, Yusef Shakur, Jerry Strez..

ANGELA KIEL

What is it?

I crochet things. I love to build things out of yarn. The piece I am submitting I have been working on for 10+ years. Something that has been traveling around with me since high school.

How did this start?

I started crocheting when I was in 3rd grade. The sweater started sometime in high school. It was a vest first. Then it became a longer vest. Then longer, then grew sleeves, then eventually grew a hood. It's been hanging in my closet for 10+ years and every now and then I pull it down and add something new.

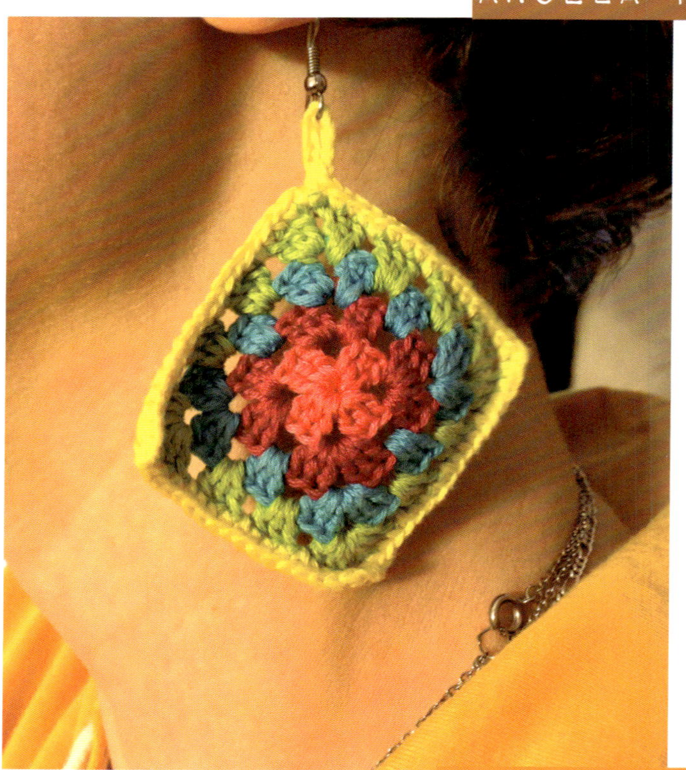

WEST VILLAGE

48214

DOLORES SLOWINSKI

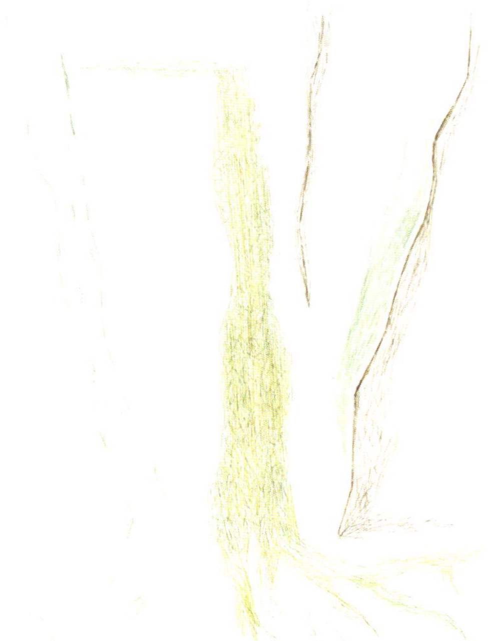

What is it?

I make handstitched abstract drawings on paper. I take large sheets of paper to the John Johnson Co., a tent and awning company in SW Detroit. I perforate random lines on the paper using a 30" long arm sewing machine. I then hand stitch textures into the areas between those large perforations.

How did this start?

I started out by making hand-embroidered greeting cards that I sent to friends and family. Then, I began doing the "cards" as drawings and had a show at Motor City Brewing Works in 2009. And then did an installation at Re:View Contemporary in 2010. I am now working out of a studio in Ferndale because I could not afford the kind of space I needed in Detroit.

Recommendations?

My husband, Bob D'Aoust, built my work-table for my studio and built a frame for my blinds in the studio. He has a shop at home. My daughter, Claire D'Aoust, is artist and an industrial designer who can design and fabricate almost anything. We are a family of makers who come from families of makers in Detroit. My husband's father and uncles were carpenters on the East side of Detroit. My father was a machine repairman for Fisher Body on the West side and could make, repair, or build anything. That generation is gone. It's up to us and our children now...to continue making things in Detroit.

AVIATION
SUBDIVISION
48228

What is it?

Fiber textiles

Fiber from different types of fabrics that are handmade such as felting, weaving, surface print designs...used in several types of forms, from sculpture, architecture productions such as theatrical backdrops, interior surfaces, and products for form or function.

How did this start?

I have been a working artist all my life but the past 20 years really developed my art form through several opportunities that include private, commercial and retail exposures. But the ICFF design show in 1995 and 1996 really started the process in a real professional arena.

Recommendations?

Yes. Audrey Franklin uses founded material and creates these incredible large motifs with paints, reusable and unusual objects.

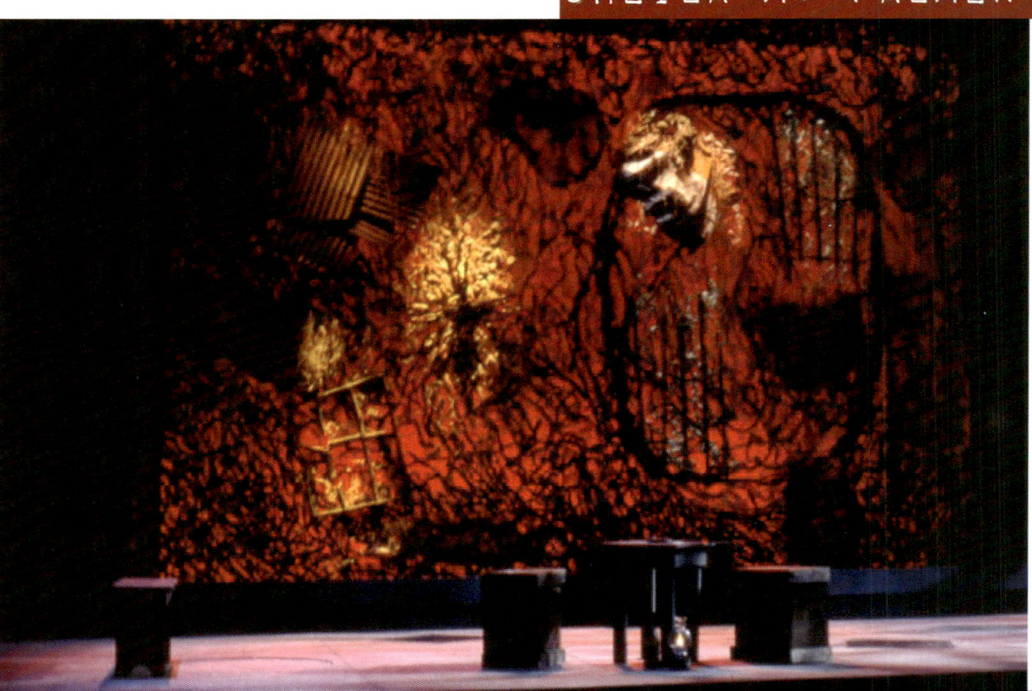

SHEILA M. PALMER

P.O. BOX: 44992
48244

SHANNON MCDONALD

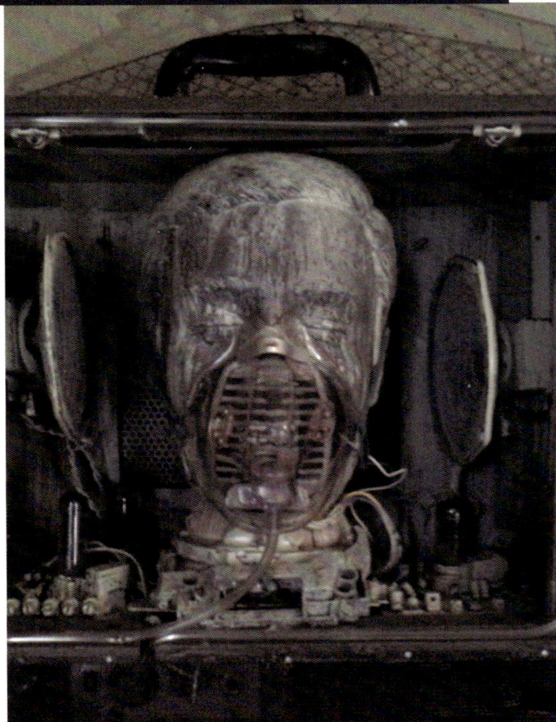

HAMTRAMCK
48212

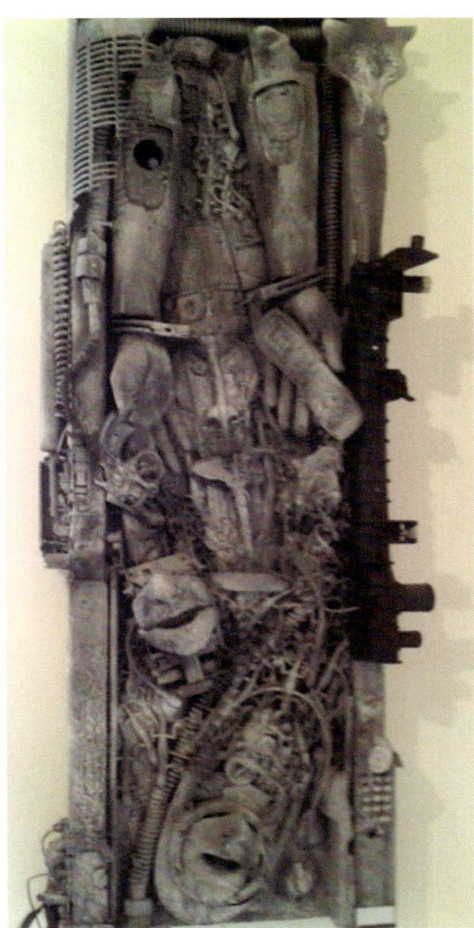

What is it?

Assemblage art

Sculptures crafted of discarded items found in Detroit.

Dramatic, industrial 3-D medium, of a lineage dating back to Heidleberg but compacted into a format for display in the home. It's a repurposing of materials from car parts to toothbrushes, from mannequins to TVs. Depicted within the sculptures are religious, social, personal, and purely whimsical images that entice the mind to imagine.

How did this start?

Started in Redford, MI, ca. 1994 among a small group of artists/friends.

JEFFRY CHIPLIS

What is it?

Neon signs/art

These signs/art are made using previously fabricated components, like tinker toys we plug in and play. If the glass tubes are not broken, chances are good they still work. Recontextulization.

How did this start?

I've been doing this for over 25 years and got started because of the color and light.

Photo Credit
Jerry Mann, Photographer
jerrymann.com

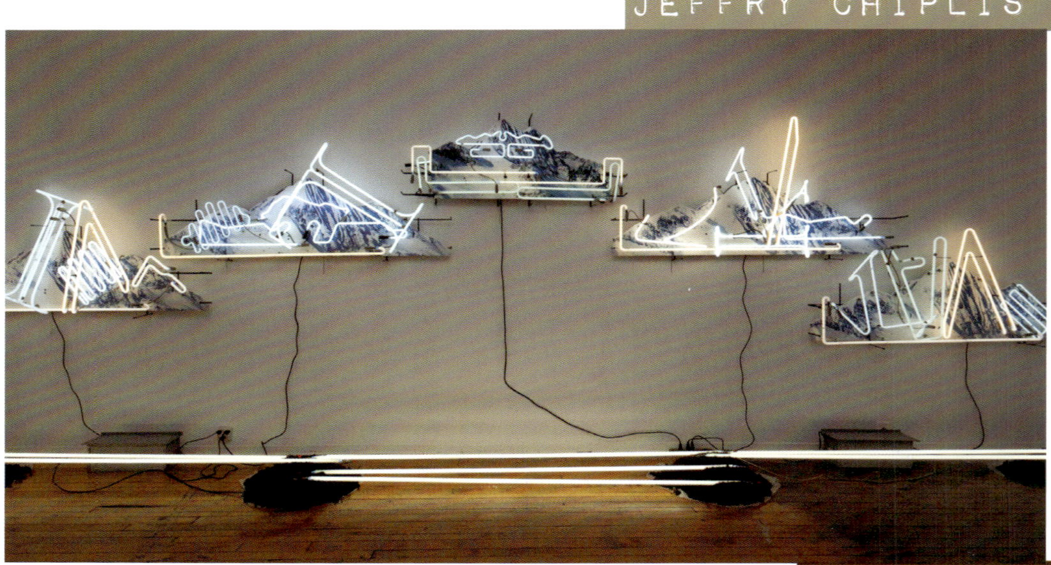

TREMONT

44113

SCOTT KLINKER

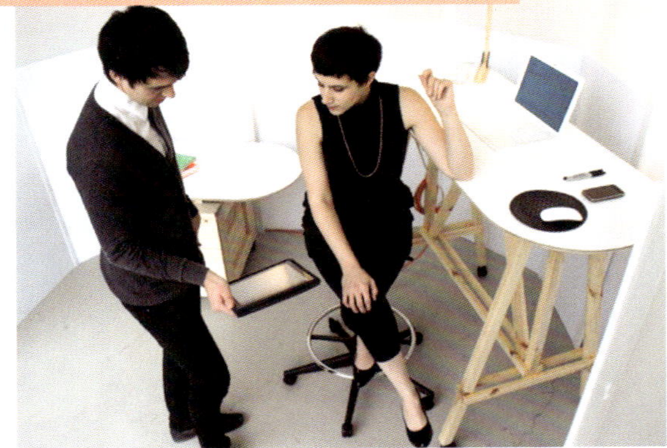

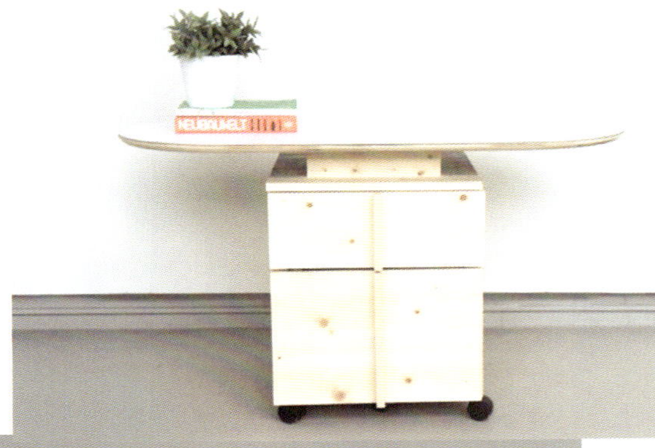

What is it?

Starter Office

Starter Office is a DIY office system to help Detroit start-up businesses convert old industrial space into new low-cost office space. It is low-tech and low-cost, yet designed to fully support new team work processes. A no-nonsense, DIY aesthetic combines simple off-the-shelf parts with everyday materials to express both professionalism and pragmatism. It offers a conceptual counterpoint to the over-priced, over-engineered products of the contract furniture world. A set of free instructions will make it an open source project for anyone to copy freely.

How did this start?

The system was originally designed for a co-working space in Detroit where young start-up companies had converted an old industrial building into new communal office space. My goal was to make a system that would be flexible, affordable, made locally, high-performance, and capable of making dynamic spaces that feel professional but suggest a new attitude toward the workplace that feels more free and improvised. The interior was not realized as planned, but the furniture system shown is the part we were able to prototype so far.

Recommendations?

Context Furniture is a local manufacturer.

BLOOMFIELD HILLS
48303

JACK CORLEY

What is it?

Tatchstiks (note magnets)

Tatchstiks are note magnets for refrigerators, office cubes & conference rooms, lockers, and toolboxes. Constructed of a small, super strong "rare earth" neodymium ring magnet and a machined anodized aluminum stud.

How did this start?

I worked for an automotive tier 2 parts manufacturer (fired after 24 years of service). We used neodymium magnets in our assemblies. They were small and strong, but frustrating to use in everyday applications. I am a frustrated industrial designer, so I began making prototypes of the magnet with an aluminum stud attached as a kind of handle. Tatchstiks is the final result.

Recommendations?

Brad Potts, Motor City Moped
motorcitymoped.com

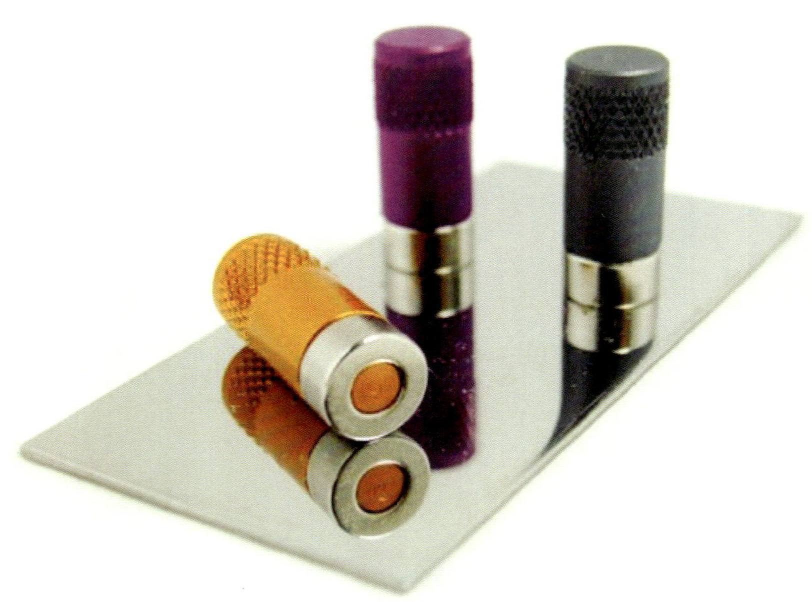

BIRMINGHAM, DETROIT
48009

CAMILLE LECOUTRE

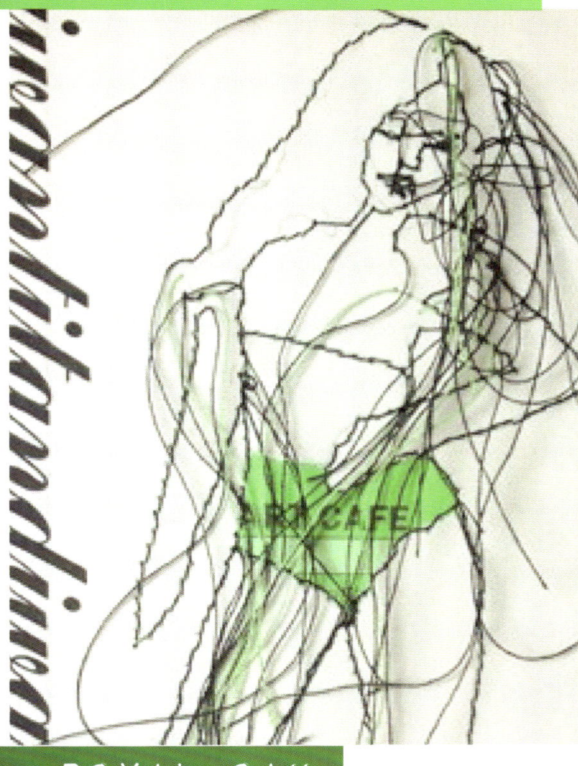

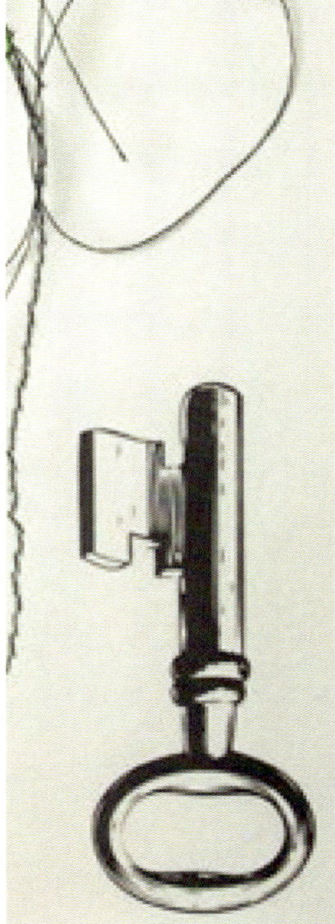

ROYAL OAK

48067

What is it?

Found object, pop culture sewn artworks

I use sewing as a prominent medium and the assemblage of mix-media into iconic images. A female figure or silhouette is always present in my work. Literature is one of my main sources of inspiration as well as popular culture and how it relates to women. My recent work explores the English language and other languages specifically idioms, clichés, metaphors and proverbs.

How did this start?

I started by making "pretty" collages with many layers and meanings. I didn't like using glue and wanted a more permanent process. Since I was sewing clothes I merged my art with my sewing. The sewing machine has a mind of its own, sometimes it works the way you want it to and sometimes not. This was a good complement to my way of working and pushed me to come up with different outcomes.

Recommendations?

Romare Bearden

What is it?

Social Relationships

I am creating a space in Detroit that hopes to bring visitors to the city together with the people who live here, under the shared premise of story-telling. It will be an artful place to sleep, learn, and collaborate - a mixed use building featuring a boutique hotel, co-working space, and sustainable mentoring program for young people.

How did this start?

Mad vision, consistant dedication, a hell of a lot of work, and love. It is still starting - we are in early planning phase targeting construction in 2013.

Recommendations?

Julia Solis at Furnace Press (which is moving to Detroit from NYC) makes books and photographs and other art things.

facebook.com/detroithotelproject

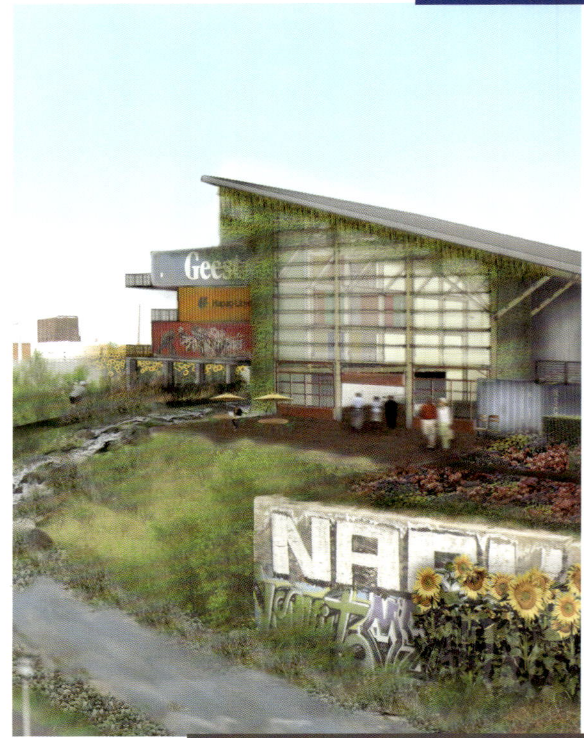

JEFFERSON CHALMERS

48215

CHiP

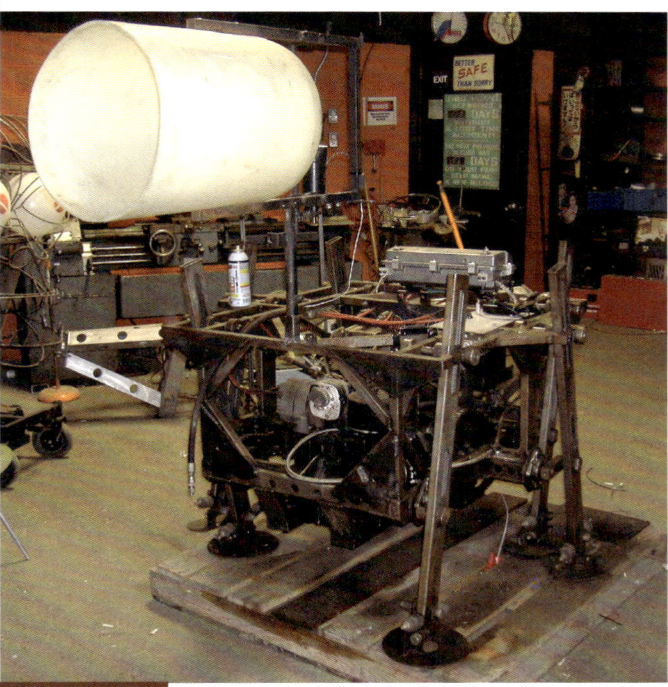

What is it?

Electromechanical devices

Robots used in a performance application.

How did this start?

Survival Research Laboratory videos.

WOODBRIDGE

48208

ELYSIA VANDENBUSSCHE

What is it?

Functional /sculptural clay objects

I make and design objects from clay, both functional and sculptural. I love minimal design and really try to focus on function and good innovative design woven together in my products.

How did this start?

I have been creating with clay since I was a child. I decided to make it my career, because I found I have a passion for making with this material. I love my craft.

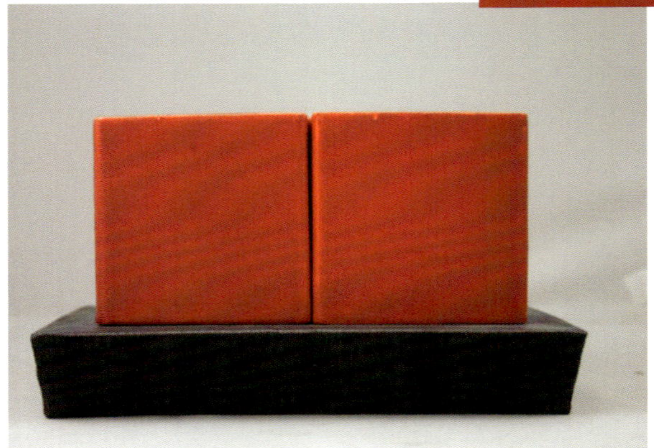

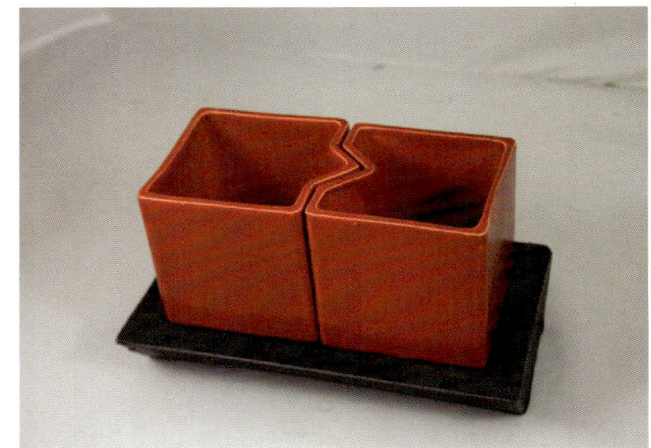

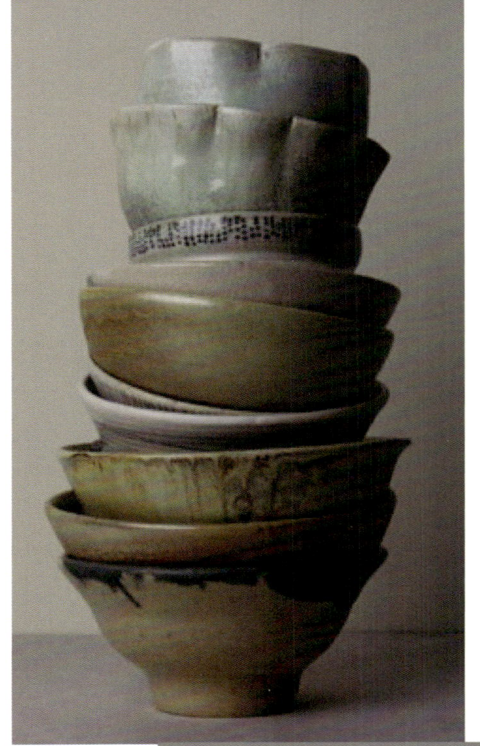

WOODBRIDGE

48208

ALLIE MALDONADO

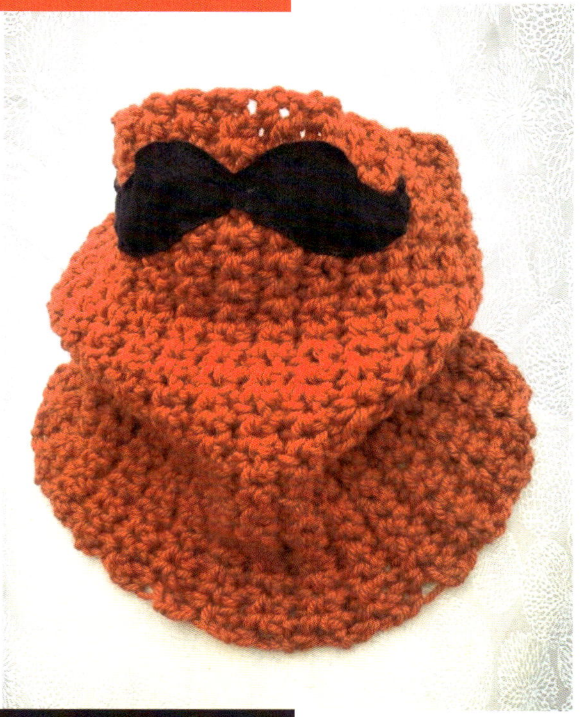

What is it?

Crochet accessories

I crochet pop culture–inspired accessories and housewares.

How did this start?

I learned to crochet at an early age from my grandmother.

Recommendations?

Check out handlebar.com

etsy.com/shop/mittenmade

DEARBORN HEIGHTS
48125

MARY BARNES

What is it?

Hats and accessories

I make hats using classical millinery blocking technique. Some are from bought supplies from millinery houses, but my favorite pieces are re-blocked, revitalized Salvation Army hats which are given new life and new style.

How did this start?

I just started making hats in January. It was something I always wanted to do and it branched out of a line of headbands and fascinators that I have been creating for some time now.

Recommendations?

All the sellers of Rust Belt Market

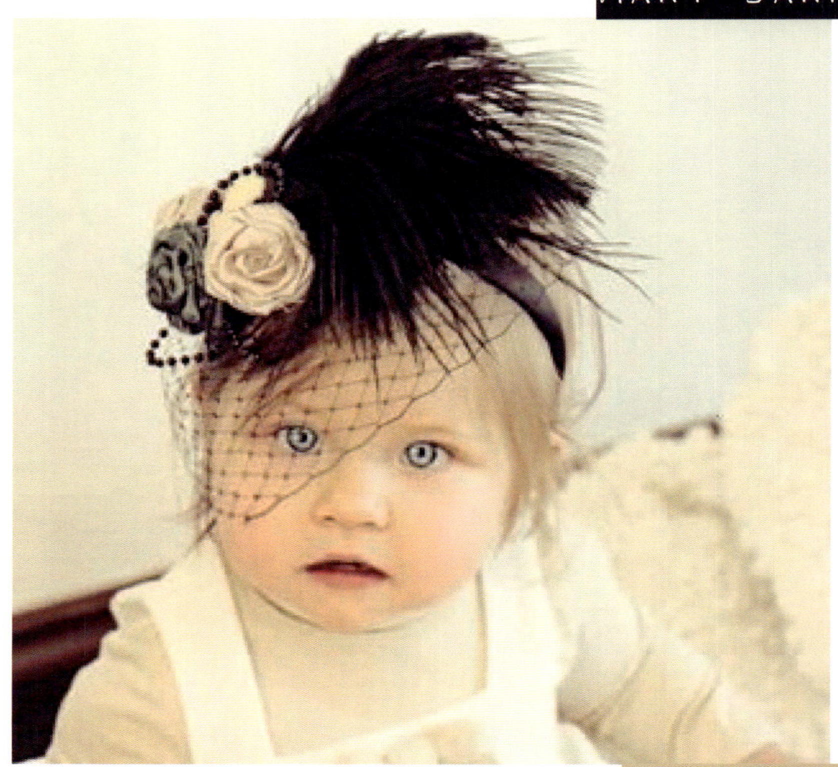

NE SUBURBS

48066

ABIGAIL RIST

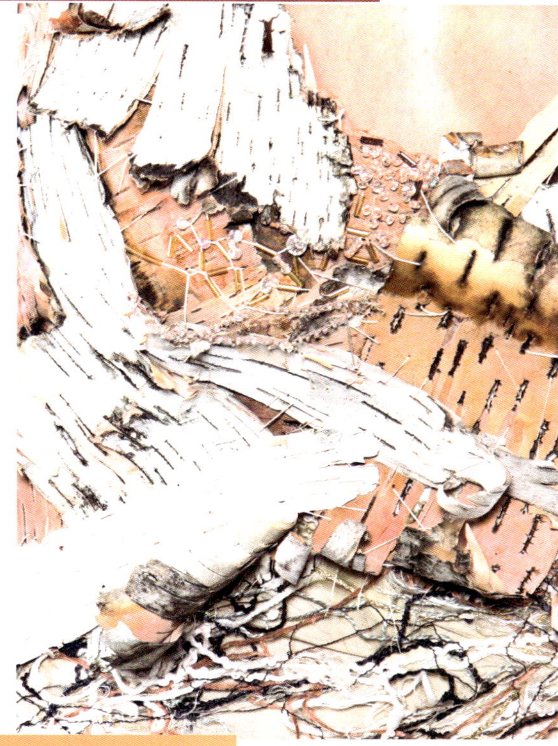

BERKLEY

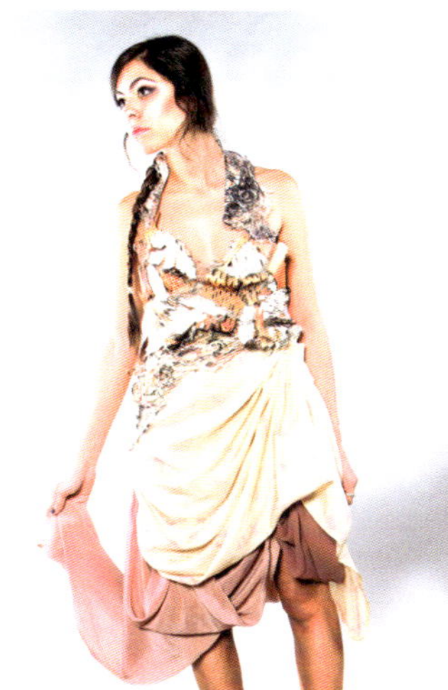

What is it?

I make wearable art from found and repurposed items.

I use many different types of materials, usually found objects, to create wearable art. Using birch bark I created a dress that was hand stitched and embroidered. Often I will create these wearables out of something common repurposed in an uncommon way. For instance, using coaxial cable I created a corset top that was woven together using a basketry technique. Each of my works is one of a kind and most aspects that are not repurposed are handmade.

How did this start?

I began to rework the idea of using unconventional materials after I learned basic sewing the summer before last. I have since been pushing the boundaries of wearable art by integrating as much mixed media into my pieces as possible. I don't like to look at an object for what its original limitations present. Instead I dream up new ways to imagine its endless potential.

Recommendations?

My friend Lakea Shepard is an amazing artist and creates very interesting accessories using found objects.

What is it?

One-of-a-kind hats

Unique hats made from recycled textiles and designer sample cuts

How did this start?

Began my business in 1992 designing and making clothing while doing hats on the side. The hats took off and now they are our main product.

Recommendations?

I sell at the Rust Belt Market in Ferndale, where there are any number of other artists and artisans. I can refer a number of them.

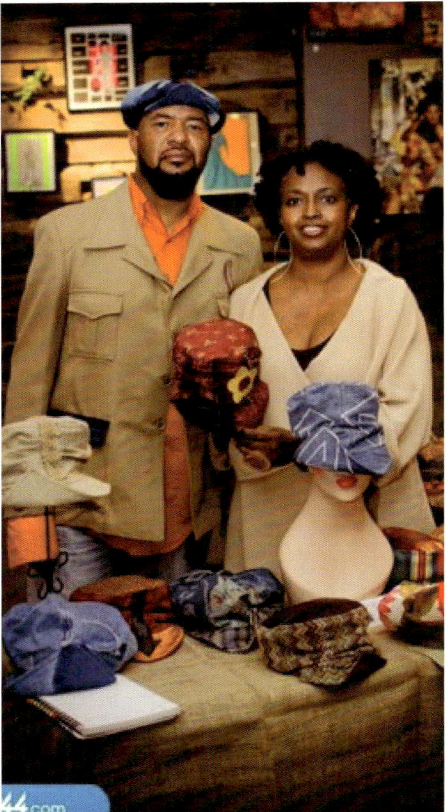

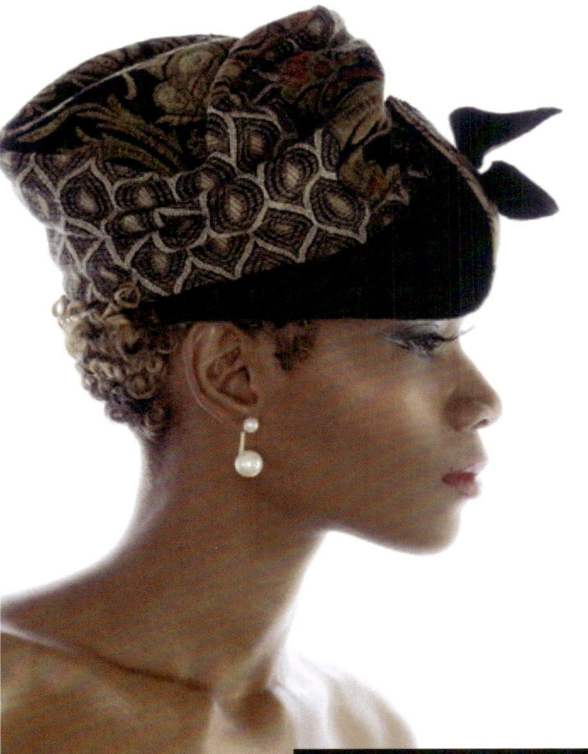

STEPHANIE DICKEY

RIVERTOWN

48207

CYNTHIA LAMAIDE

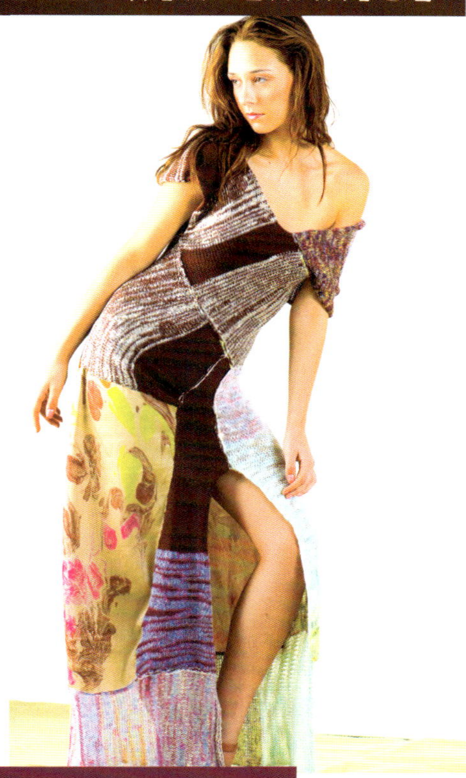

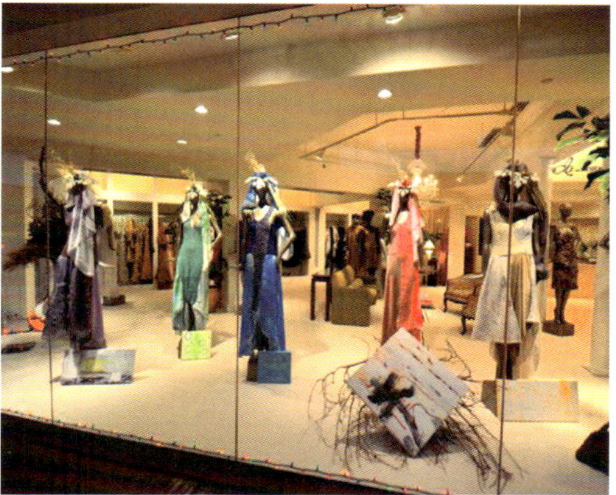

What is it?

I create one of a kind clothing

I make the fabrics and designs for my clothing. I use uncommon materials in the garments with the goal to always enhance the body.

How did this start?

There is a need for clothing and I want to make it beautiful in different and unusual ways.

Recommendations?

Rick Gage

ROCHESTER

48306

What is it?

DJ, Fiber Artist

I am a DJ. I also knit and crochet and macrame. I create my own patterns and exhibit in various art shows and galleries. This year I have taken fiber arts to another level and have begun yarn bombing, which is grafitti with yarn. I am involved in various yarn bombing projects and installations this year.

How did this start?

I learned how to knit and crochet at age 6. My grandmother taught me. I spent my youth living with her and taking care of her. She was the best teacher in my life. I named my business after her. I began doing art shows 4 years ago. This year I will be back at the E. Market Artisan Village and my work is also at The Yellow Door and various other galleries throughout the Metro-Detroit area.

Recommendations?

Ron Olson, graphic designer,
fix-it man, DJ

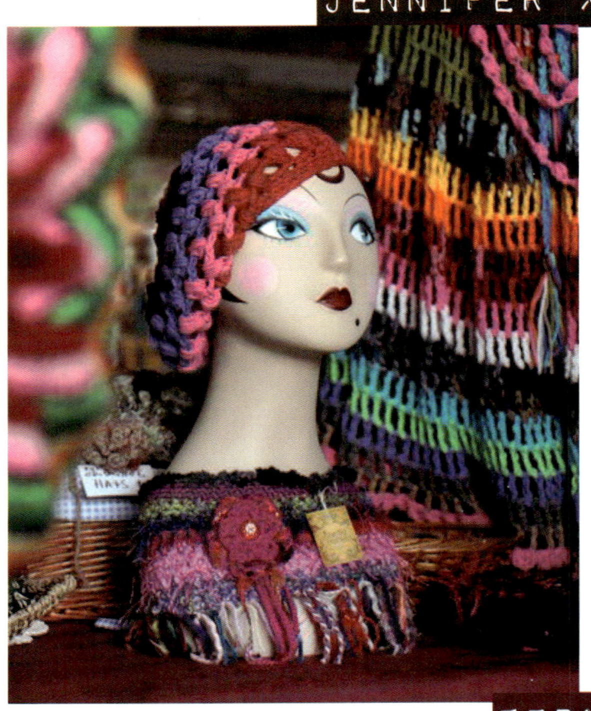

JENNIFER XERRI

FERNDALE

48220

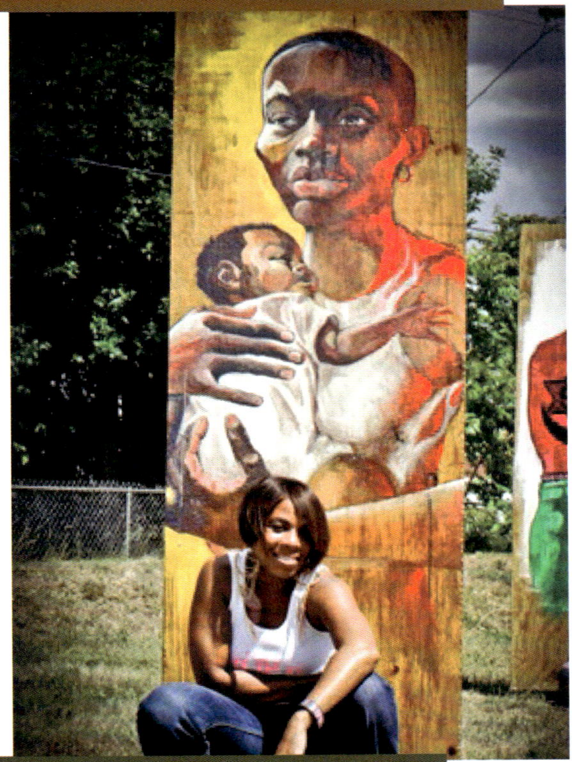

What is it?

Vacant lots

Inspired by the North End Community garden created by fellow artist and friend Halima Cassells.

How did this start?

I returned to my hometown of Detroit from Los Angeles with hopes of change. I, along with Halima, took over a vacant lot in my neighborhood, Conant Gardens, because it was an eyesore and the perfect picture of despair. We transformed the litter and weed-filled space into a beautiful outdoor gallery and garden, erecting six 7 ft wooden panels from the ground in which 6 visual artists including myself painted fine art–type paintings. We filled the lot with vegetation and flowers for all to enjoy. This garden has inspired neighbors, community churches, and the local Girl Scout troops to get involved in the property's maintenance.

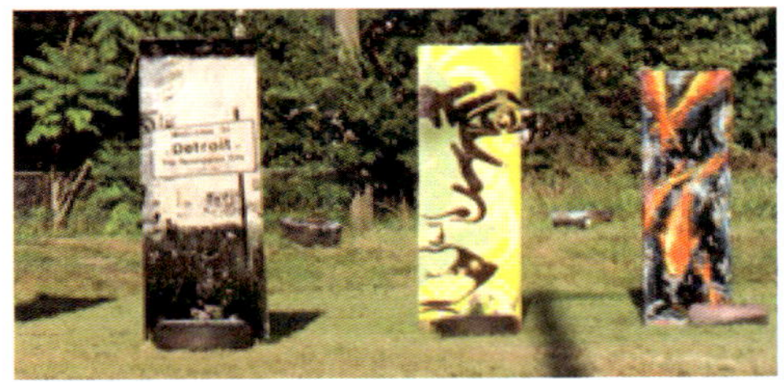

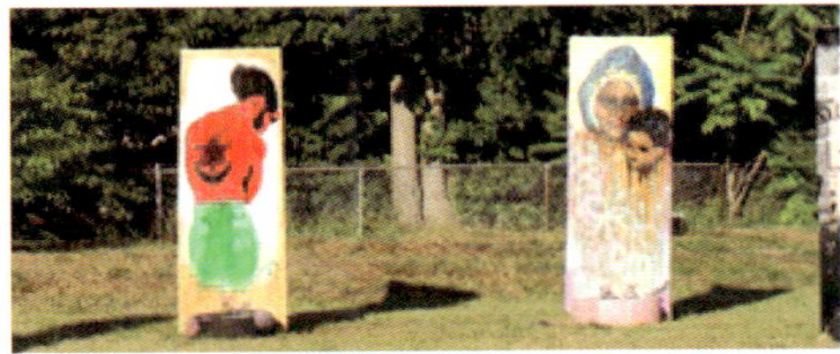

I was inspired by Halima Cassell's takeover of a vacant lot in her neighborhood, the North End. She spearheaded a transformation of the lot into a community garden on the North End of Detroit.

Recommendations?

Lamar Landers
Halima Cassells

MARY WRIGHT

What is it?

Wool felt hats

Using wool – oftentimes from animals raised in Michigan - I create felt and design hats.

How did this start?

I inherited a hat block and wool roving from my late sister's design studio. I dove in and taught myself.

Recommendations?

Pat Roan Judd - storytelling

Brandon Trenz - writer and musician

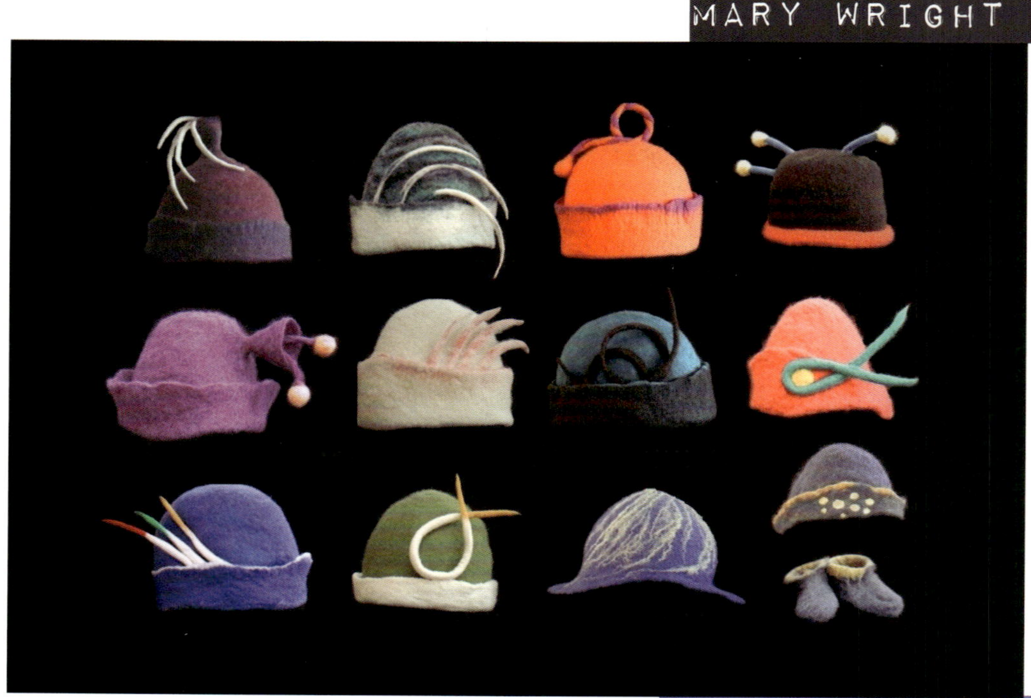

FRANKLIN, MI
48025

56

BRIAN MUNCE

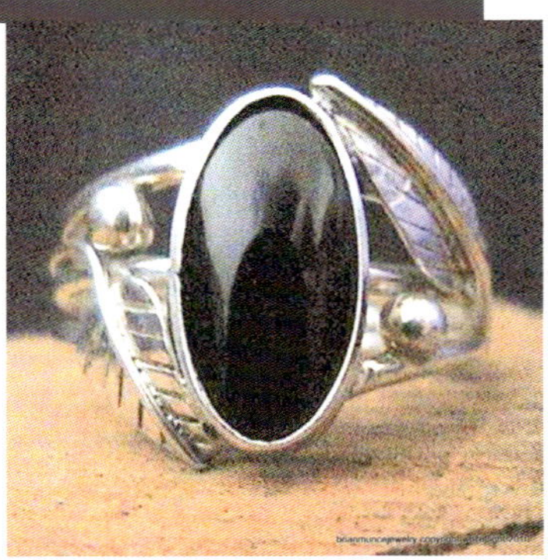

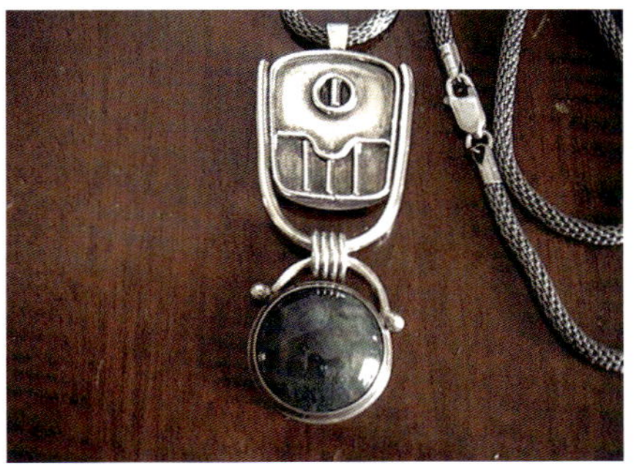

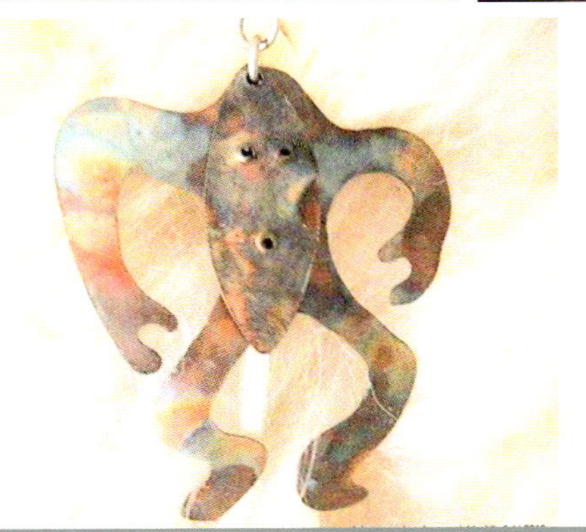

PONTIAC, SYLVAN LAKE
48341

What is it?

Primarily metals

I have been making jewelry for over 40 years using both construction method and in carving wax modeling for castings, steel and bronze residential and commercial gates, railings, screens, large outdoor sculptures. Also, active in painting on board, canvas, and paper.

How did this start?

I first got interested in ceramic artwork in Jr. High School. Most everything else has come from picking other artist's brains and being self-taught.

Recommendations?

Carolyn Masnari - a portrait artist /friend, Jay Lefkowitz–stone / steel artist

What is it?

Thoughts

I am a fabricator and manipulator of ideas and paradigms and wholly committed to freeing souls from their frangible and rotting "human" costume.

How did this start?

After the universe's initial expansion from a singularity, it cooled sufficiently to allow energy to be converted into various subatomic particles, including protons, neutrons, electrons, and perhaps most significantly, me.

Recommendations?

Every Italian male in my "human" family.

EITAN SUSSMAN

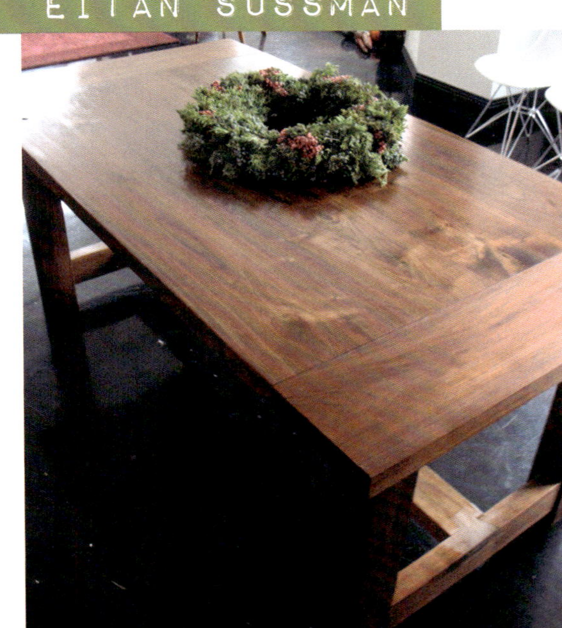

CORKTOWN
48226

What is it?

Wood and metal furniture and housewares

Tables, chairs, cutting boards,
beautiful objects

How did this start?

Once upon a time, there was a tall, proud tree growing in one of Michigan's vast hardwood forests. This tree lived a full life producing oxygen and habitat for living things. Right before the tree died, its last wish was to be transformed into delightful furniture and objects to continue adding to the beauty of the world. I was walking through the forest and heard this tree's last whispers, and promised to do my part helping to fulfill its dream.

Recommendations?

Hm. I consider most of my friends to be talented in these regards.

JANNA BISSETT

What is it?

Jewelry made out of vintage machine and auto parts

How did this start?

I take apart vintage and antique machines such as cash registers, typewriters, and also auto parts. I shine them up and then combine them by soldering and wiring them, sometimes adding Swarovski crystals or semi-precious stones. My goal is to combine industrial with delicate and find the perfect balance. I have a background in fashion and I try to make them as chic and modern as possible.

Recommendations?

I got a hold of a 1950s cash register and took it apart merely because I was curious. Then I started shining up the little pieces inside and started making jewelry. Now I have a collection of old typewriters and have expanded into auto parts.

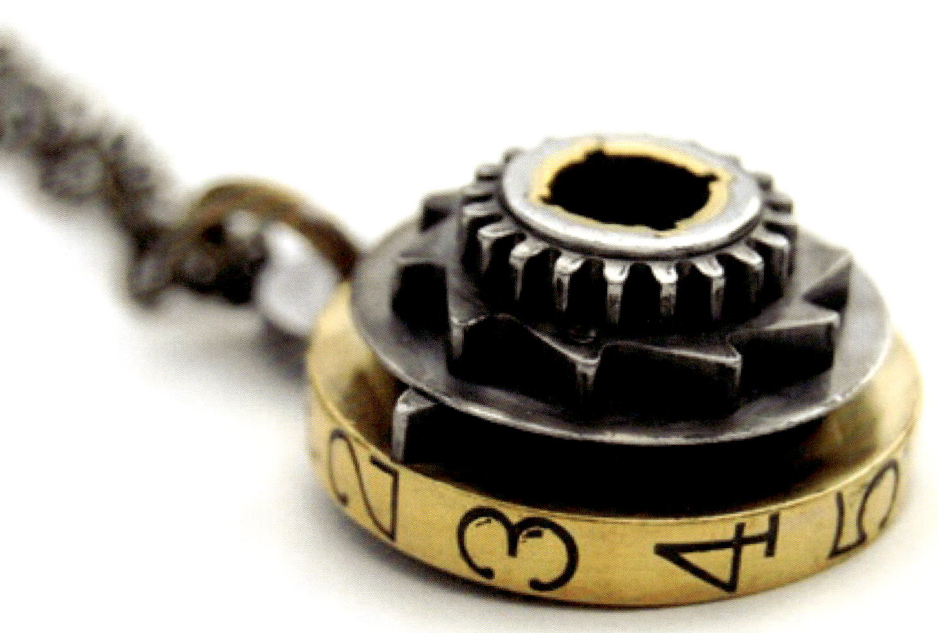

CLAWSON
48017

RACHEL GERVAIS

MIDTOWN
48202

A. WILL YOU DRAW WHAT YOU MAKE?
OR ATTACH A PHOTO?

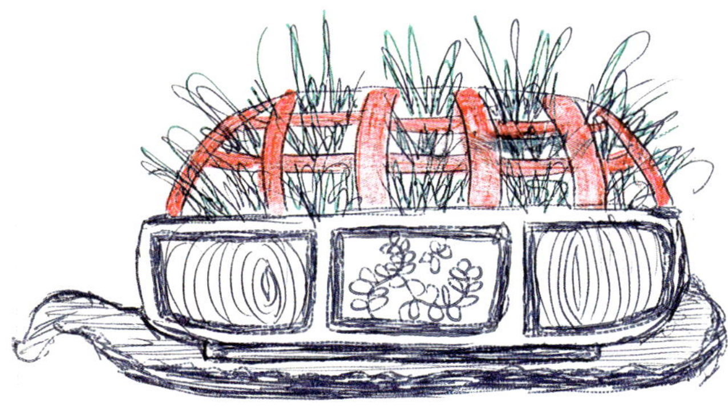

P.S. - Or someone from MOCAD bought this!

B. WHAT DO YOU MAKE, MODIFY, IMPROVE OR REPAIR?
PLEASE DESCRIBE!

I make ceramic artwork.
I draw my inspiration from nature and my surroundings.

C. HOW DID THIS START?

I enjoy making things, and it brings joy to my heart when people buy my things and tell me how much they like them. Its nice to know people are supportive of what I do

LINDSAY JEWELL

B. WHAT DO YOU MAKE, MODIFY, IMPROVE OR REPAIR?
PLEASE DESCRIBE! I IMPROVE GARBAGE.
to make ART B FASHION thru
trash = TRASHION. I Am the
TRASHION PARLOUR: Art installations
& experiences in creativity.
INTERACTIVE

C. HOW DID THIS START?
WASTE is ugly. Art is BEAUTIFUL
TAKING something that is
visually depressing and turning
it into something that is visually
stunning is magic. Detroit needs
a lot more magic.

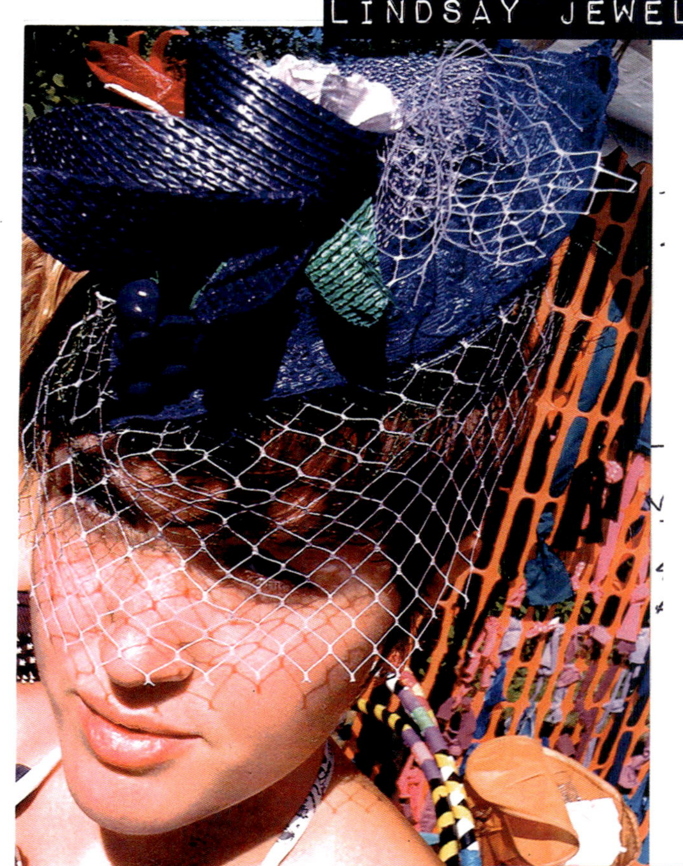

ALL CITY
48208

FRED ELLISON

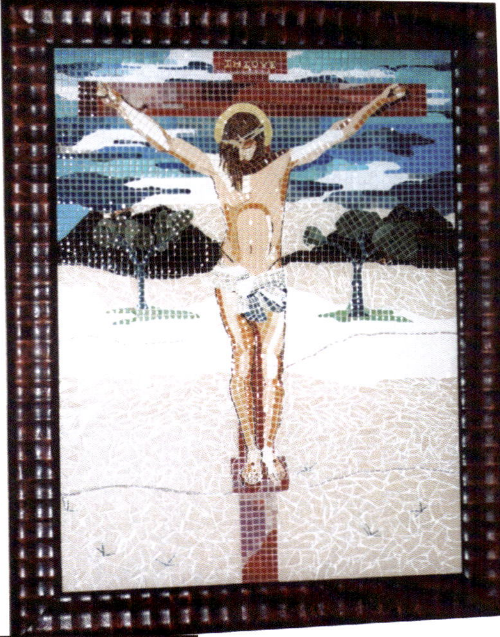

BANGLATOWN

48212

Mosaics
Paintings
Drawings
Sculptures

it just
Started

B. WHAT DO YOU MAKE, MODIFY, IMPROVE OR REPAIR?
PLEASE DESCRIBE!

I BUILD BAMBOO BIKE TRAILERS, WORKING WITH HIGH SCHOOL STUDENTS IN/AT D.C.S. BRIGHTMOOR. WE USE TRADITIONAL JOINERY + WHEELS FROM KID BIKES

C. HOW DID THIS START?

1. LOTS OF PEOPLE USE THEIR BIKES FOR WORK.
2. LET'S MAKE IT SO OUR BIKES REALLY CAN WORK WITH US.

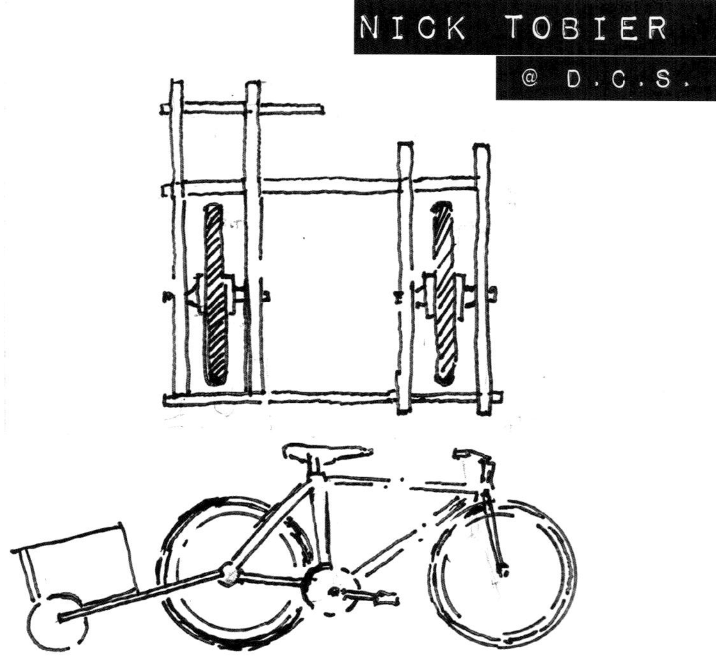

EVELYN PINKARD

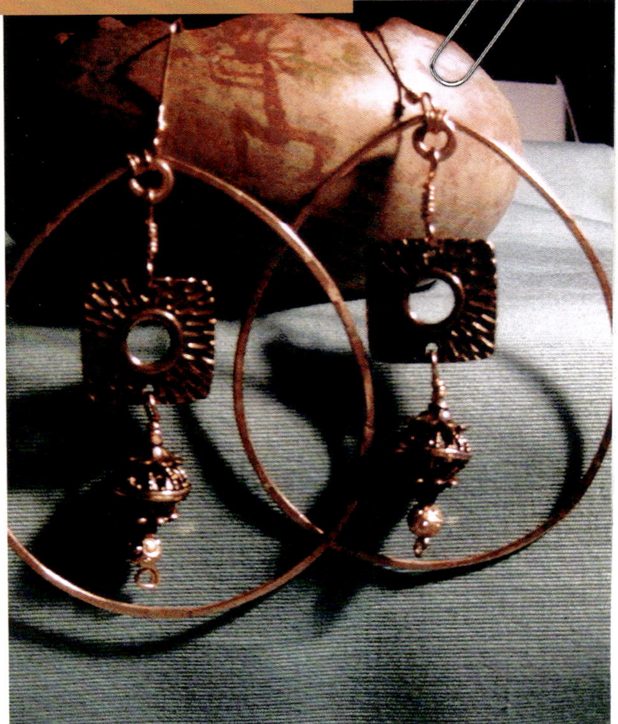

I make, repair, and redesign Jewelry. I make soft Sculpture dolls, wearable art, home and personal accessories. I use Natural materals and repurpose Wherever and ~~Whever~~ whenever I can.

C. HOW DID THIS START?

I started making doll clothes at the age of 5. When my family moved to Detroit in the late 60's I was introduced to the sewing maching and art classes in Jr and High School. Always having an .entreprenureal spirit, being a Single parent, and taking care of elderly parent ~~fac~~ facilitated my working from home.

EAST-SIDE
GRATIOT, VAN DYKE
48214

SUMARAH YAA K. SMITH

B. WHAT DO YOU MAKE, MODIFY, IMPROVE OR REPAIR?
PLEASE DESCRIBE! I make soft-body stuffed dolls with my sister-friend, Evelyn Pinkard. We facilitate doll-making (with focused dialogue) with young girls, their moms, adult women in all phases of life, as a tool/format for identifying strengths, inner beauty and shaping self-perception. It is crazy fun and very rewarding.

C. HOW DID THIS START?
Evelyn & I were instructors with a grass roots entrepreneurial project & enjoyed the collaboration beyond the termination of funding. By meeting weekly in-studio we supported each other and shared skills, which led to desire to share what we love about creativity and its meaningful expression.

NORTHWESTSIDE/
LIVERNOIS, GR. RIVER
48204

A. WILL YOU DRAW WHAT YOU MAKE?
OR ATTACH A PHOTO?

ALAN KANIARZ

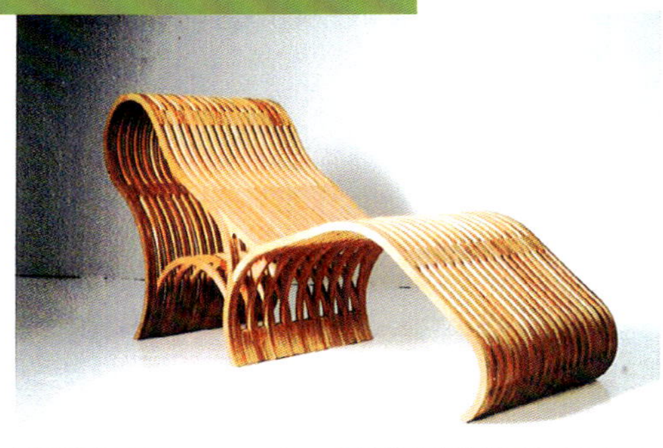

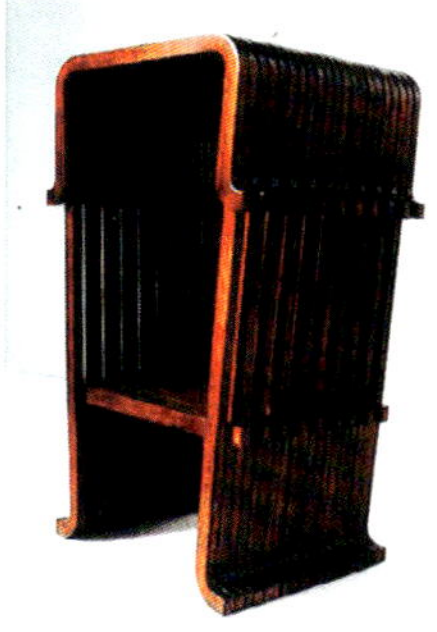

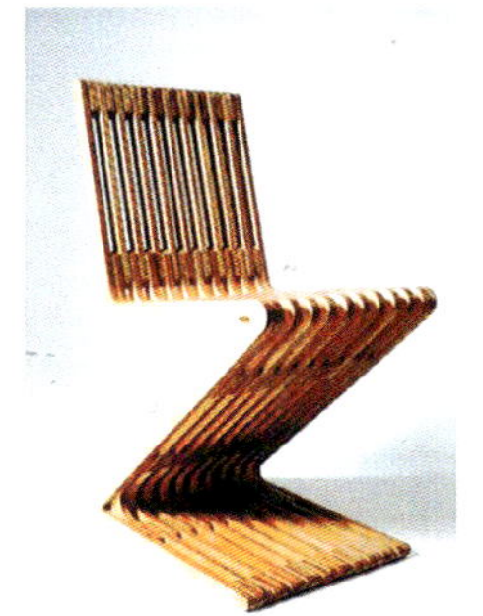

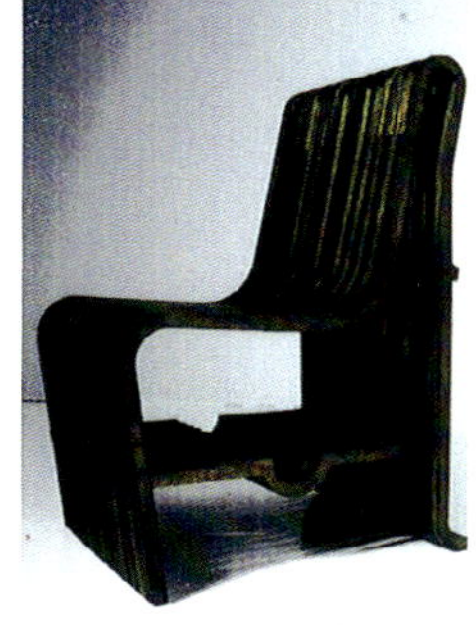

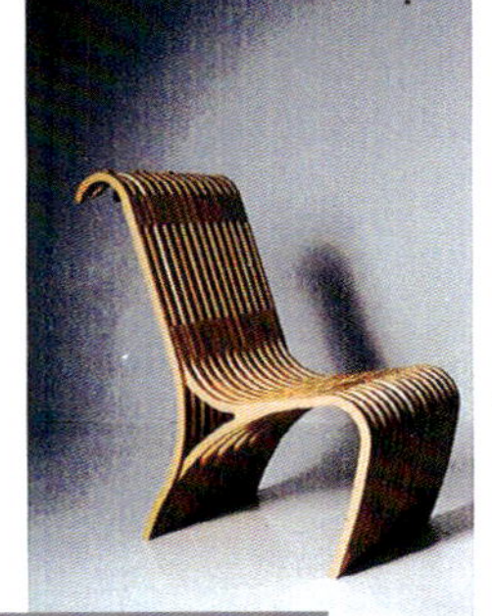

RUSSELL INDUSTRIAL CENTER
48211

B. WHAT DO YOU MAKE, MODIFY, IMPROVE OR REPAIR?
PLEASE DESCRIBE! I'VE DEVELOPED A LINE OF FURNITURE WHICH IS CNC CUT FROM BALTIC BIRCH PLYWOOD. I CAN CUT MOST, BUT NOT ALL OF THESE PIECES FROM A SINGLE 4'X8' SHEET OF PLYWOOD; IN SOME CASES, LESS THAN 1 SHEET.

C. HOW DID THIS START? I WAS WORKING ON SOME PLYWOOD ART PIECES FOR BEN HALL, LIKED THE INTERPLAY BETWEEN THE PLIES; THE VOIDS, THE LIGHT AND DARK AREAS AND; AS A RESULT, SKETCHED MY FIRST CHAIR; THEN MADE IT AND OTHERS

ROBERT BRIAN CRONIN

B. WHAT DO YOU MAKE, MODIFY, IMPROVE OR REPAIR?
PLEASE DESCRIBE!

I make ART objects called paintings. I sense a certain approach or attitude to follow, rather than having a clear, defined strategy. Interested in the organic and the plastic working together in imaginary landscapes.

C. HOW DID THIS START?

Revisited paintings that I was doing in 1997-98.

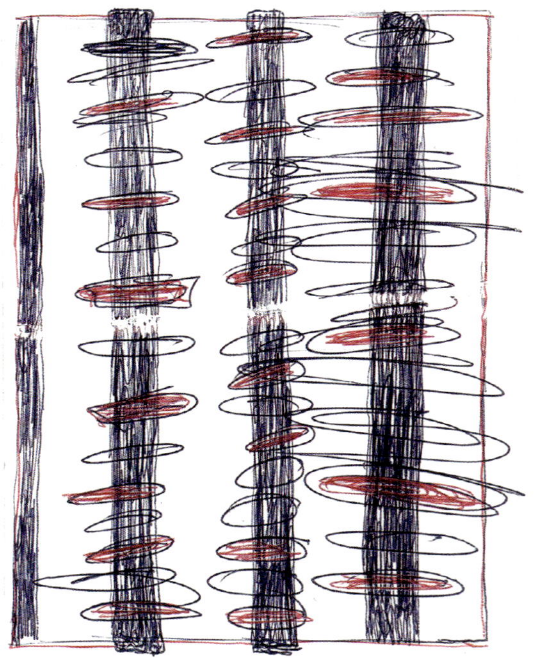

WOODBRIDGE
48208

JUANA MOORE

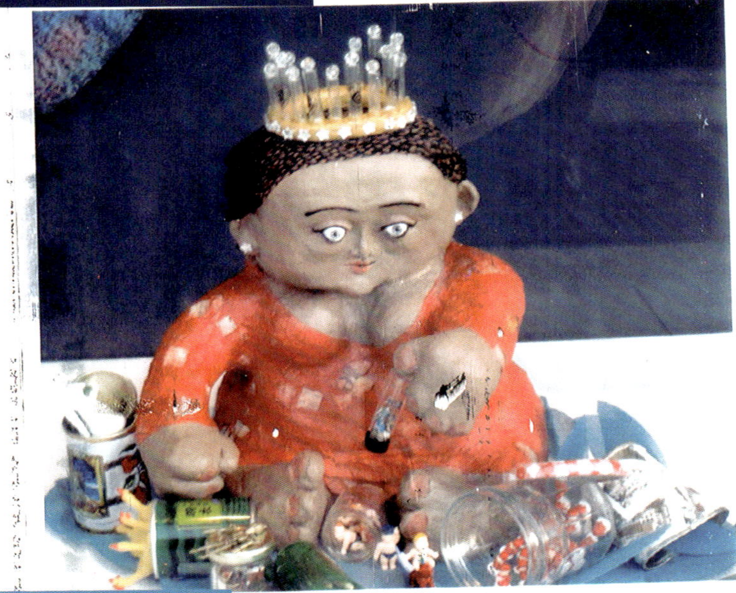

FERNDALE
48220

PHOTO ATTACHED —
"THE QUEEN OF CANS & JARS" AIRDRY CLAY AND
FOUND OBJECTS OVER SCAVANGED FOAM PACKING.

B. WHAT DO YOU MAKE, MODIFY, IMPROVE OR REPAIR?
PLEASE DESCRIBE! I MAKE TOYS AND DOLLS USING
RECYCLED AND FOUND/ALTERED OBJECTS, ALSO
JEWELRY AND PERSONAL PORTABLE SHRINES
AND TRIBUTES. THE PIECE IN THE PHOTO
USES JARS, CANS, & PERFUME VIALS, AS
WELL AS PLASTIC SPACERS AND
BROKEN TOYS

C. HOW DID THIS START? I'VE BEEN DOING PAPER
COLLAGE FOR OVER FORTY YEARS, AND AS
I LEARN TO WORK WITH NEW MATERIALS
IT ENABLES ME TO WORK WITH MORE
ODD, OUTCAST ITEMS AS WELL.

B. WHAT DO YOU MAKE, MODIFY, IMPROVE OR REPAIR? PLEASE DESCRIBE!

I WRITE POEMS, STORIES & STORYBOOKS FOR MY FAMILY. I LIVE IN DOWNTOWN DETROIT. THAT'S ME ON THE LEFT, MY SON TODD, MY DAUGHTER-IN-LAW TAMAKI & GRANDDAUGHTER SIENA.

C. HOW DID THIS START? ALWAYS DID IT FOR FAMILY HOLIDAYS BUT NOW, MORE THAN EVER, BECAUSE OUR FIRST GRANDCHILD, SIENA, WAS BORN 4-24-2011. THE LATEST IS THIS THANKSGIVING BOOK.

JOANNE MCNARY

3-26-2012

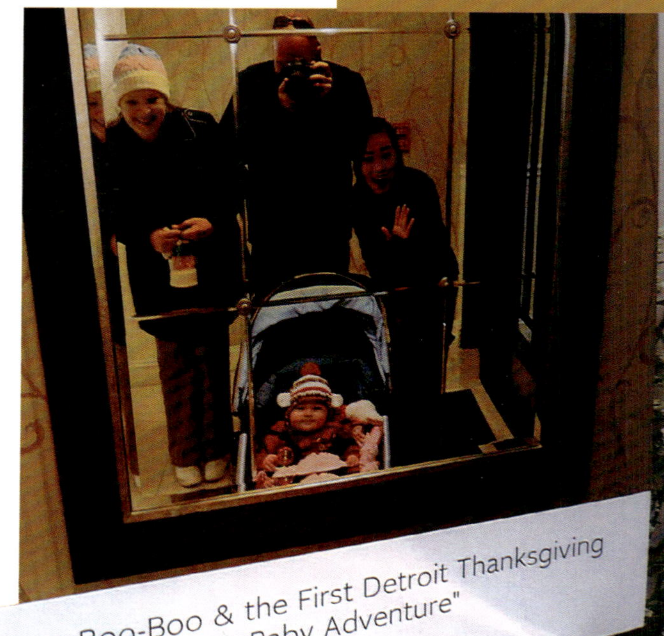

Siena chan Boo-Boo & the First Detroit Thanksgiving "A Detroit Baby Adventure"

DETROIT
48226

A. WILL YOU DRAW WHAT YOU MAKE?
OR ATTACH A PHOTO?

JON BRUMIT

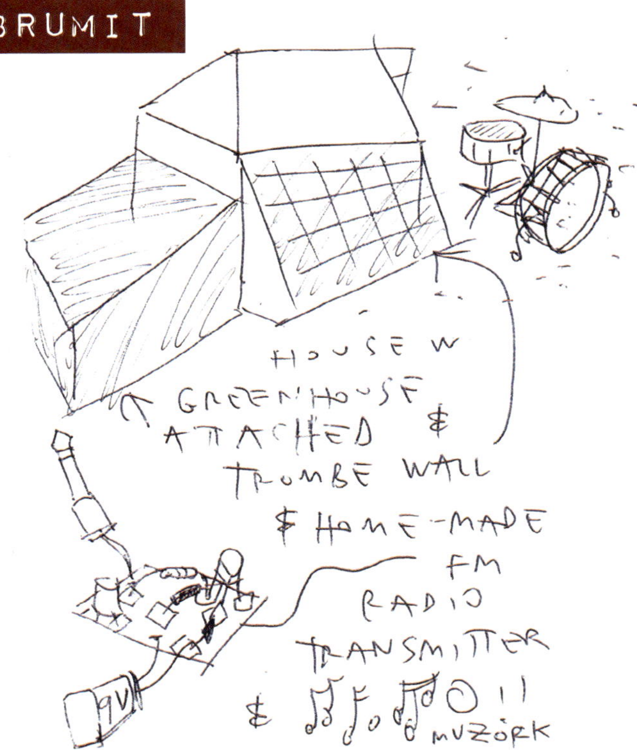

B. WHAT DO YOU MAKE, MODIFY, IMPROVE OR REPAIR?
PLEASE DESCRIBE!

OH & A HUGE-ISH GATE THAT BLOCKS OFF THE ALLEY WHEN I OPEN IT UP... YES!

C. HOW DID THIS START?

BUYING A CRAP HOUSE BUT ALSO ALWAYS TAKING THINGS APART

BANGLATOWN
48212

B. WHAT DO YOU MAKE, MODIFY, IMPROVE OR REPAIR?
PLEASE DESCRIBE! I modify found objects, texts and imagery. These become small sculptures and images with manipulated data. They are part of the project "Grey Zone", which explores Nuclear energy, its problems/ disasters, and the public's reaction.

C. HOW DID THIS START? It started with my long-standing interest in the Chernobyl accident, and its ties to my upbringing. This interest continued when I compared the accident to the social disaster of poverty in Detroit.

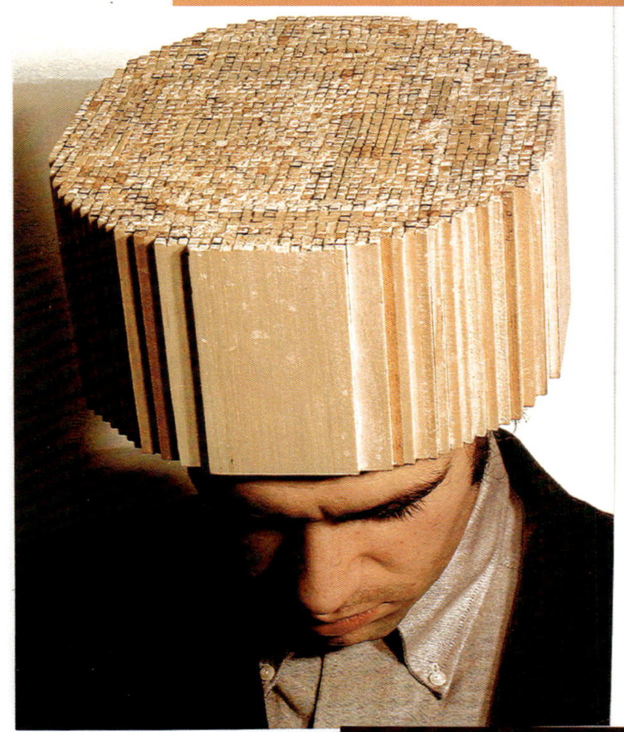

MARAT PARANSKY

OAK PARK
48237

RICHIE CAMPBELL

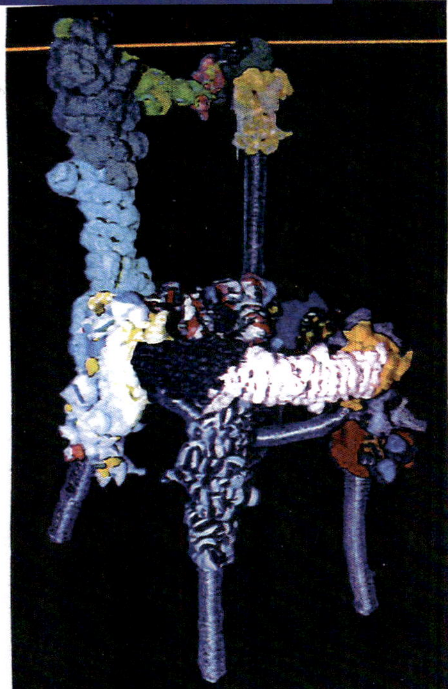

B. WHAT DO YOU MAKE, MODIFY, IMPROVE OR REPAIR?
PLEASE DESCRIBE!

Description: The chair, seat removed, is wrapped with twisted and knotted cloth of many colors and textures and with silver wire.

C. HOW DID THIS START?

A quilter gave me some cloth!

Artist Biography: Richie left the confines of canvas to tackle structural sculpture with non-traditional materials. Her work reflects her love of dance with its twists and turns. Richie has attended Marygrove as well as Arizona State University and Los Angeles Community College. She has exhibited her work extensively in the Detroit area.

ALEX STCHEKINE

What is it?

Functional, sculptural metal work

I create gates, bridges, stair rails, bicycle frames, eyeglasses, tables and many more items . The image that I have submitted is of a zinc clad steel gate with a simple latch mechanism. The latch is inspired by the "volume knob" found on digital devices like iPhones. The gates are installed in Good Hart MI, at the northernmost tip of the state.

How did this start?

My interest in steel bicycle frames has led me on a creative path, learning all sorts of metal fabrication techniques. Studied at WSU, worked as a concept car maker and ultimately opened my own creative studio.

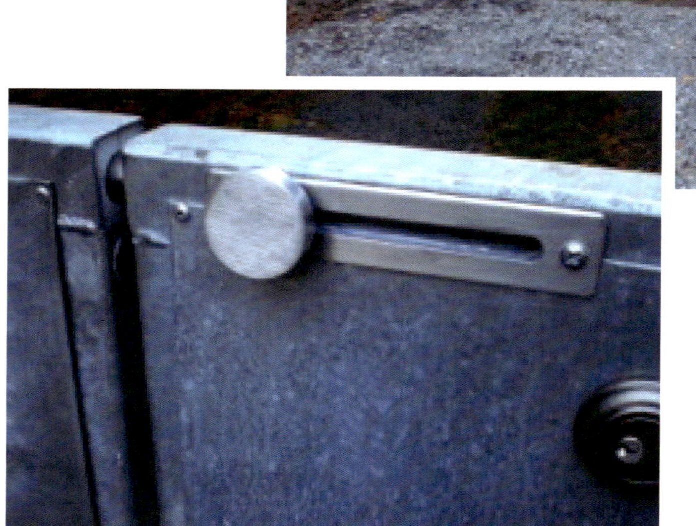

MIDTOWN
48202

MARY BETH CAROLAN

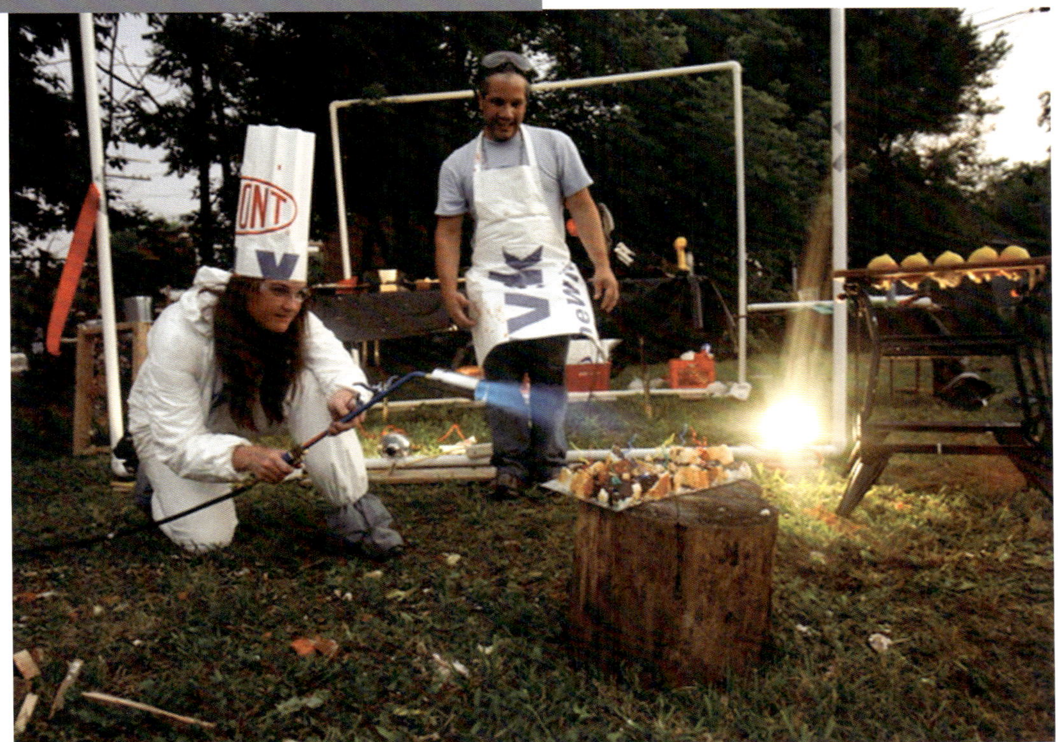

What is it?

Performative Sculpture, Home Renovation, Urban Intervention

Drawing from 'real life' experience in Detroit I make projects that attempt to solve the unsolvable. Cooking With Power Tools, Soft Scrap Show, Flag Parade, Bailout, Drawing Power, Light Interventions, and Redlining all serve to challenge the norm, one party at a time.

How did this start?

I first moved to Detroit in 2001. A friend asked if I would contribute to a fashion show at the Detroit MONA. In a couple months Pas/Cal, Bem, and I had created an interactive extravaganza of a fashion show/live band/party we called Five Walks.

Recommendations?

Kathy Leisen

CANDICE EVERETT

What is it?

I repurpose t-shirts

I take t-shirts and find ways to reuse the material and create something new and useful.

How did this start?

I have always been a jeans and t-shirt girl. I found that even after my favorite t-shirts were past the point of being acceptable to wear in public, I still couldn't let go. I decided to use my creative skills to find another use for the shirts so I didn't have to part with them.

Recommendations?

Ida Hawkins is a local artist and teacher. She's the one that told me about this MOCAD project.

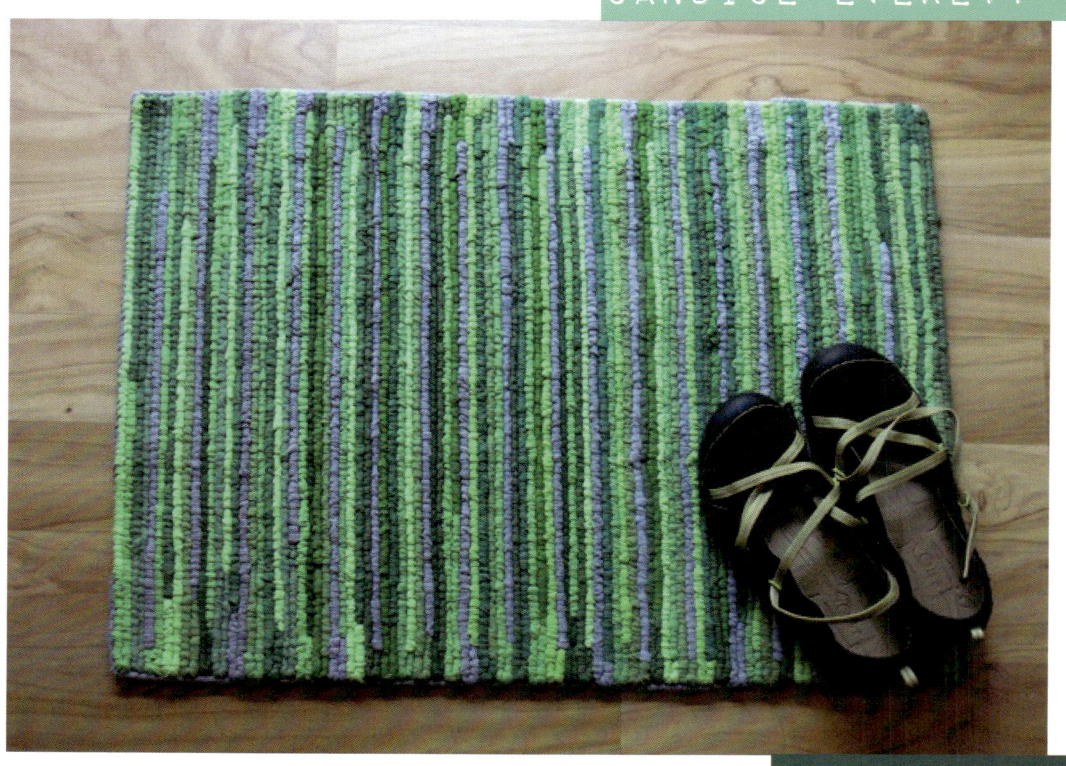

YPSILANTI
48219

LARRY ZDEB

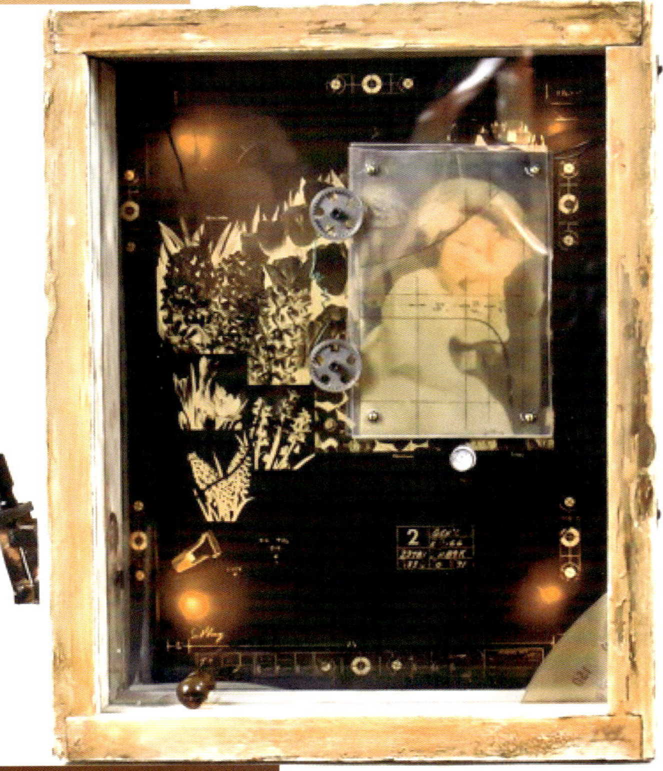

TROY, MICHIGAN
48098

What is it?

I make art objects using found objects. Many of which have battery powered lighting! The art of Larry Zdeb employs the use of found objects and recycled paint. Many constructions are developed by the kind of detritus discovered. He never sketches anything out; he has the parts, the instructions are in his head and he puts them together! The use of "obvious" items is avoided. The items in his work are juxtaposed in such a way that the viewer might ask, "WHAT IS THAT!"

How did this start?

I am a fan of Robert Rauschenberg and Joseph Cornell. I always felt that it is natural for an artist to use found objects, so I do! The mistake I used to make is to add too many found items to a piece of art. My work started getting better when I removed items from earlier works, totally reworking them!

LESS IS MORE in now my theme!

What is it?

The human spirit

Shetroit.com: Women Dreaming Detroit (shetroit rhymes with Detroit) is a digital nonprofit project that helps create an enriching space in which the women of Detroit can weave community. Shetroit's vision is that by bringing women together to support each other in realizing their self-worth and recognizing their strengths, new heights of feminine leadership can emerge.

How did this start?

Launched in December 2011, we're in beta-mode and toddling (we do stay standing longer these days!). Shetroit was conceived with the intention to encourage the shift toward a new paradigm of feminine leadership, partnership and collaboration woven together with intercultural dialogue and action in Detroit. It was birthed by wise women of varying ages who put into practice their heart-centered leadership skills. They believe that the world can be a better place when more women accept their rightful place in leadership, but the kind of leadership that is rooted in the heart and supports respect and honoring of themselves and each other.

Recommendations?

Desiree Cooper
Detroit Snob wear (detroitsnob.com)

Ron Williams
happyfrogdetroit.com

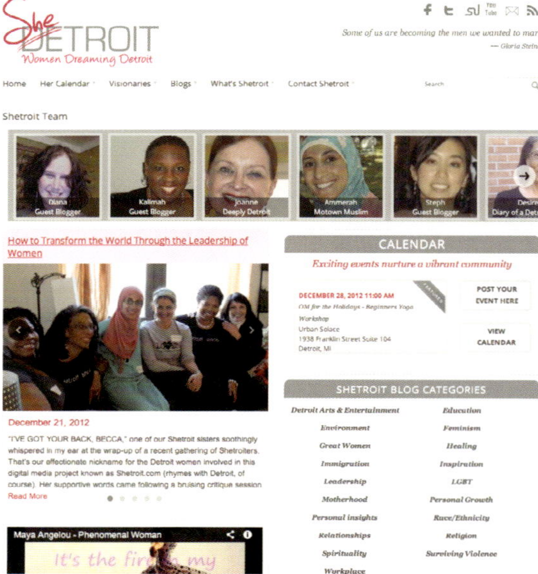

JANICE DEGEN

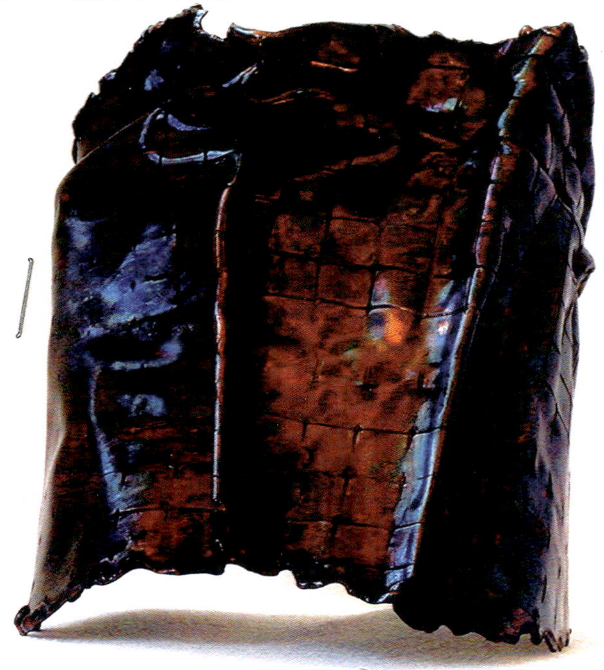

I make & sell organic looking cuffs, belt buckles, rings — all _wearable art!_

with an idea and a little creativity

BLOOMFIELD HILLS
48301

B. WHAT DO YOU MAKE, MODIFY, IMPROVE OR REPAIR?
PLEASE DESCRIBE! _DANCE NOUCE_, a
modern dance company presents
original choreography that is pro-
vocative and fun as well as thought-
ful. Athleticism, innovative concepts
and artistry meld to provide
the audience with the wonder
of themselves and their world.

C. HOW DID THIS START? W I F H A -
When I first tread about - evolved
through a culmination of heart-wrech-
ing events. It started w/ 9/11, then
an earthquake, volcano eruption and
a tsunami. People coped & went
forward. Humankind is the
inspiration.

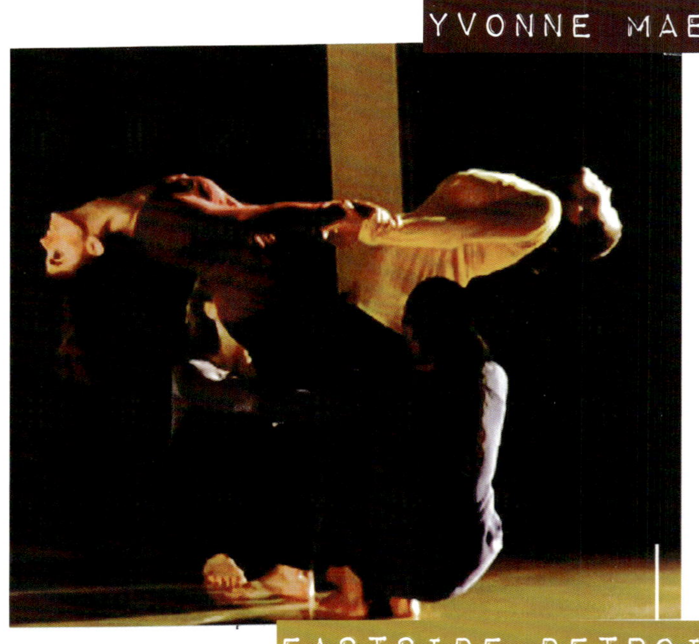

HARRIET BERG

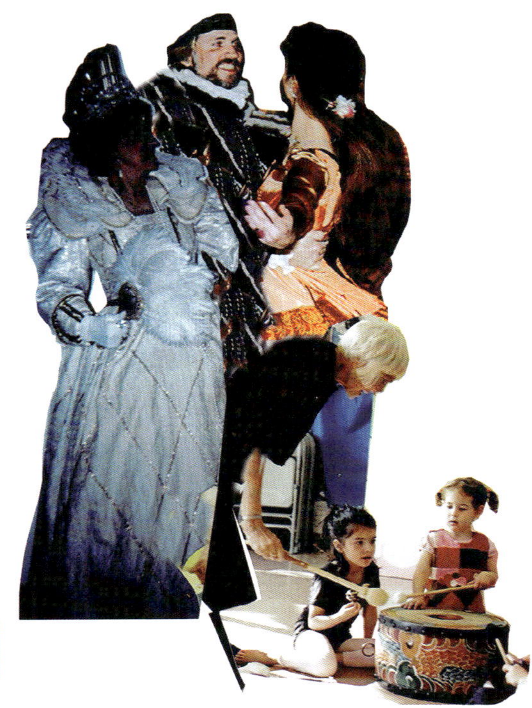

MIDTOWN

48202

B. WHAT DO YOU MAKE, MODIFY, IMPROVE OR REPAIR?
PLEASE DESCRIBE! I Make dances: Ethnic, historical, modern, contemporary, choreographed, improvised, written; for children, teens, adults, senior citizens; for studio, stage, film, video and public spaces.

C. HOW DID THIS START?
When I took modern dance @ WU 60 years ago. Directed Dance wkshops there. Did Wassail Fest 25 yrs @ DIA. Directed & Choreographed @ JCC of M.D. for 50 yrs. Festival Dancers for 40 yrs so. Dance Thru History Co. for 30 years (current) Studied with the greats in New York but did all my work in Detroit.

SHARLA AHMED

**B. WHAT DO YOU MAKE, MODIFY, IMPROVE OR REPAIR?
PLEASE DESCRIBE!** I create modern dog art for local pet resorts, vetrenarians and local animal rescues for their auctions. My specialty skills are taking a pet photo and turning into a creative piece of digital art. I am also the creator of a local dog blog linked with the macomb daily, to help local dog

C. HOW DID THIS START? businesses get attention and updates. my art work has been published in a nation wide magazine 6 times for it's creativity. Please google me for my info lollypupgirl dog blogs

lollypupgirl Pet Art
Creator of modern pet art for local animal rescues to stay in business.
Lollypupgirl Dog Blogs

Creator of lolly pupgirl dog blogs for helping local rescues, adoptions agencies, and animal owners keep updated on latest events and recalls. dog news I hope to make Michigan a great place for dogs and dog business with my art and dog blogs.

BLOOMFIELD HILLS
48302

GABRIELA JIMENEZ

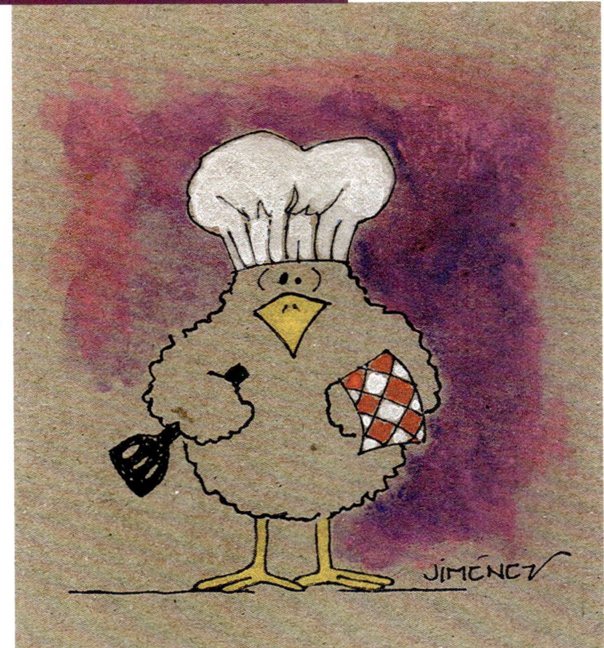

I DRAW CARTOONS ON RECYCLED CARDBOARD (SEE EXAMPLE) I USE WATERCOLOR, INK & PASTEL AND MOSTLY ANIMALS AND CHILDREN IN FUN SITUATIONS.

WHEN I WAS TRYING TO DECORATE MY KITCHEN WITH ORIGINAL PIECES OF ART, I DECIDED TO DRAW WHAT I WANTED.

ROCHESTER HILLS
48307

JON PICKELL

B. WHAT DO YOU MAKE, MODIFY, IMPROVE OR REPAIR?
PLEASE DESCRIBE!

deconstructed and reassembled
polaroid sx-70's

C. HOW DID THIS START?

as a means of exploring the
intersection of image and object

photo attached

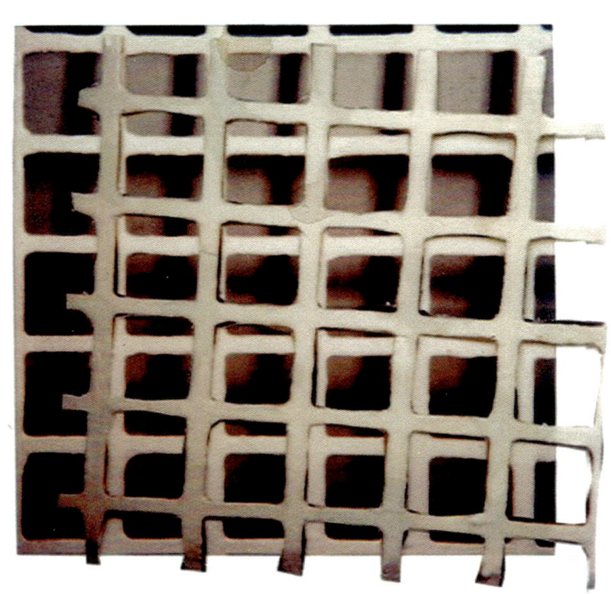

WOODWARD NORTH
48070

NNEKA JACKSON

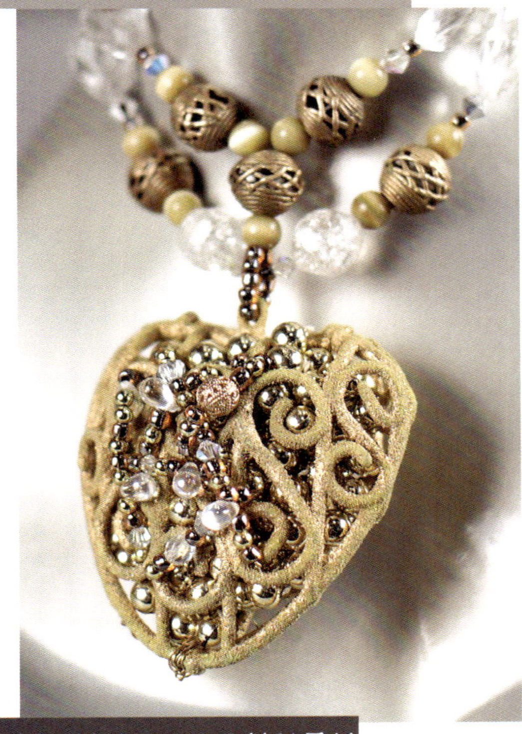

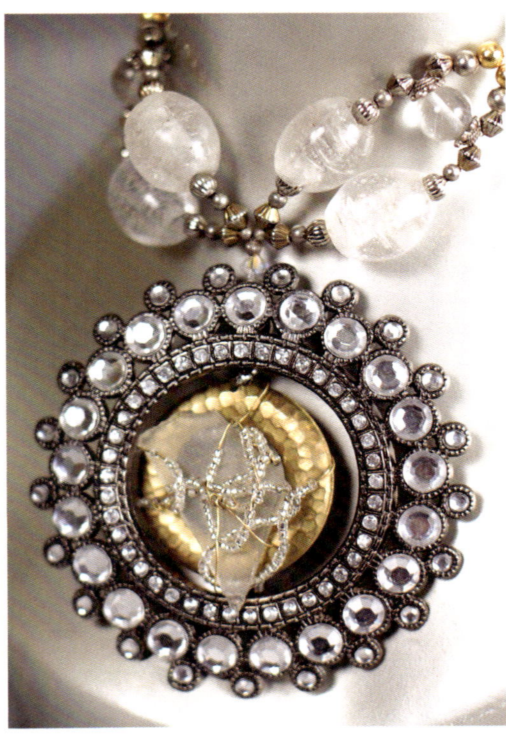

What is it?

Jewelry, wearable masks and wings

I create jewelry, wearable masks and wings. I include beads, feathers and sometimes found objects in my jewelry. I sew the fabric together in the construction of my masks and wings.

How did this start?

I have been creating jewelry and many forms of art since I was a little girl.

Recommendations?

Ralph Taylor creates costumes for Carabana and Mardi Gras

WAYNE COUNTY
48203

What is it?

Mostly glass, but whatever I can get my hands on.

I mostly blow glass, but have experience with a wide range of materials. Clay, metal, sound, wood, paint, pencil, pen, paper, etc.

How did this start?

A bead-making glass that led to a furnace glass class that led to a B.F.A. in Craft.

Recommendations?

Anyone and everyone who creates in this city is worth checking out. Chocolate Cake Design Collective, Michigan Hot Glass, Axiom, Jackline Studios, Ben Warner, Studio Black, TechShop, all great people and places.

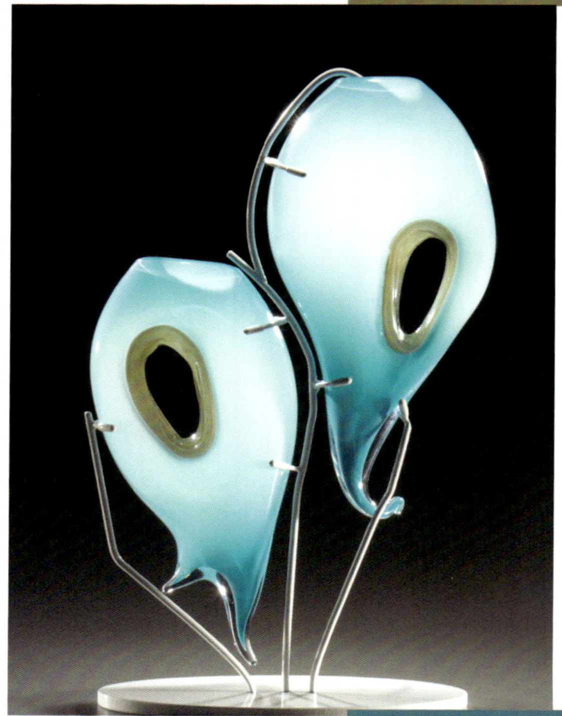

JIMMY FACKERT

CASS CORRIDOR
48201

86

JASON JAY STEVENS

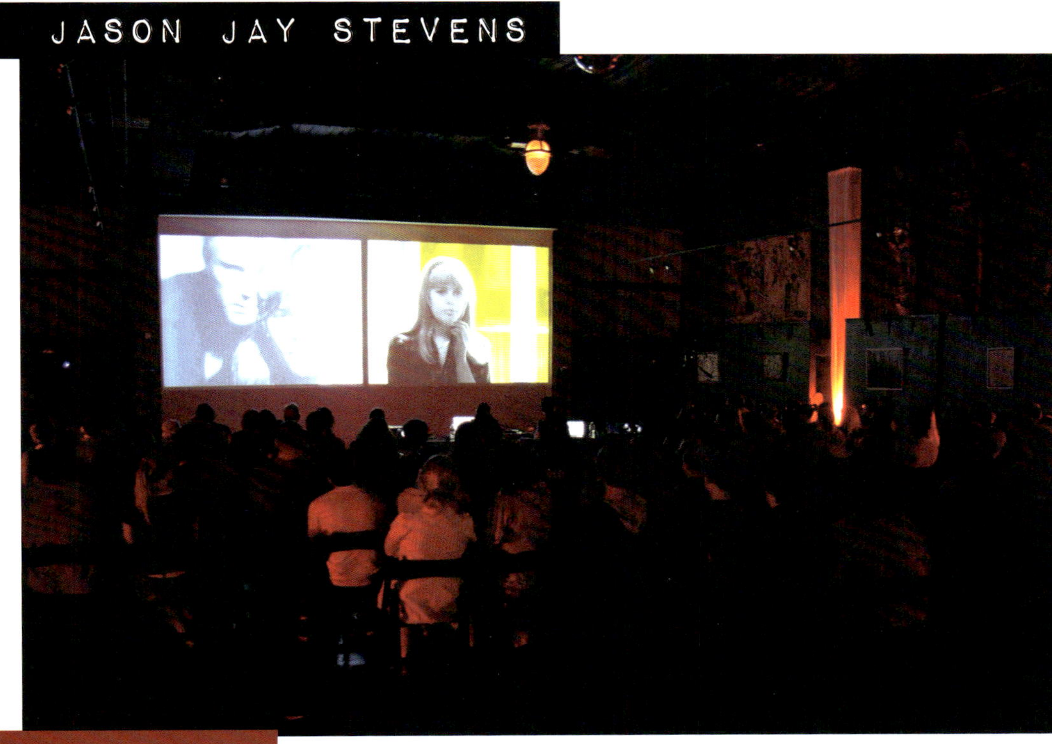

DETROIT
48221

What is it?

I create science–themed interactive public art.

I sculpt experiences that are intuitive to discover and which cultivate wonder via hands-on interactions with enigmatic spectacles of science. Each of my works feature shared-control interfaces to foster an organic sense of community in public spaces through cooperative play.

How did this start?

I was laid off from my job as a high school science teacher and my best friend challenged me to reimagine my ideal job.

potterbelmar.org
flutterwow.com
myspace.com/spokenine
whodoowoowei.blogspot.com
potterbelmar.blogspot.com
myspace.com/potterbelmarlabs

What is it?

I make maple syrup from the sap of local trees and I raise chickens for their eggs.

How did this start?

I'm a farmer, I've done this for a long time.

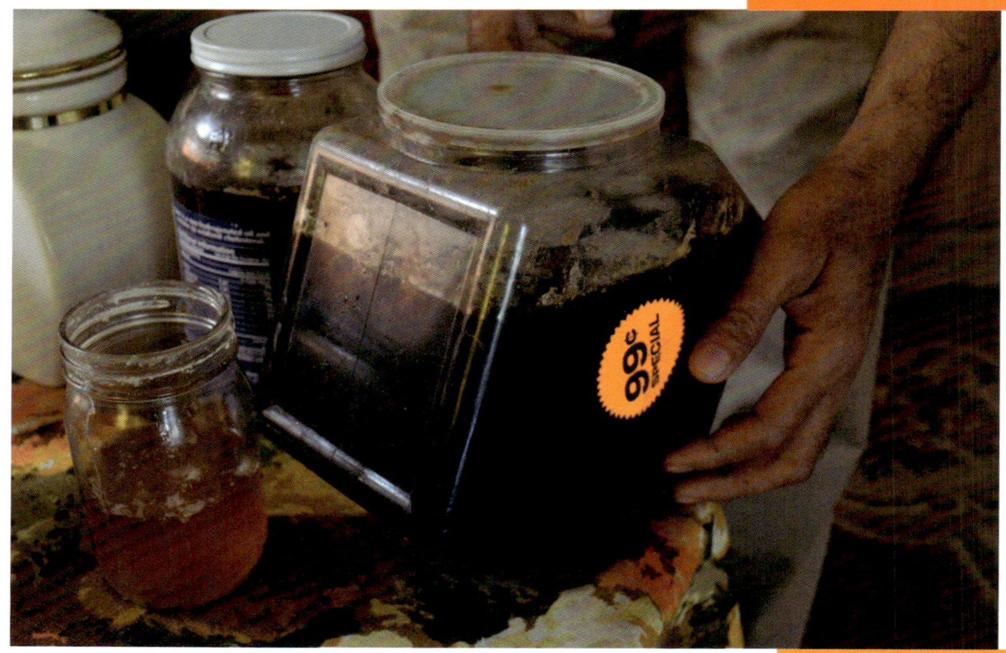

HAMTRAMCK
48212

JOYCE GOTTLIEB

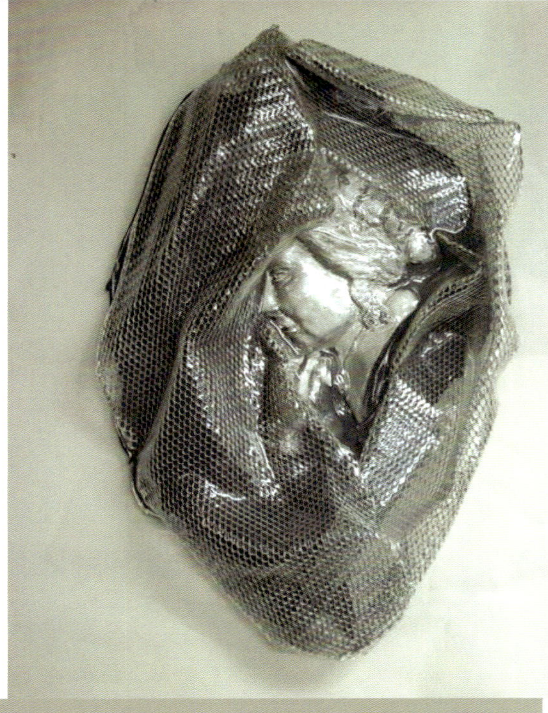

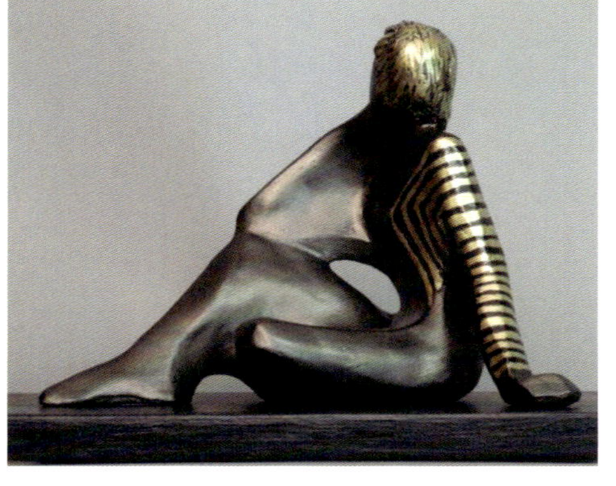

What is it?

I make relief sculptures and 3D sculptures in clay, glass, bronze and polyurethane.

I am a figurative sculptor. The figures and reliefs are fired in clay, or I make molds and cast my work in glass, bronze or polyurethane. My abstract glass pieces are slumped over metal mesh and vary in size from very small to three feet high, many are wall hung.

How did this start?

The figure was always a passion of mine and I chose to pursue forming it when the opportunity occured. Abstract glass came through experimentation with the media.

My Website is:
portfoliosforartists.com/joycegottlieb

WEST BLOOMFIELD, MI
48323

ADWOA MUWZEA

B. WHAT DO YOU MAKE, MODIFY, IMPROVE OR REPAIR?
PLEASE DESCRIBE! I make gift cards and bookmarks using gift wrapping, scraps of paper, ribbon, crayons, watercolor and acrylics. I create small, fine art collages out of card stock, to gift or sell. The idea of small works comes from an interest inanimation as an independent filmmaker.

C. HOW DID THIS START? My penchant for collecting unique, manufactured papers and my desire to freely express myself as an artist drove me to focus on collage. My time constraints cause me to work on small items.

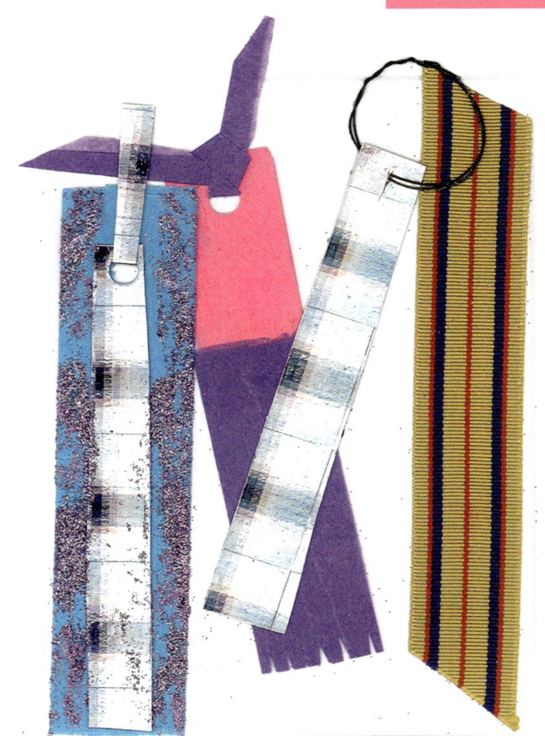

CONANT GARDENS

48234

RICK PRUCKLER

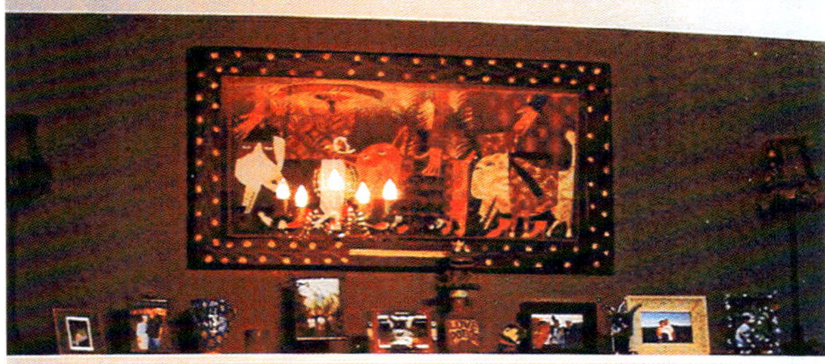

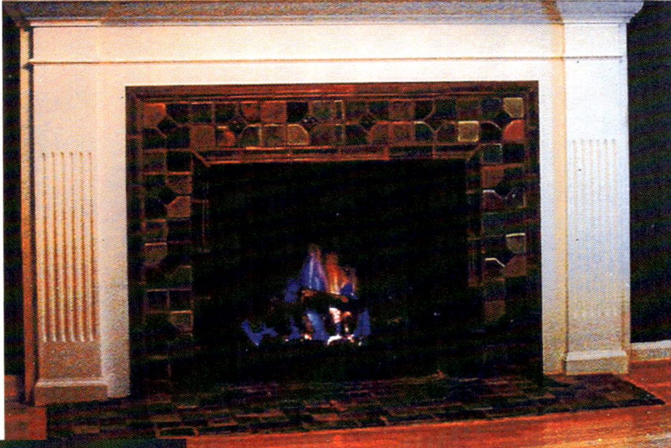

FERNDALE
48220

B. WHAT DO YOU MAKE, MODIFY, IMPROVE OR REPAIR?
PLEASE DESCRIBE!

Murals and Handmade Architectural tile in custom glaze Colors and shapes.

C. HOW DID THIS START?

I began making custom tile in 1987 while working as a designer for Pewabic Pottery in Detroit

B. WHAT DO YOU MAKE, MODIFY, IMPROVE OR REPAIR?
PLEASE DESCRIBE!

BUILT AND SUCCESSFULLY
FLEW FULL SCALE REPLICA
OF LARGEST ROCKET
POLAND FLEW

C. HOW DID THIS START?

END RESULT OF
ROCKETRY HOBBY

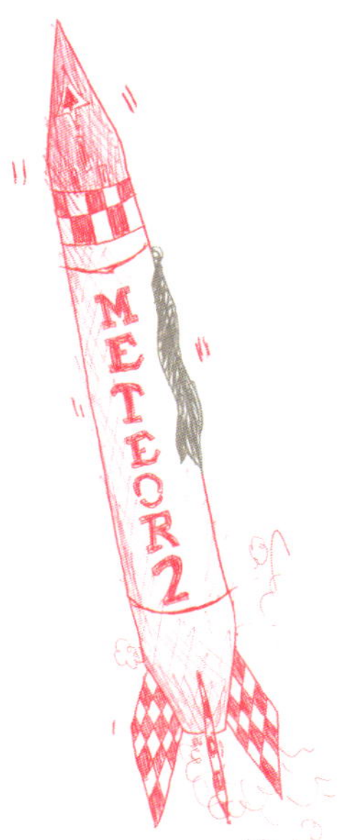

BILL KOZY

INDIAN
VILLAGE
48214

STEVEN KUYPERS

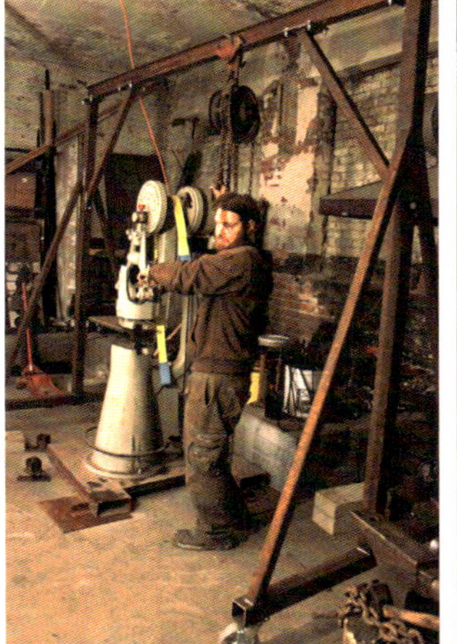

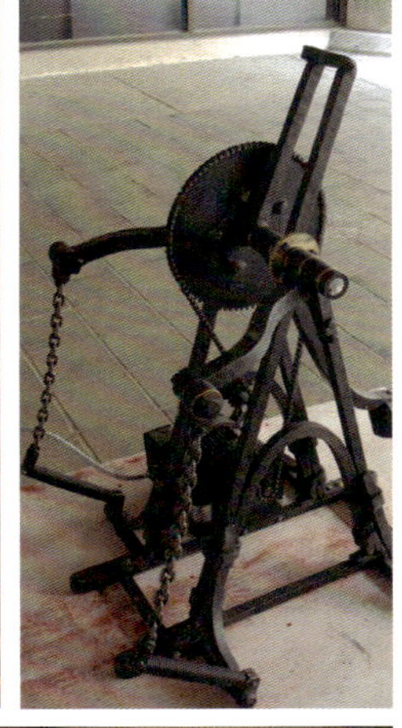

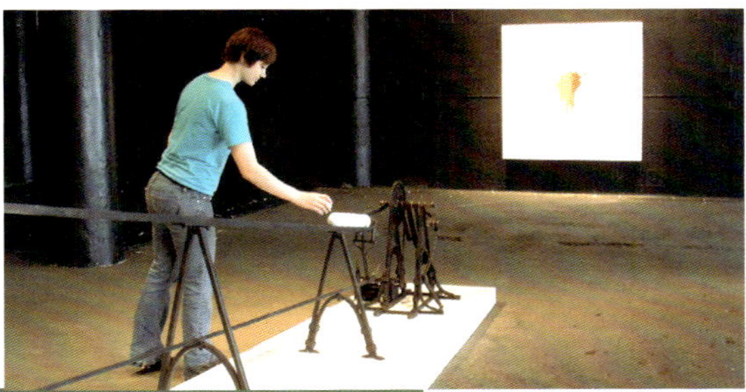

What is it?

I make the mundane spectacular.

One example would be a roto-caster that I made to create hollow castings which I later turned into the basis for a catapult painting machine. Or a paddle boat using a neglected duck boat and MG differential. Currently I'm working on a large scale work that will utilize batteries and solar power to move around a predetermined path. Outside of my art I have Fortress Studios, a live work space that currently hosts ten artists. We have a full metal shop, blacksmith studio, ceramic studio, as well as equipment for foundry and wood work.

How did this start?

I've always been making things, building mini-bikes, tinkering with my old VWs. I later focused my energy after attending the College for Creative Studies. Being an artist justifies my obsession with how things work allowing me to learn while creating. I'm lucky to be surrounded by people that make things.

Recommendations?

The College for Creative Studies, Fortress Studios and TechShop are all great places to meet people that pride themselves on the things they make.

www.sculptureguy.com

ELAINE REED

B. WHAT DO YOU MAKE, MODIFY, IMPROVE OR REPAIR?
PLEASE DESCRIBE!

Robots from wood,
metal and piano parts.

C. HOW DID THIS START?

The love and fear
of robots and pianos
at a very young
age.

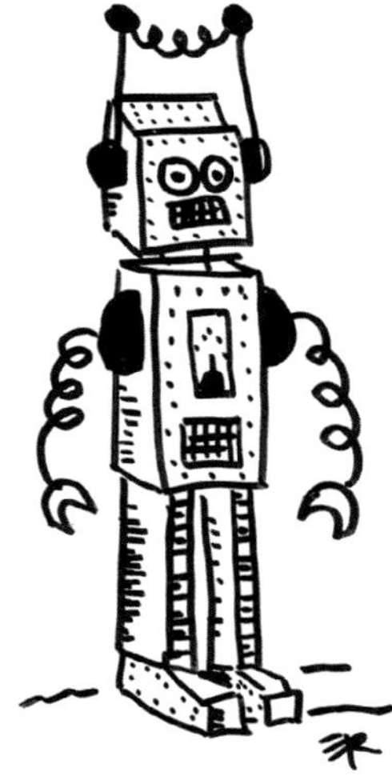

ANN ARBOR
48103

CHRISTOPHER
I.GIRARD (4FR)

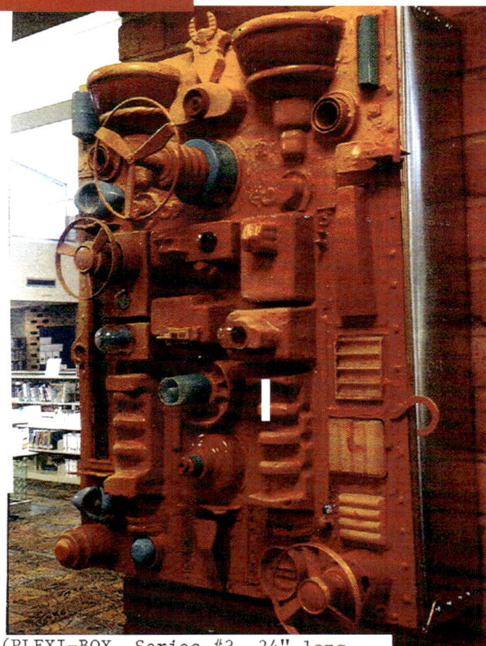

(PLEXI-BOX, Series #3, 24" long,
18 1/2" wide and 10" deep.4FRc2010

title- "SAND: Central Access Point"

Produced object is a type of wall-hanging
piece called a "PLEXI-BOX". Materials are
manufactured plastic(recycled), acrylic paint,
plexiglass, aluminum, steel screws, floures-
cent light.

C. HOW DID THIS START?

A childhood interest in Science Fiction
(movies, books, sounds, etc.).

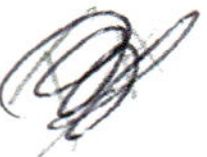

ROYAL OAK/FERNDALE

BERKLEY   48067

95

What is it?

Stovetops, beehives, meringues.

I like to modify existing industrial objects. I like to use focused fire to fabricate, like CNC plasma cutters and laser CAMMs.

How did this start?

Moving between Milwaukee, Oakland and Detroit will leave a girl no other choice but to try to soften the post industrial landscape.

Recommendations?

Many of my colleagues at Cranbrook Academy of Art make beautiful modifications to existing objects.

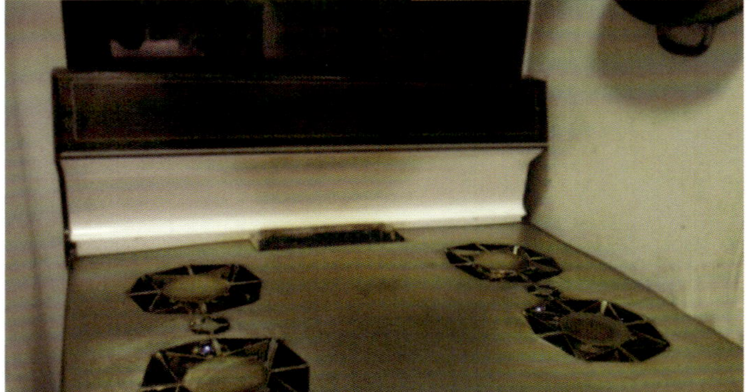

KELLY GUY

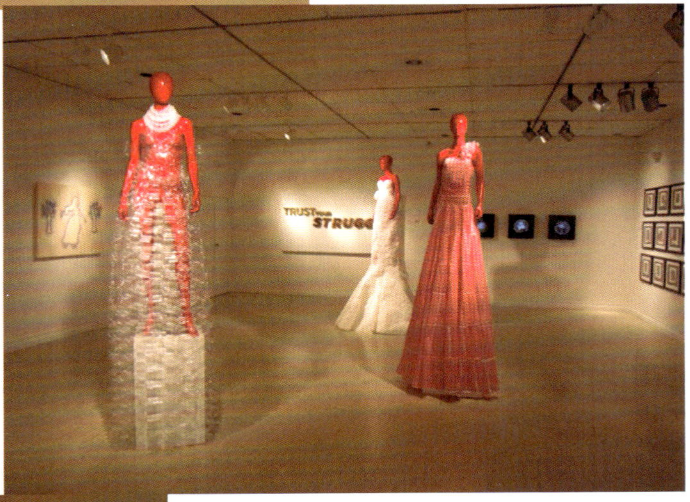
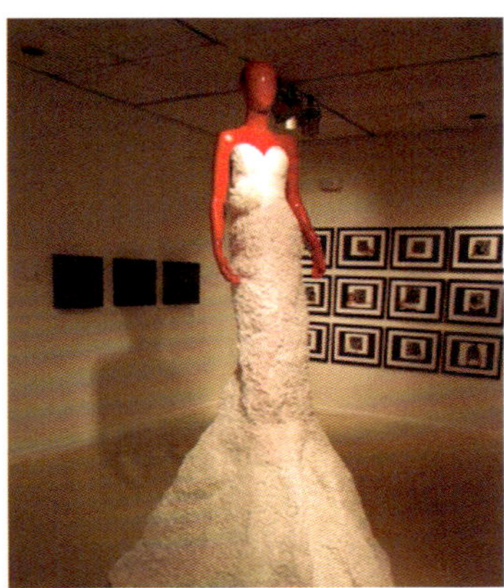

TROY

48085

What is it?

I make fashion sculptures out of recycled and repurposed objects.

I use items like plastic water bottles, target bags, and coffee filters as fabric for my sculptures. I alter each item using a set of techniques I have developed. I deconstruct, experiment and reconstruct these objects to give them a new meaning. It is the transformation of something ugly such as the garbage we throw away into something beautiful and high-cultured.

How did this start?

This body of work began with an assignment to create a wedding dress out of newspaper in high school. It continued into college, where it became a full body of work. It is the focus of my senior thesis.

Recommendations?

Janna Bissett, she makes jewelry from parts of old machines like typewriters and car parts.

97

What is it?

Furniture that makes art and sometimes other furniture

I designed and built a CNC machine out of MDF, roller skate bearings, aluminum and steel.

How did this start?

I designed the machine digitally and then printed paper patterns at Kinkos. Because the design was so successful, I was flooded with requests for the plans. I have since compiled a document set on how I did it and sell it online to people all over the world who wish to build their own CNC machine. I am currently in the process of developing a bent steel and aluminum machine that I have codenamed 'Project Rustbelt'. I am sourcing the parts from the rustbelt region (Indiana, Ohio, Illinois, and Michigan) with most of the fabrication done here in the Detroit area. I am hoping to promote this CNC as an open source kit and a platform for the development of additional functionality such as plasma and laser cutting. I hope to eventually use it as an educational tool for introducing people to digital fabrication and home manufacturing.

The decision to design and build my town CNC machine came out of my frustration with developing ideas in napkin sketches or on the computer and having to abandon them untested and unfulfilled. To me, a CNC machine represented an opportunity to play with forms and test ideas, bringing things to life that would otherwise just live in my sketchbook. I believe that access to technology drives innovation.

Recommendations?

Anyone at Omnicorp Detroit Hackerspace Daniela Hellmich, my partner in Grunblau Design Studio at www.grunblau.com

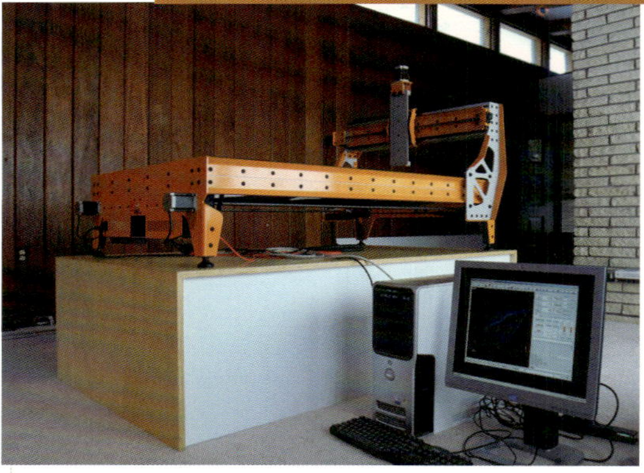

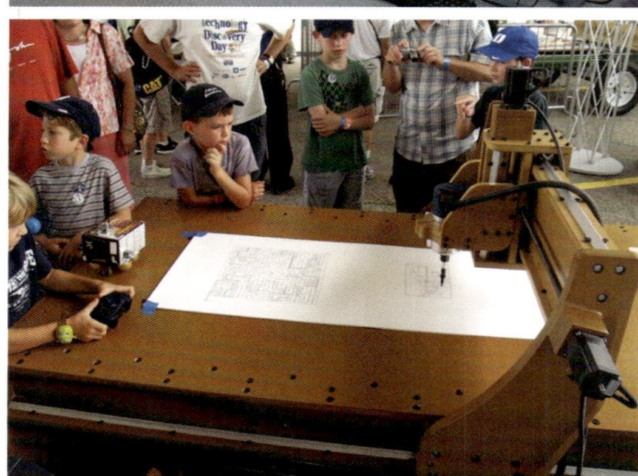

SHERI KASH

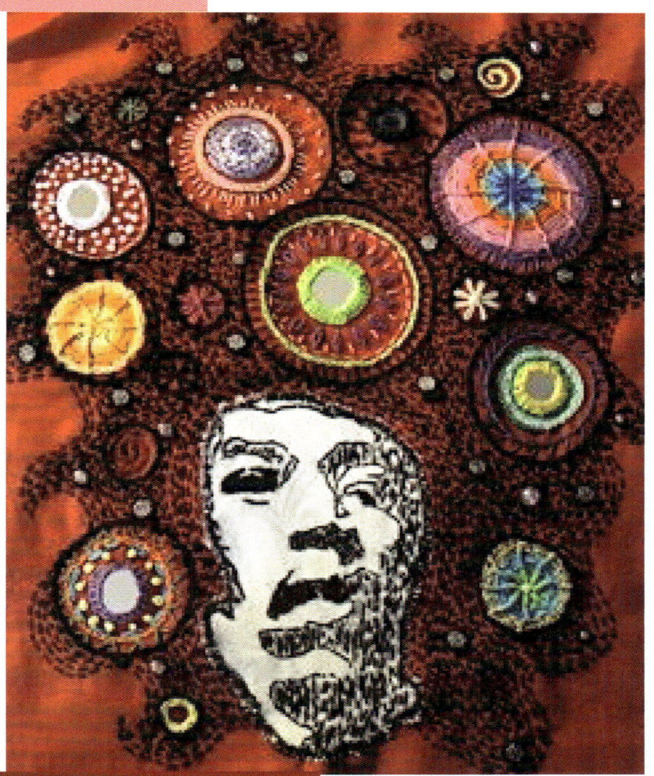

What is it?

Embroidery

Embroider my heros, inspirations, religious iconography, vegetables...things that move me.

How did this start?

My mother bought me tiny embroidery kits with hoops when I was 5.

Recommendations?

Paul Belleau, blown glass

WEST BLOOMFIELD
48322

What is it?

Discards turned adornment, auto glass brooches, Larceny turned Luminary.

I've created a collection of brooches from gleaned auto glass. Comprised of repurposed "Detroit Diamonds," the brooch turns broken glass into a beautiful pendant, looks great mixed in with the band pins on a leather lapel, or alone on the top button of a favorite silk blouse. This piece was designed as a way for one to wear their Detroit pride on their sleeve (or collar) as it represents what we do best here, taking what we're given and spinning it into a new chapter. Of course, these brooches can be enjoyed by any social alchemist who appreciates the hard work of turning dirt into diamonds. Brooch is 1" in circumference, sealed in rock-solid resin, with a small (but sturdy!) pin backing. I've created them in both blue glass, and black privacy glass.

How did this start?

I've always been interested in dichotomies, how one better exists with the other.

Both in my artwork, and my life in Detroit, I've only been interested in dual-part ideas. There is no beauty without danger, there is no luxury without hard work. I wanted to make something that represented a harsher reality of city life and turn it into something beautiful. Something that said, yeah that happens, but so does this.

Recommendations?

So many people in Detroit take the rich landscape we have and spin it into new ideas! I've been particularly impressed with the work of Omnicorp Detroit in Eastern Market. Their workspace is outstanding and it's a great sense of community when you walk in. You can learn the basics of anything there, and then learn how to make basic ideas even better.

ASH NOWAK

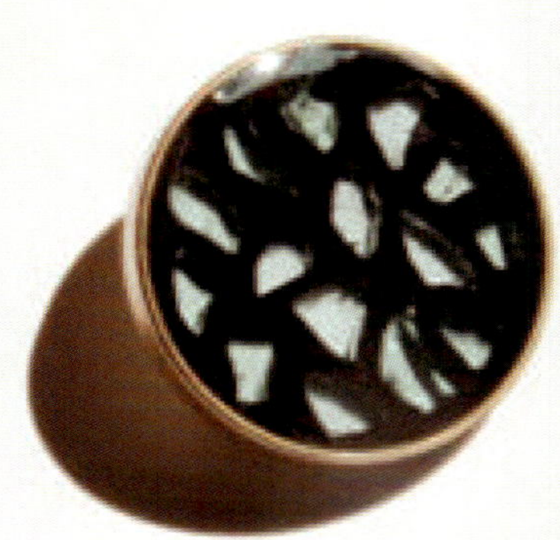

CORKTOWN, DETROIT
48216

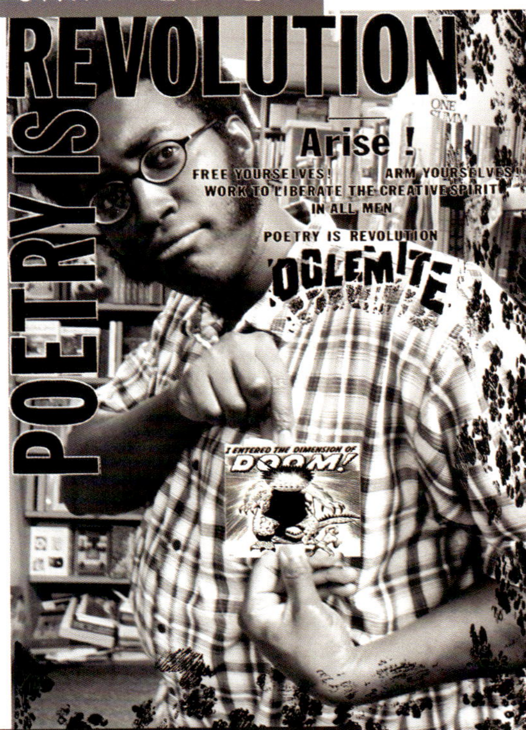

What is it?

Music, records, films, books, zines, photographs, documents, archives

Films: Blood of God, Elmo the Geek, Grow Live Monsters, Banzai Detroit, Ah! Sunflower, others 1970-Destroy All Monsters magazines 1976-1979 Nightcrawlerz #1-9 1979-1989 DAM, Xanadu, Monster Island (see discography, The End is Here, Black Hole Records 1975-2009) Jeffery Silverthorne Photographs (book Gallery A/ Book Beat, 1991) Backyard Monstertube & Pig (Time Stereo cassette & End is Here CD, 1995/1998) This is Our Music by John Sinclair (reprint, poetry book, Book Beat 1999) Music is Revolution (docutext CD 1999) Dream Tiger (Peyotemind w/John Sinclair (End is Here, CD 2001) Children of Mu (Monster Island 12", 2007) Sextet (DAM 12" Printed Matter) Destroy All Monsters Magazine (book, Primary Information 2011) Return of the Repressed (contributor, Picture Box studio, 2011) Hungry for Death (editor, Boston University 2011)

How did this start?

I began making films in high school, then more activity came out of being in art collectives; "Destroy All Monsters" 1973-, "Nightcrawlerz" 1979-, "Monster Island" 1995- and through the Book Beat bookstore beginning in 1982.

Recommendations?

Dennis Tiechman (publisher), John Sinclair (poet), Bill Harris (poet, playwright), Vievee Francis (poet), Susanne Hilberry (gallerist), Nancy Barr (curator, DIA), Nancy Sojka (curator DIA), Naomi Long Madgett (poet, publisher), Mariela Griffor (publisher, poet), Gordon Newton (artist),Matthew MCR Ellison (illustrator/film), Barry Roth (poet, artist), Jimbo Easter (artist), Sean Barry (filmmaker, actor) , Oren Goldenberg (filmmaker) , Maurice Greenia (artist) , Janet Kelman (glass artist), Tom Carey (artist, bookmaker) , Gabby Buckay (artist, silkscreener) , Tracy Gallup (dollmaker, illustrator), Andrew Zago (architect) , Tom Stoye (photographer)…

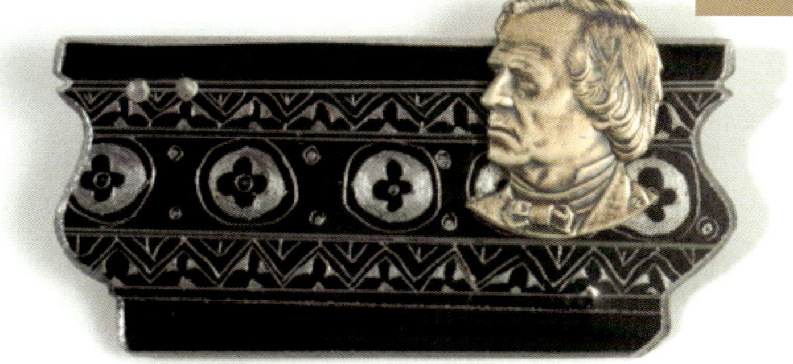

What is it?

Jewelry and functional metal objects

In late 2011 I began work on 'Pattern Anthology,' a series of jewelry objects made from locally sourced recycled materials. The series combines my interests in ethical material sourcing and historical decorative patterning. The patterns are interpretations of architectural and decorative arts ornament from various historical periods, but especially take their influence from Romanesque and Gothic stone and woodwork.

Recommendations?

Bryan Christopher Baker (Stukenborg Press), Henry Crissman, Adam Shirley, James Viste

gabrielcraigmetalsmith.com

How did this start?

This strategy of remixing (reappropriating and interpreting) historical motifs was prevalent in the work of many 19th century designers including my heroes A.W.N. Pugin and H.H. Richardson. The series is made exclusively from recycled material, including a salvaged filing cabinet, recycled silver, discarded silk cord and coins. I have been a metalsmith for about ten years, having recently returned to Detroit where I grew up. I am very interested in using ethically sourced materials and have found that there is an abundance of locally discarded metal that can be used to make my work.

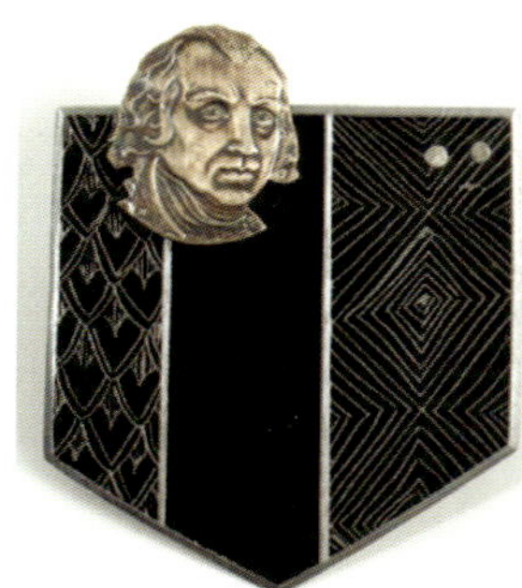

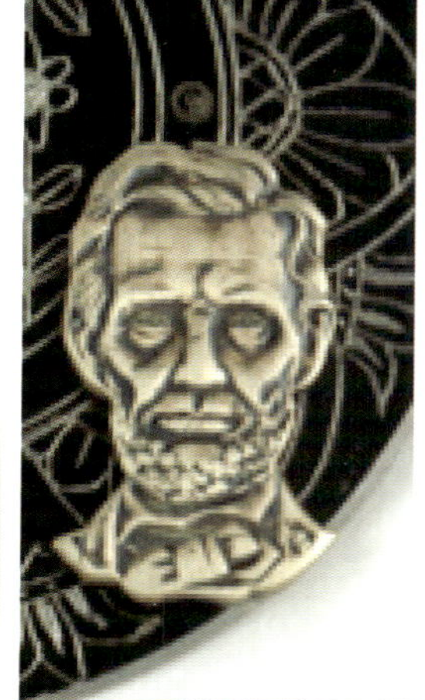

CHRISTOPHER GIDEON

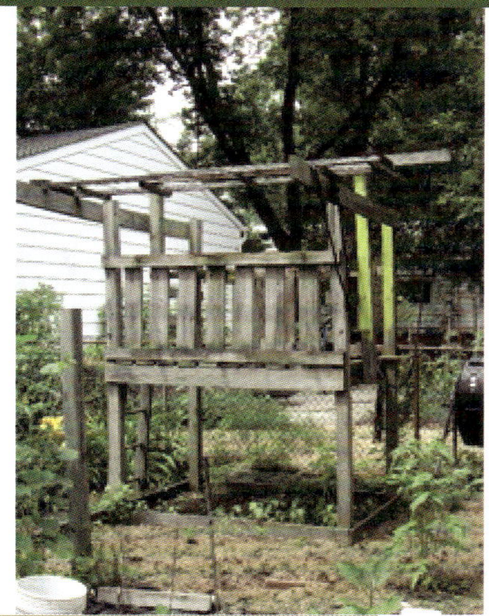
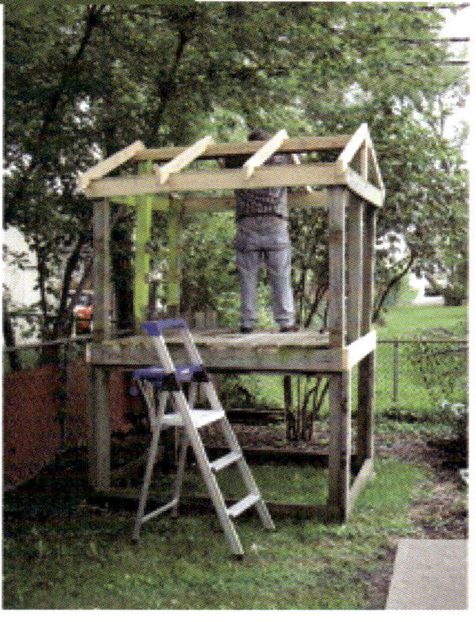
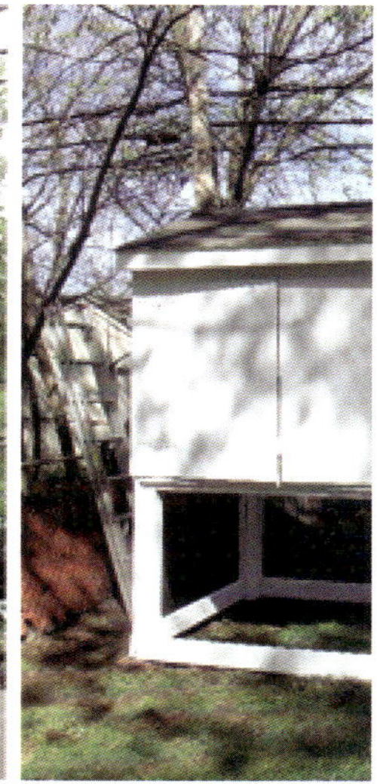

ROYAL OAK
48073

What is it?

Chicken Coops

We took our neighbor's old, unused play structure and are re-purposing it into a chicken coop.

Recommendations?

We were tired of buying eggs shipped from some distant location. There's nothing more local than your backyard.

How did this start?

James Connor - artist and custom flooring specialist.

christophergideon.com

What is it?

Ojibwe Language Books

We use a collaborative format to write and self publish kids' books in the Ojibwe language. All illustrations, stories and translation are by us. The current capitalist structure of society does not mass produce books in languages that are not prevalent in society because it will not draw a profit. So we make them.

Recommendations?

The entire Native American Community has always made things - way before hipsters and hippies.

four-colours.com

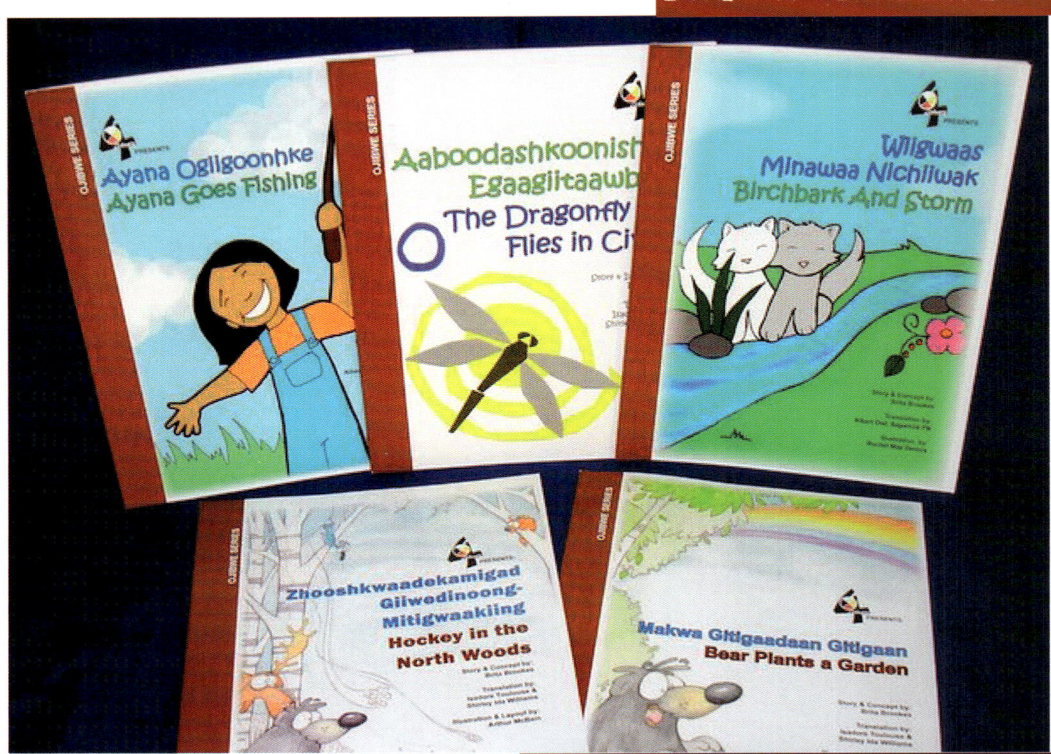

BRITA BROOKES

ALL OF US & CANADA

48220

104

CAREY GUSTAFSON

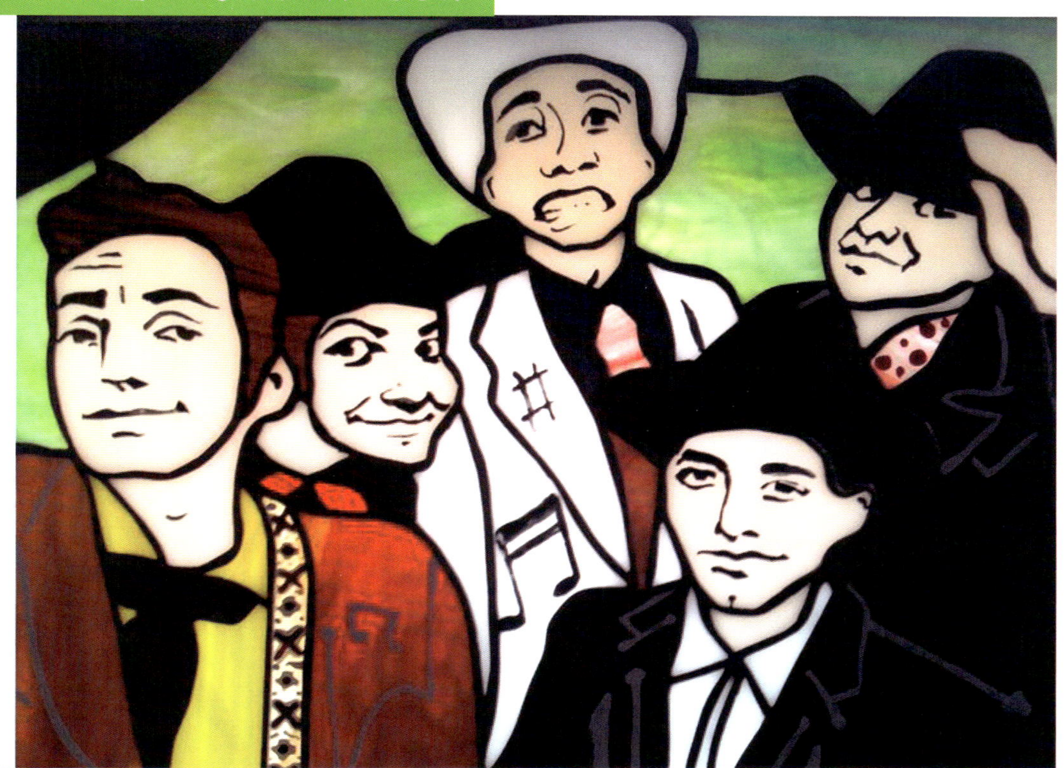

What is it?

Stained Glass

I have a home studio called Glass Action! in which I make stained glass nightlights, ornaments, jewelry and more.

How did this start?

I was laid off in 2005 and decided to work on projects randomly to help supplement my income. It grew from there!

FERNDALE
48220

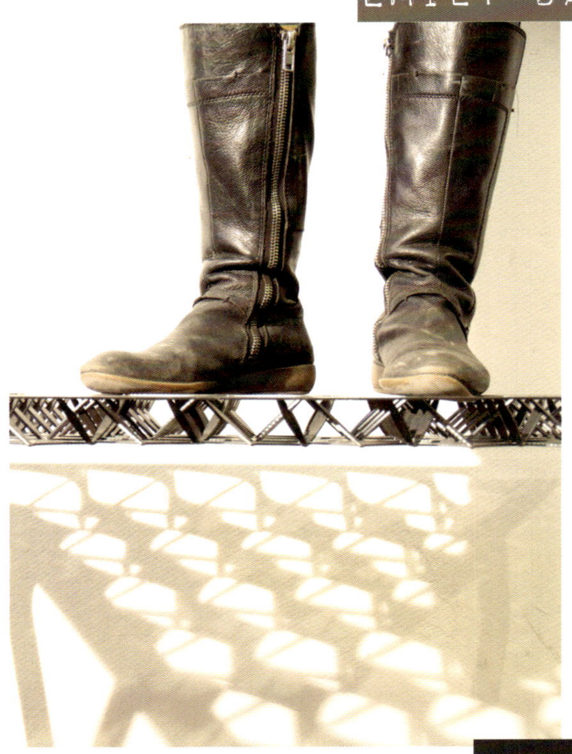

What is it?

Architectural fabrications in steel/glass.

Student at Cranbrook employing CNC plasma cutting to make experimental constructions and structural art.

How did this start?

Systems for expanding/folding the steel have been invented through the use of this minimally explored technology. Access to CNC plasma technology led to a series of tests and trials that resulted in several working systems.

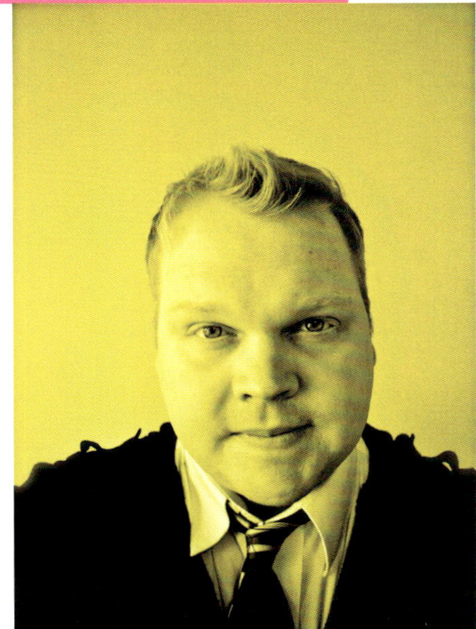

What is it?

Stories, articles, and ideas

As a poet, editor, storyteller and news anchor, I'm always writing up and conjuring ways to best bring people information in a way that's as entertaining as it is informative and appealing across generations.

How did this start?

Making up ghost stories at sleepovers as a youngin'; coming up the various personas to impress girls in cities that weren't my own as a teenager; writing poetry in hopes to impress older people and have them take me seriously in college; writing and editing under various names and in multiple voices for local and national publications.

Recommendations?

Chris Everhart is the best designer I know and he's also one hell of a 3D graphic animator.

What is it?

I create video, animations, and machine art that generate artistic spectacle.

For additional crafty fun, I upcycle sweaters to create blankets, toys, and clothes. I make hybrid, time-based artworks that generate artistic spectacle in order to visualize the unseen: memories, thinking patterns, emotions, compulsions. These have included: narrative intimate installations (video projection and 19th century "cinema machines") that tell little known stories, electronic wearables (women's clothes with custom electronics), mechanical girls legs sculptures, and stop motion animations, as well as animations using motion graphics software. All of my work is grounded in the theatrical and uses the visual language of gestures, behaviors, and role-playing.

By placing simple actions within a constructed environment (nuclear family, school, prison), I use art to demonstrate how small gestures, even the most private and poetic, can become political acts.

How did this start?

I started my creative habits as a chemist, photographer and radio DJ in college. When photography started to feel too "still," I started to build up sequences of them until they became very short films and film loops. When the behavior of these objects and images started to feel too predictable, I began to use simple electronics and a small amount of programming to create more responsive artworks, artworks that could change with the user and context. A few years ago, at Maker Faire Detroit, I saw a woman and her family selling beautiful blankets made from upcycled sweaters. They made a strong impression on me, and I recently invested the time and energy into teaching myself basic sewing and felting methods.

Recommendations?

Michael Flynn, Matt Shlian, Osman Khan, Matt Kenyon, Emilia Javanica, Thea Eck, Anne Mondro, Adrianne Finelli.

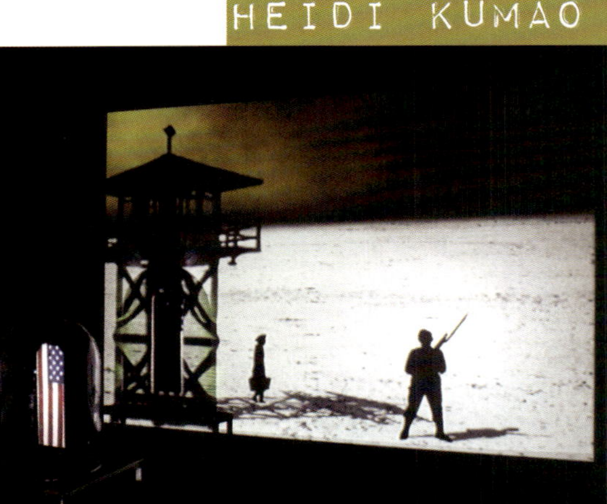

JESSICA FRELINGHUYSEN

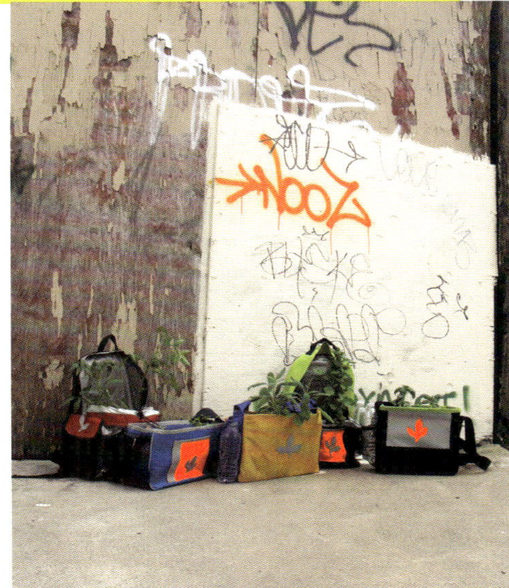

HAMTRAMCK
48212

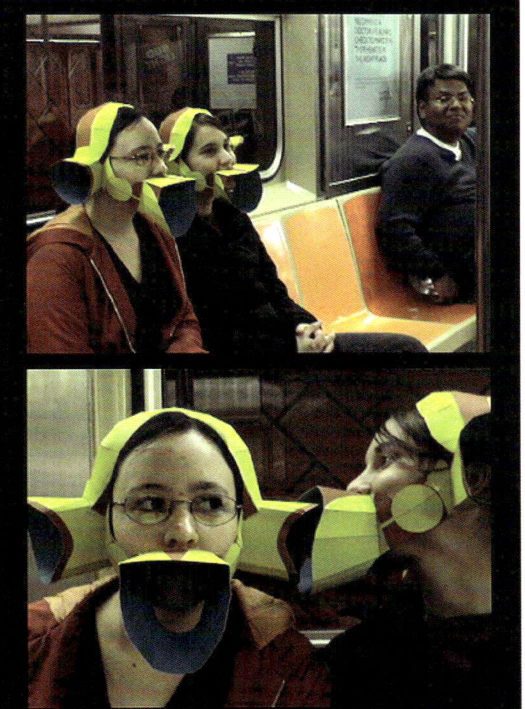

What is it?

Objects

I fix awkward social situations through art objects.

How did this start?

As a way of life.

What is it?

Sculpture, Glass Art, Video & Performance, Lighting & Installation

Detroit Glass House is a Detroit based business run by Andrea Oleniczak and Taylor Kurrle. Detroit Glass House focuses on developing a contemporary vocabulary of glass, merging historical techniques of the medium with modern production processes. Bringing what was old, current with industrial applications.

How did this start?

After spending years of intense study in glass learning in the traditional craft approach of apprenticeship, we now are hands on learning 3D modeling & printing, CNC machines, water jet cutting and many other industrial machines and processes. Detroit Glass House recently teamed up with Locke Wetters Inc. Interiors to install lighting for Catalyst Restaurant in Cambridge, MA. This project included 5 chandeliers and pendant lighting.

Andrea Oleniczak creates sculpture, performance, video, installation and design. Andrea has taught at Ox-Bow School of Art and has exhibited at the Grand Rapids Art Museum, Heller Gallery New York, & Sydney College of Art and Design Australia. She also spent a brief time hiding in the mountains of North Carolina studying glassblowing under Venetian glassblowing artist Kenny Peiper.

Recommendations?

Taylor Kurrle creates sculpture, installation & design. Taylor has worked at Ox-Bow School of Art as a glass technician and ran the only glass studio in Jaco, Costa Rica. Andrea and Taylor met at College for Creative Studies in the glass department, a shared interest and passion grew into Detroit Glass House. Both Andrea & Taylor work at TechShop Detroit, a local DIY workshop. There are hundreds of artists, makers, tinkers, designers, scientists, experimental machinists and many others around us daily.

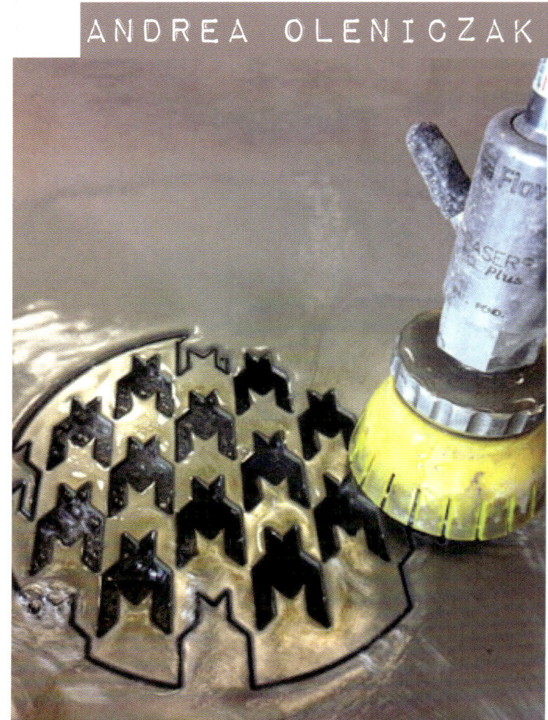

DAVID COLE

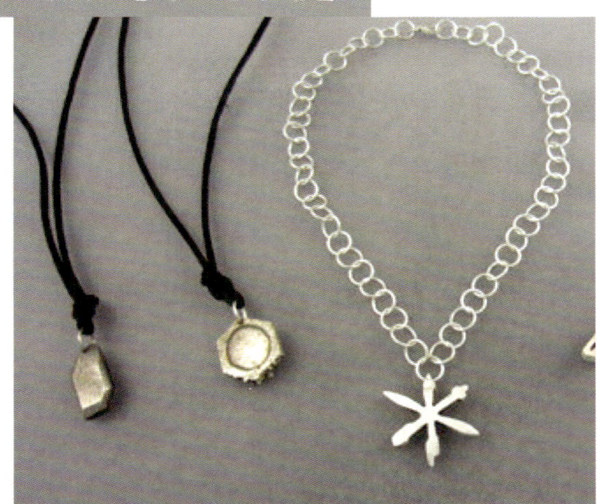

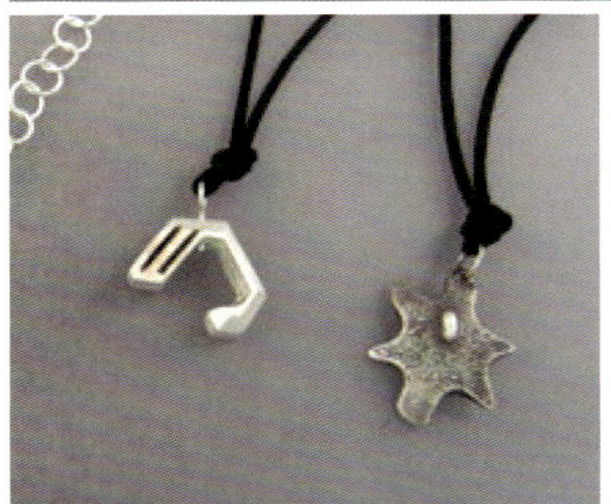

What is it?

Jewelry, sculpture, and other metal objects.

Acid Winter is currently both a sculpture and a jewelry series. The project is composed of forms taken from electron microscope images of snow crystal samples that have been naturally eroded by wind or sun and then remelted in snow pack. The forms were cast in shibuichi (an alloy of silver and copper) and then acid etched to mimic the unnatural erosive effects of acid precipitation on outdoor public artworks and architecture.

How did this start?

Acid Winter was realized though techniques common in the mass production of jewelry and other small scale products such as toys and consumer products. Despite this "mass" production, each individual piece is unique and retains the qualities of a handmade object. As a sculpture, it was part of the inaugural Wayne State sculpture installation competition in 2011. As jewelry, a friend of mine mentioned that it would be cool to have one of the forms as a pendant, which proved to be a great way for people to relate to the sculpture.

Recommendations?

Rose Rivard, jewelry

Heather Zayne-Mitchell, charms

What is it?

Fabricating welder

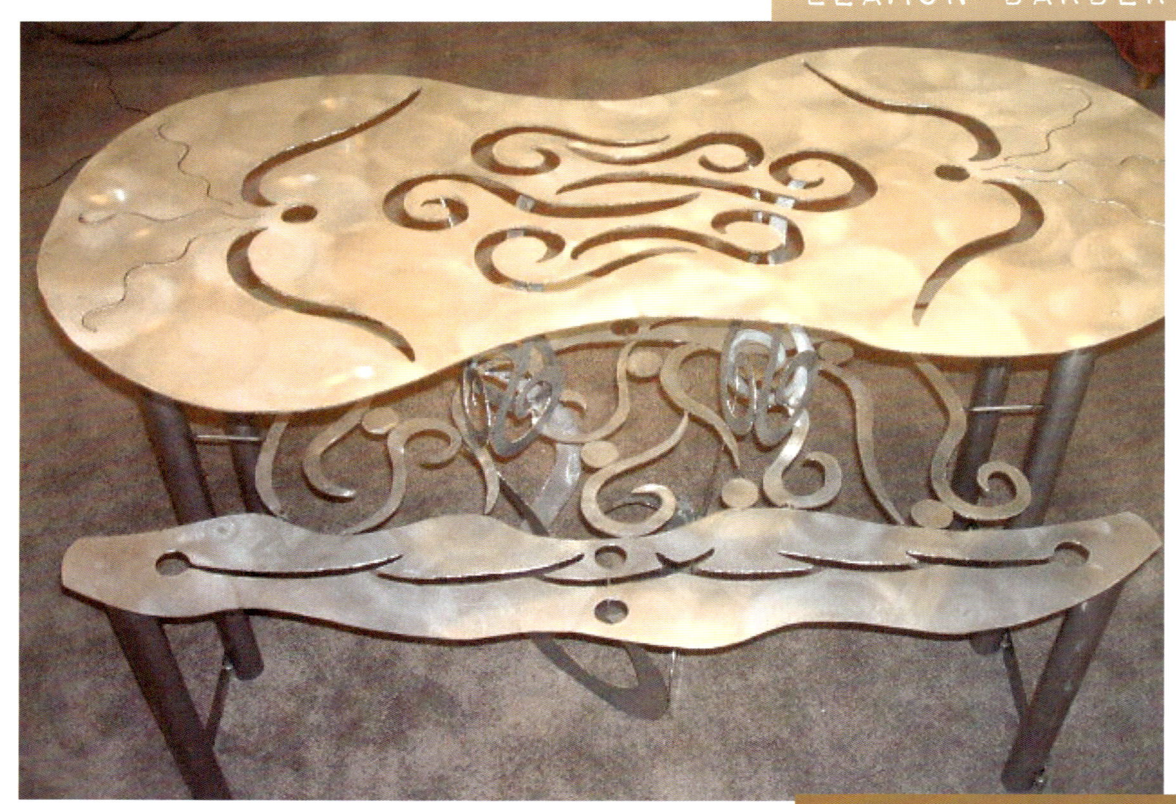

JOCELYN RAINEY

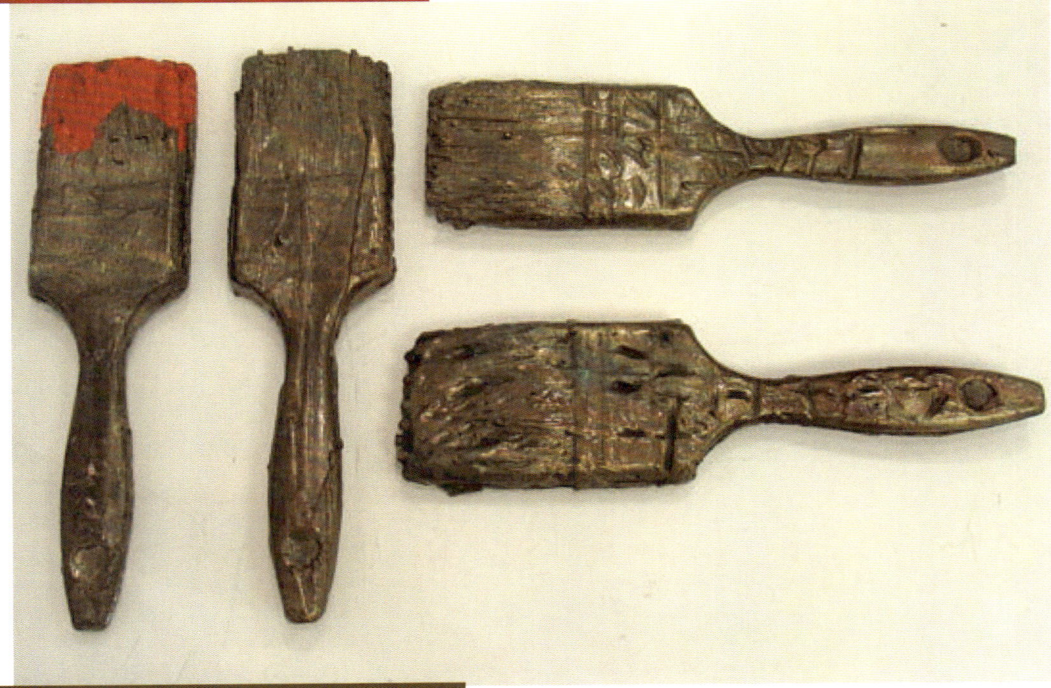

What is it?

Paintbrushes cast in bronze

I select an assortment of brushes and cast them in bronze metal and further embellish the patina with paint on the brush tips and handles.

How did this start?

It started by me wanting to preserve the objects after usage, transforming my studio tools into sculpture.

EASTSIDE DETROIT
48224

BARRY ROTH

What is it?

I make pictures and small constructions

The constructions are made out of common materials I find or have around the house. I use wood, plastic, cardboard, tape, wire, glue. They are table top size. Some of them I photograph or scan and make 11"x14" exhibition quality prints.

How did this start?

I started this body of work in 1975 when I was working on my MFA in Photography at Cranbrook Academy of Art. It started with exploring the idea of constructing the subject matter of a photograph and experimenting with how the look of things are transformed in the final print.

Recommendations?

Cary Loren

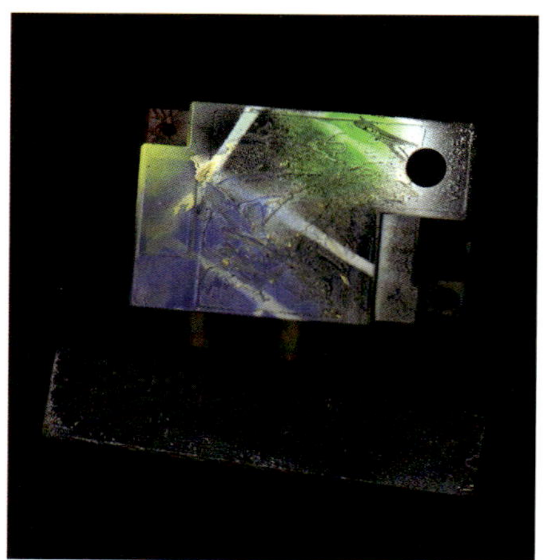

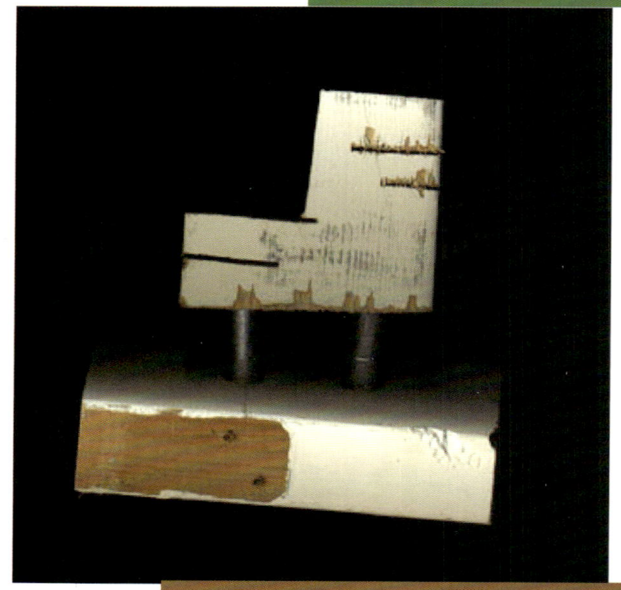

HUNTINGTON WOODS

48070

LISA L. GRIX

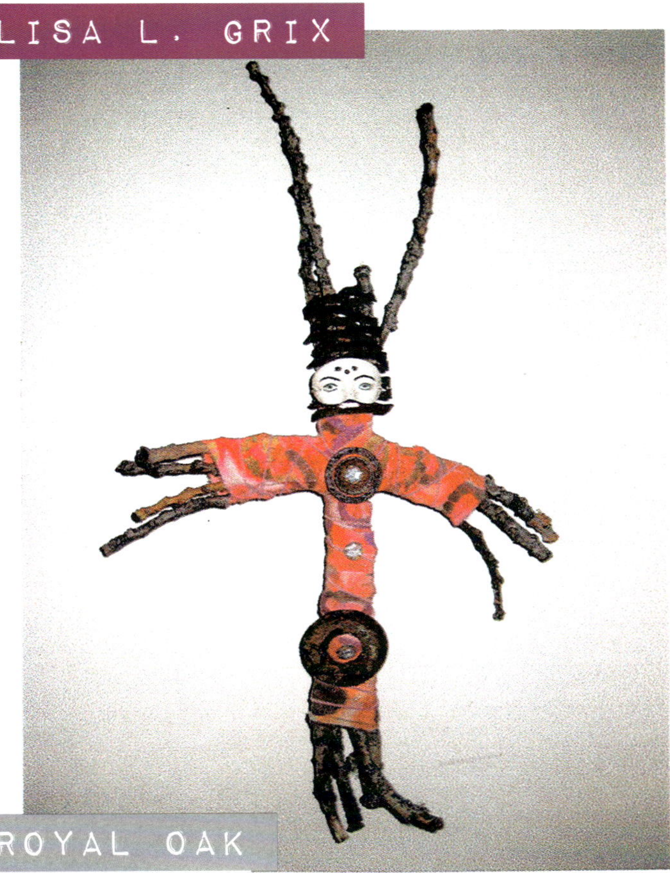

ROYAL OAK

48067

B. WHAT DO YOU MAKE, MODIFY, IMPROVE OR REPAIR?
PLEASE DESCRIBE! MY WORK IS CALLED GRIXDOLLS, LOOSELY BASED ON AFRICAN TALISMAN DOLLS. MANY OF MY DOLLS/MIXED MEDIA PIECES ARE MADE OF REPURPOSED STICKS, PINE NEEDLES, FABRICS, AMULETS AND FOUND OBJECTS AND ARE INSPIRED BY VARIOUS ENERGIES.

C. HOW DID THIS START? IT STARTED IN 2005 WHEN I WANTED TO USE SOME OF THE MATERIALS I COLLECTED. I ACTUALLY WAS INSPIRED BY THE STICKS AND FRONDS AND PINE NEEDLES. I HAVE ALWAYS BEEN INSPIRED BY BEADS AND RUSTY FOUND TRINKETS. I DECIDED TO COMBINE ALL OF MY COLLECTIONS INTO A MIXED MEDIA ART OBJECT.

What is it?

Musical instruments: guitars, mandolins, ukuleles, etc

I am a builder of high-end fretted musical instruments that are made to the unique specifications of each of my customers. I have built approximately 300 instruments in a wide range of styles.

How did this start?

Around 1978 I wanted a new guitar and could not afford one, so I decided to try to build one. I had no training in instrument building and had to learn as I went along, often making significant mistakes. I continue to be self-taught, but now have customers around the world who are players and collectors of fine musical instruments.

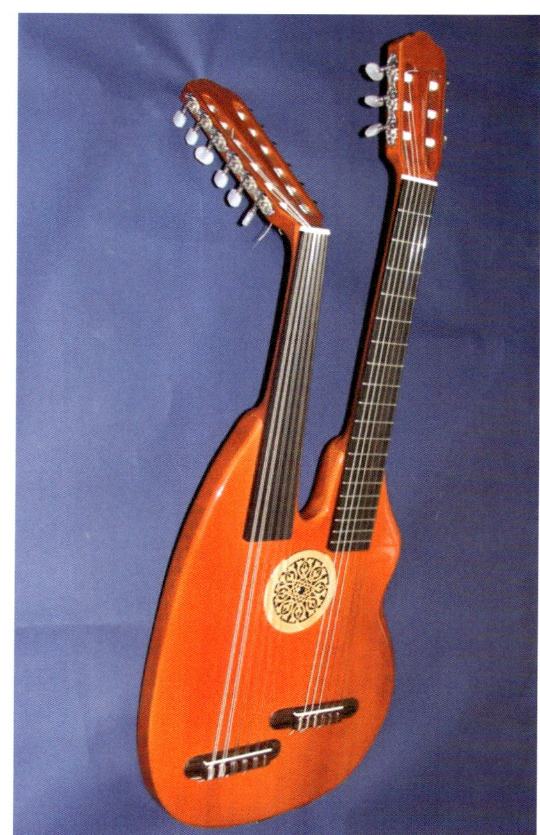

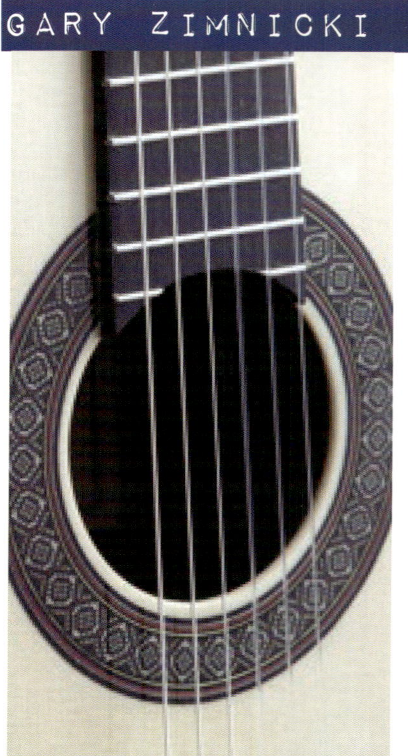

BILL HARRIS

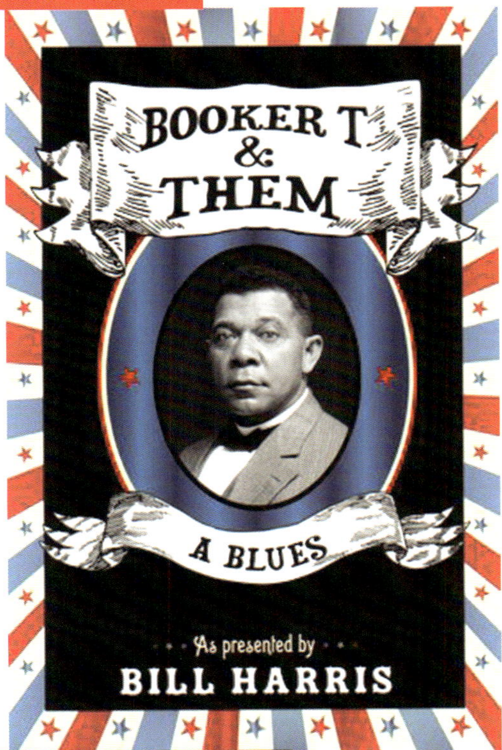

What is it?

Poems, plays, historical investigations, critical reviews

I write historical bio-poems, American history critiques, and full length plays centering around African American life and issues.

How did this start?

When I discovered that I had the ability to do the above.

Recommendations?

Almost all of the people that I know.

CULTURAL CENTER
48202

What is it?

Clothes and lights

My boyfriend and I made a jacket fitted with twenty multi-colored LEDs. He's made lamps, and I've been getting into making lamp shades recently. He's been into electronics and I've been into textiles since we were both young.

How did this start?

One day, he said he wanted to build something that would be fun for concerts. He came up with the idea and the design for the jacket, and I did all the fitting and wiring. We've been designing stuff together since.

Recommendations?

As for other people, all I know is what I've read. The Detroit Fire Guild is involved in making skill toys (poi/hoops/etc.). Probably a good amount of maker activity there.

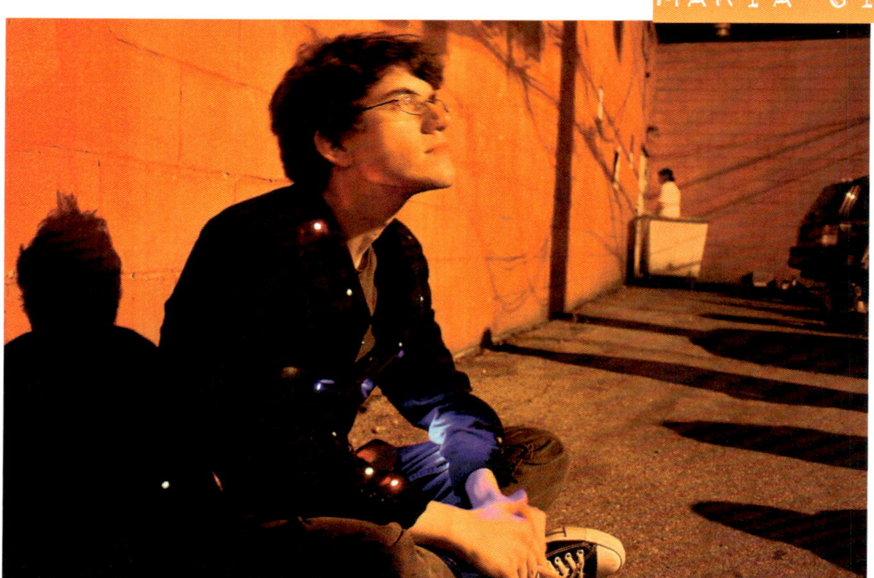

GABBY BUCKAY

DETROIT

48226

What is it?

Signs, murals, clothing

Silkscreening, stencilling,
drawing, handlettering,
painting, all media.

How did this start?

I started at Avalon doing their signs in
2001.

Recommendations?

Tom Carey, Sarah Burger, Emily Linn,
Mike Williams

What is it?

I make books housed in assembled boxes.

The books contain my poetry. The book and box works are collaged and assembled from pictorial fragments depicting my family's history.

How did this start?

The box works began in the early 1990s when I exhibited an initial work in the exhibition "Coast to Coast: Women of Color."

Recommendations?

Senghor Reid
Tannisha Reid
Jocelyn Rainey
Valeria Fair
Evangeline Montgomery

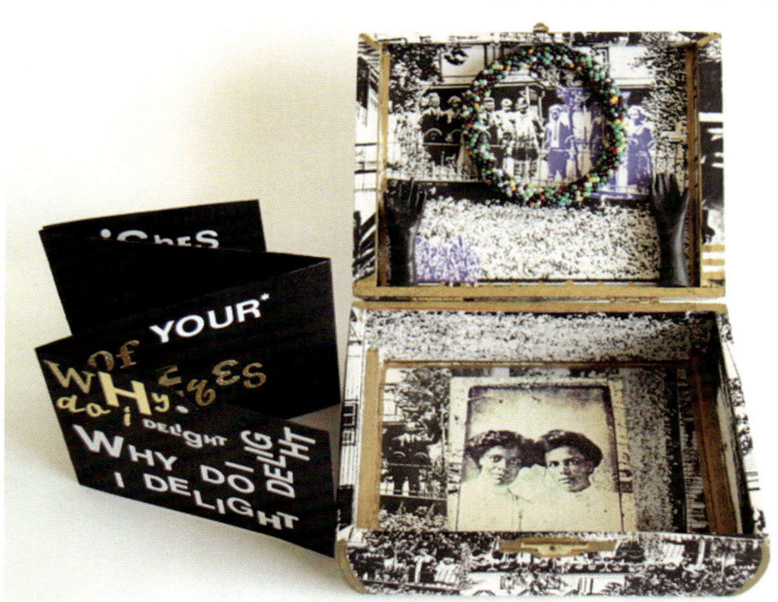

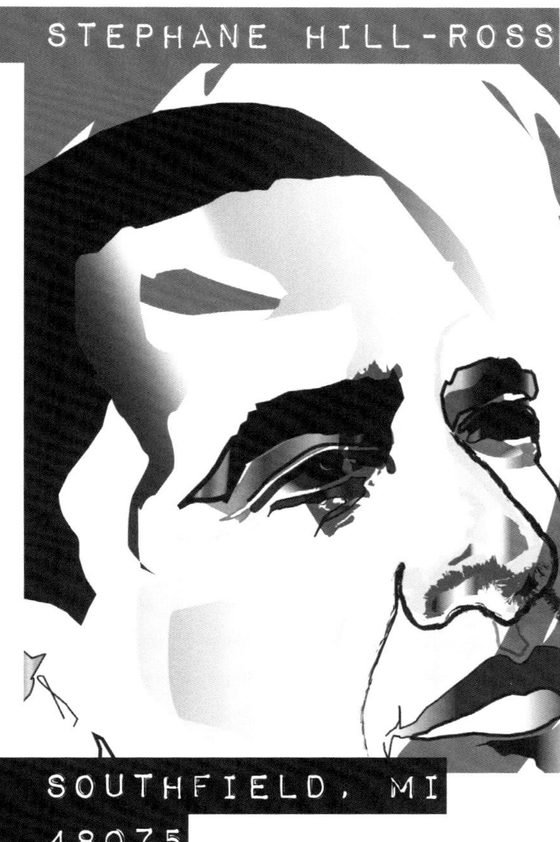

What is it?

Digital paintings and illustrations

I am a local artist that does manual works of art (illustration, paintings, etc) and I also do non-digital artworks.

How did this start?

I began noodling with a Wacom tablet and a Mac at a friend's home about 15 years ago. I loved it because there was no toxic spraying or paper wasted and if you made a mistake, you could just clear the part you don't want and continue on and save it to a file on the computer. About 2000, I finally got my own Mac and Illustrator software with a tablet and I just started experimenting with certain pieces and thought these would make cool reprints if I could only find the right printer. I went on line and researched the process of Giclee printing. I was in the Las Vegas Art Expo back in 2007, so I had to get 3 large prints made up and shipped to the facility. Another friend of mine found a local printer that did Giclees as it was not too many that did this process at the 30" x 40" size. I was truly in awe of this process. The difficulty that I find now is that many of the "old school" artisans disregard this type of artistry, feeling that it's cheating, but I disagree. We live in a digital age now so the art world must be more aware of the digital surroundings, save our environment (less trees used and no toxic sprays) and make room for this wonderful genre of art.

Recommendations?

Various members of a local art group that I am a member of - The National Conference of Artists/Michigan Chapter. There are so many talented people with me in this organization. At our last meeting in early April, one of our members passed this information to us.

What is it?

Jonathan Austin Accessories

In the near near future I want to establish my own line of menswear clothing and travel items. I began "Jonathan Austin" in 2011 producing small accessories such as portfolios and coin pouches. Then I began to progress to larger travel items, such as bookbags.

How did this start?

I've always been interested in fashion and plan to pursue a fashion career studying at Savannah College of Art and Design. Starting my own label has been a dream and passion for a years now.

Recommendations?

DOPE CVLTVRE: Steph Dorsey, Aaron Johnson, Shanice Brown, Etim Eniang and Dante Rionda.

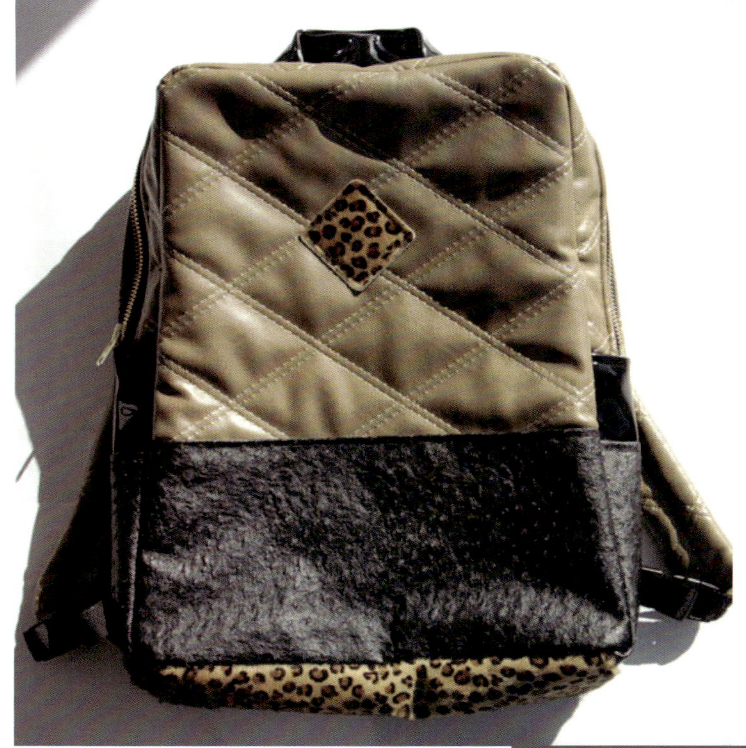

KRISTEN TRANCHIDA

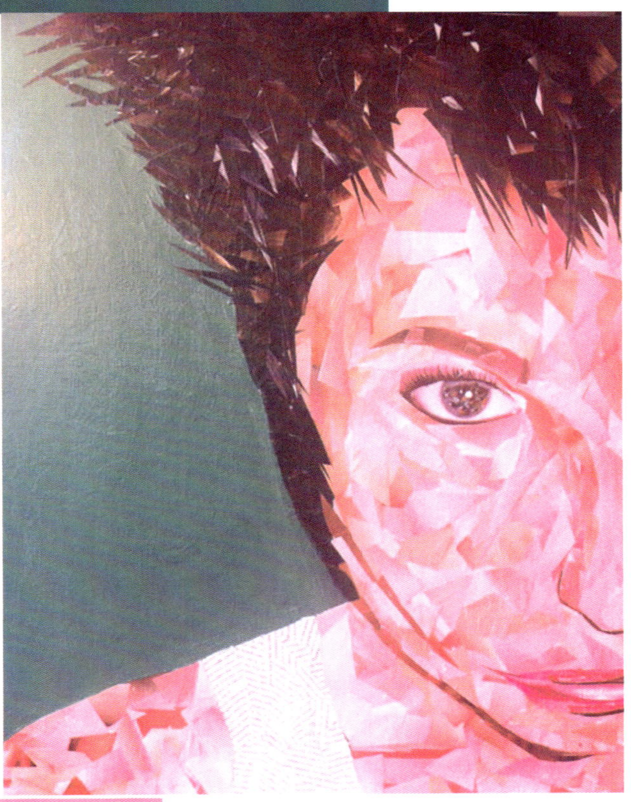

What is it?

Art from repurposed media materials

In an effort to combat mainstream gender representations (ex. very feminine women and hyper-masculine men), I created a collage from fashion magazines of an androgynous individual to encourage people to break free of gender presentations that may constrain them. By using the medium of mainstream fashion magazines, my intent was to repurpose the messages regarding gender we subconsciously receive every day and turn it into something beautiful and unique.

How did this start?

I took a graduate course on gender and education at Eastern Michigan University and turned my theoretical knowledge gained from the readings into a visual art piece.

YPSILANTI
48197

AARON JOHNSON JR.

What is it?

Jewelry

The name of my line is A-Craft which stands for Artistic Crafts. I make rings, bracelets, pins, medallions and pendants, all from cardboard!

How did this start?

I always liked jewelry but I could never afford any, so i thought, "what if I just made some?" So people saw all of the different pieces I was wearing and they wanted me to make them jewelry, too.

Recommendations?

DOPE CVLTVRE, Austin Nelson (Jonathan Austin), Stefanie Perkins (Live Loud)

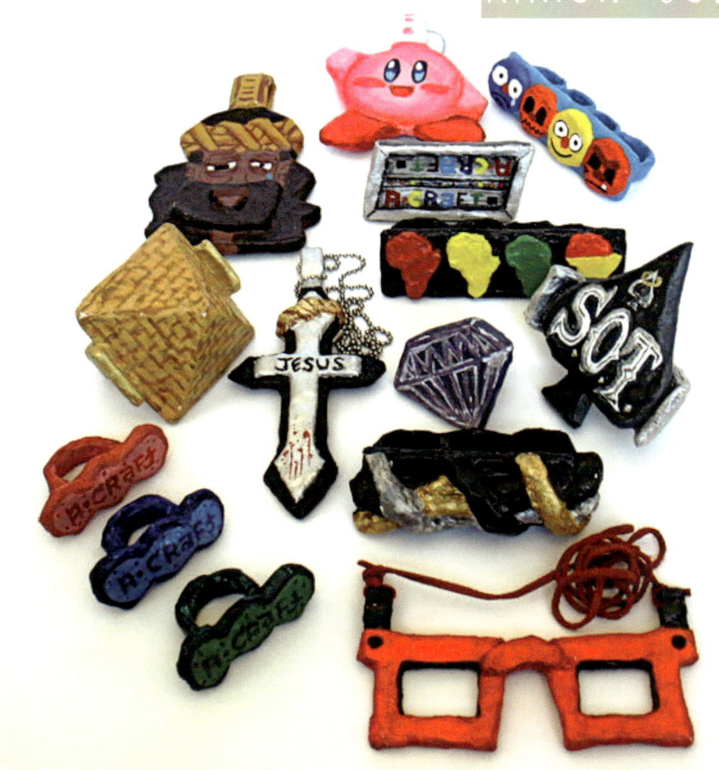

METRO DETROIT
48207

JOE FOERG

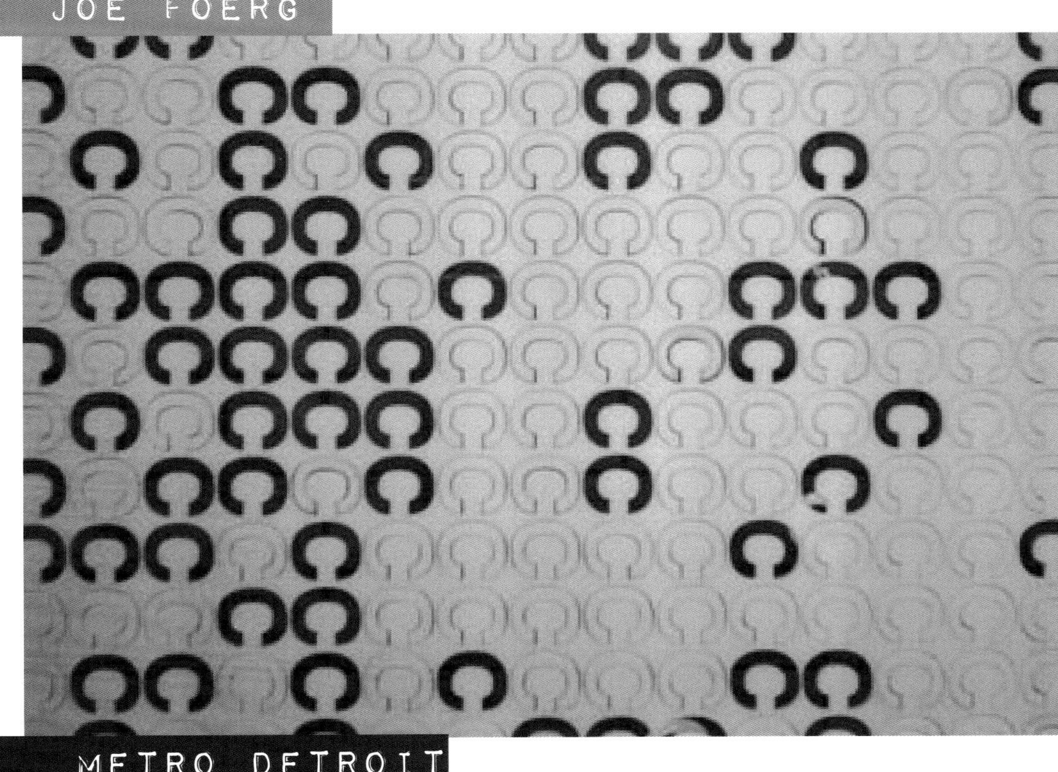

METRO DETROIT

What is it?

Tactile signs for low vision and blind individuals per the Americans with Disabilities Act

How did this start?

This is a sheet of letters cut out on a laser for signs.

What is it?

Comic books and books about comic books

Tool Publications is an independent Detroit comic book company distributed by Diamond Comics that is uncompromising in its approach to the comic marketplace. Tool Publications is known for *The Journal of MADness*, a magazine about *MAD* Magazine and its influential artists and writers. Tool Publications also champions many local artists and writers of comic books and graphic novelists by bringing them to a world-wide audience. Publications include CCS graduate Ken Krekeler's graphic novels "Colodin Project", "Dry Spell", and "Westward" and Eastern Michigan grad Jesse Rubenfeld's "Into the Dust". Tool Publications has continued the underground comic tradition with "THWAK!", "Jokester", and "Southern Fried Comix". These titles have proven to be launching pads for their artists and writers as they moved on to *MAD*, *Cracked*, movies, and television. Tool Publications is artist and writer controlled with no thought given to demographic trends. Yet, the product is distributed worldwide within the Marvel and DC Comics system.

How did this start?

The company was started by longtime Detroit punk rocker John E. Hett, alias Ron Tool, also a partner in Detroit's Phonetic Records, to promote quality writing in the comic book genre. Tool Publications started in 1997 as a single fanzine and in 1998 was awarded a coveted Diamond International Comic Book distribution contract allowing access to a marketplace often closed to artists and self-publishers.

Recommendations?

Ken Krekeler, writer and artist

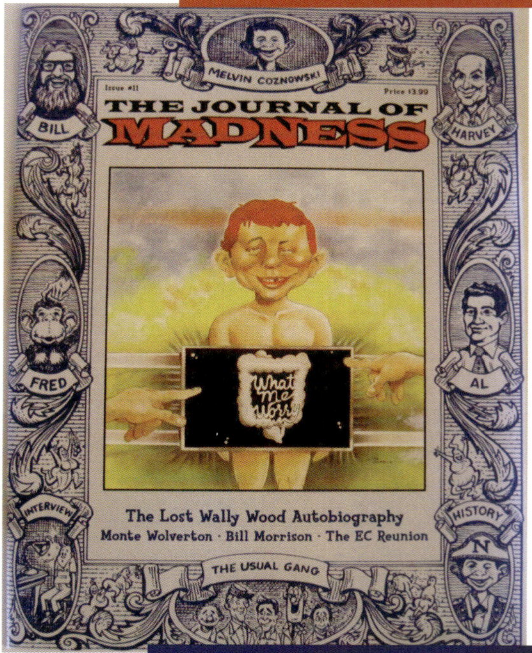

SENGHOR REID

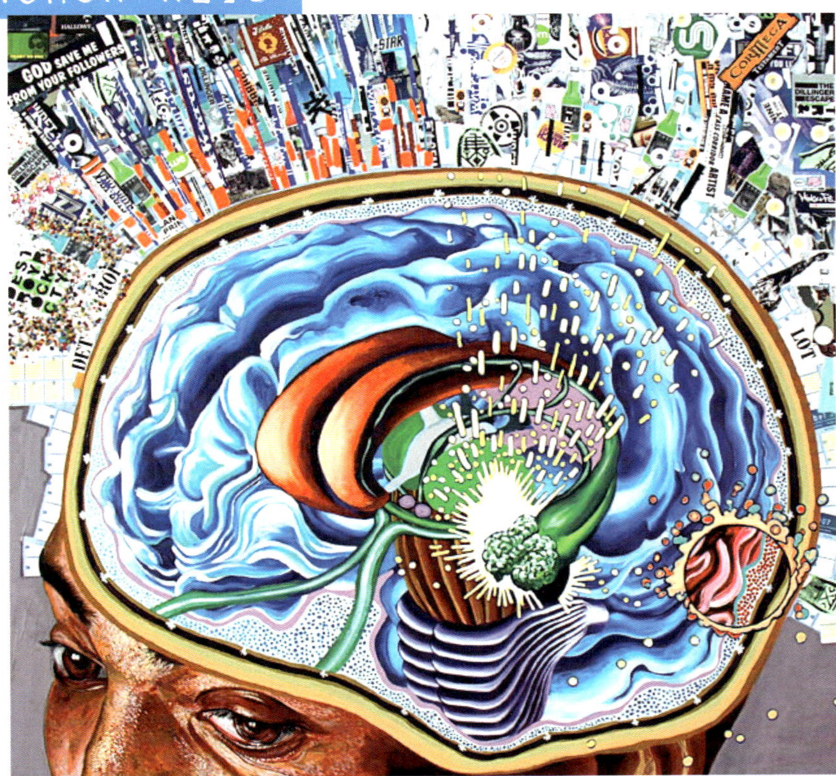

What is it?

Painting

I am an artist who uses a variety of media to describe my reactions to living in a post-industrial environment.

How did this start?

I have been making art since I was a child. My mother, Shirley Woodson, is an artist and she taught me everything.

Recommendations?

Shirley Woodson

AVIATION SUBDIVISION
48204

ROB HENDERSON

What is it?

Outdoor Art + Landscaping

The muses of nature and excitement of found objects blend with an African/Asian aesthetic within my sculpture.

How did this start?

Initially I started out as an arborist. Time progressed, I delved into landscaping, founded Sage Treeworks, and before I knew it stones and plants would find me. The outdoor sculptural art is an extension of the fusion of myself and nature.

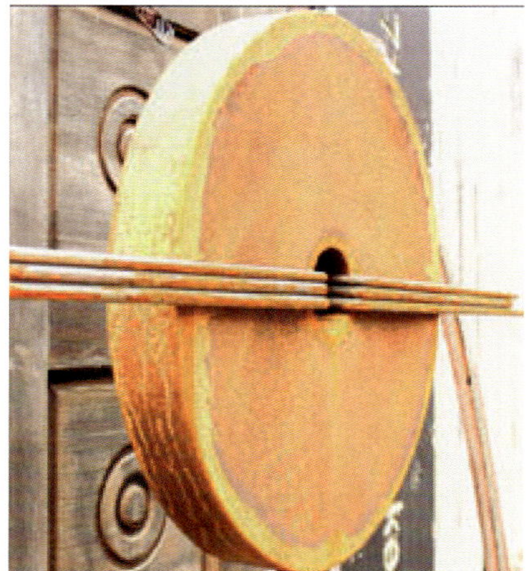

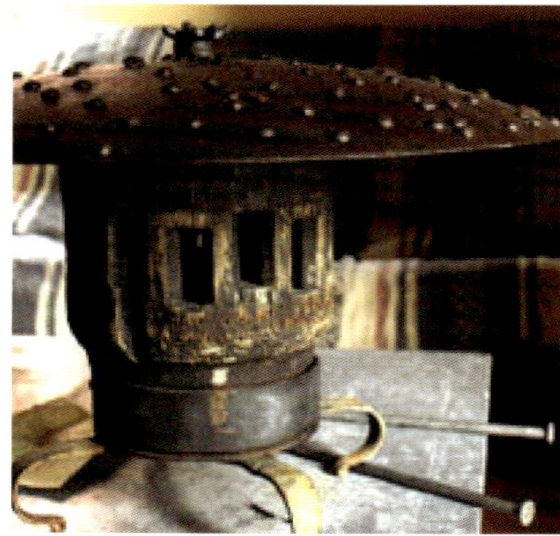

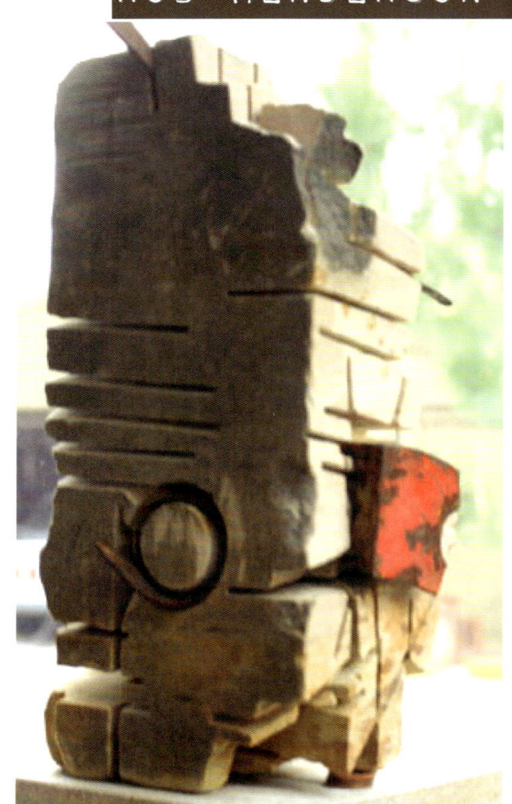

NORTH ROSEDALE

48235

RIMMA ISAYEVA

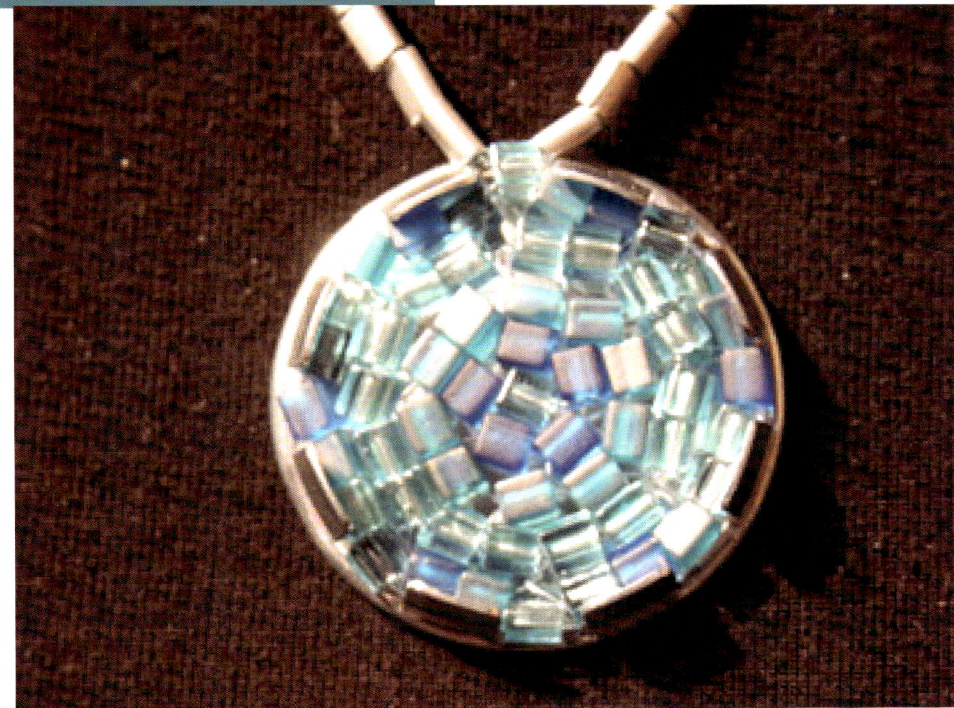

What is it?

Beaded jewelry

I make beaded bracelets, necklaces, and earrings for friends and family whenever I have free time. I collect discarded, interesting-looking objects that resemble jewelry with a goal of incorporating them into my pieces.

How did this start?

When I was 10 years old, my friend showed me how to put beads on a fishing line. I was hooked since then.

Recommendations?

Marat Paransky, Chris Girard, Lisa Grix

FARMINGTON HILLS
48334

What is it?

Pathway Patterns:
hand painted wood design modules

I am the designer and maker of Pathway Patterns, an interactive medium and process that brings people together with art to explore relationships, discover pathways, and build temporary patterns one part at a time on walls, tabletops and floors in a variety of settings. The parts include 367 geometric designs handpainted in twelve color sets on wood or canvas panel modules in several sizes. I also designed and manufacture Flip Parts, a boxed set of 96 cards with two sided designs.

How did this start?

Pathway Patterns evolved from my love of geometric art and bright colors, and a lifelong interest in patterns. I received my first set of geometric modules when I was nine, and continue to collect similar sets to facilitate pattern building. I made the first set of parts on paper as a personal creative outlet, but soon discovered their universal appeal to others. Several thousand parts in a variety of designs and colors compose the Pathway Patterns "road show" that travels to provide creative entertainment for participants in interactive exhibits and at community meeting centers. Flip Parts are sold in galleries and online from my website to promote pattern building at home.

Recommendations?

Theresa Peterson, Andy Malone

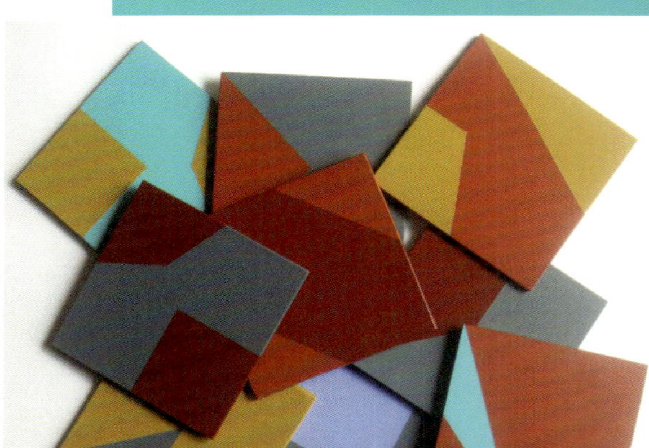

GRIND KAI JAPERA

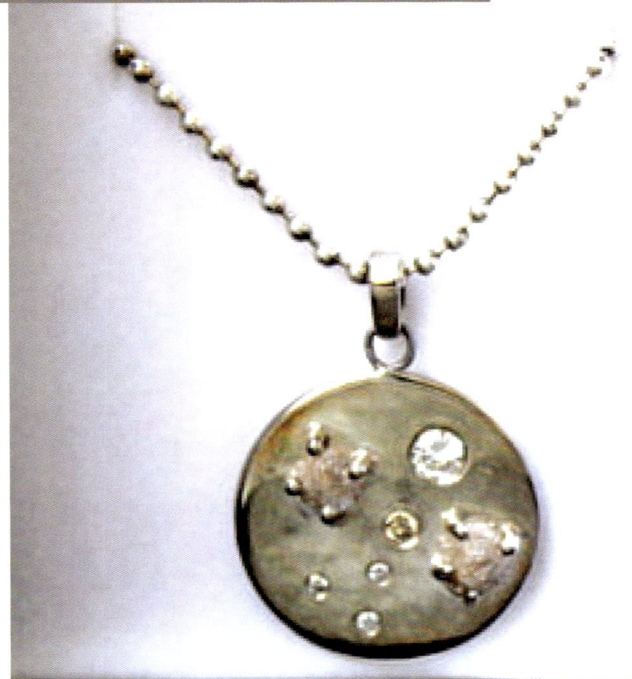

NORTH END

48202

What is it?

Jewelry

I design and create jewelry with a variety of precious metals and diamonds, and gemstones that enhance the wearer's attitude and aura. As an Accredited Jewelry Professional, I founded Japera Jewelry Co. which also offers jewelry consultation.

How did this start?

Since the age of seven I have enjoyed designing and creating jewelry from a home office. My newest pieces incorporate uncut rough and polished diamonds to represent the appreciation of raw beauty with respect to progression. I was really just being a copycat! I just wanted to be like my big sister, Halima, who at the time made jewelry.

Recommendations?

Sydney James
Grind

KELLY HARTSFIELD

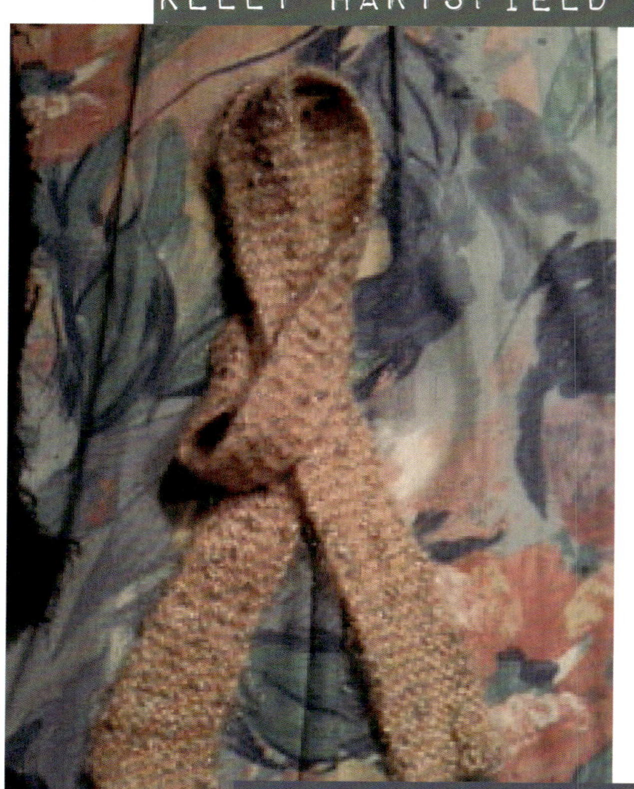

What is it?

Crochet and knit scarves

Different grades of yarn are used to crochet and knit the scarves. Some scarves are made thin and some thick.

How did this start?

Began making scarves when I was 9, learning from my grandmother.

Recommendations?

Halima Cassell

METRO DETROIT

48033

DAUNE SMITH

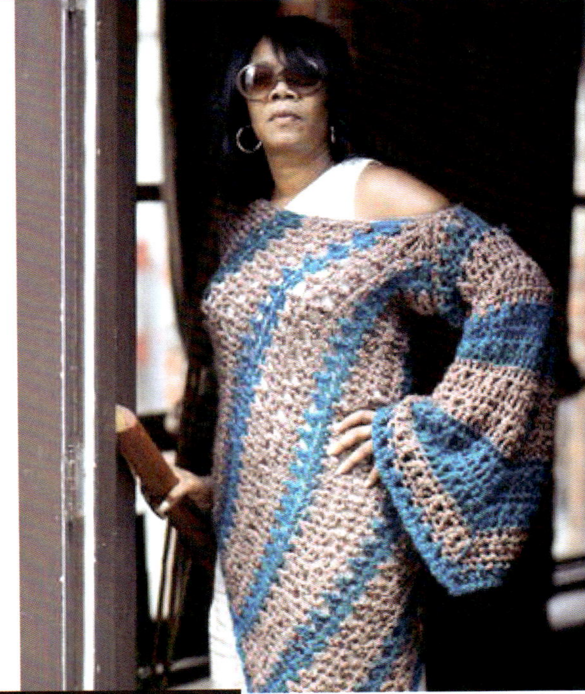

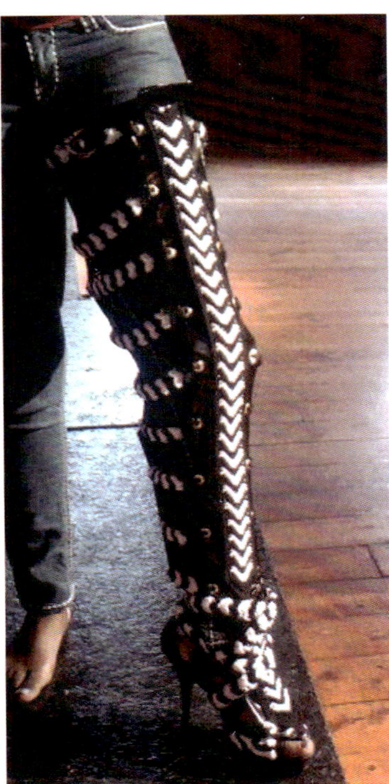

What is it?

Crochet clothing

One Sleeved Poncho, Crochet Boots

How did this start?
by crocheting items for a boutique.

DETROIT
48206

133

What is it?

Visual Art + Opportunity

Create, connect, collaborate, repeat.

A life-long visual artist and native Detroiter, I returned after spending the decade following Cass Tech in other cities. Currently, I paint and experiment with mixed media fusion and create art with community.

How did this start?

I established the Detroit Mural Factory in 2009 as a way to connect artists, youth, and community, address our landscape via authentically engaged public art.

Recommendations?

detroitmuralfactory.com to see more.

ifoma, daune smith, juan martinez, chazz, sabrina nelson

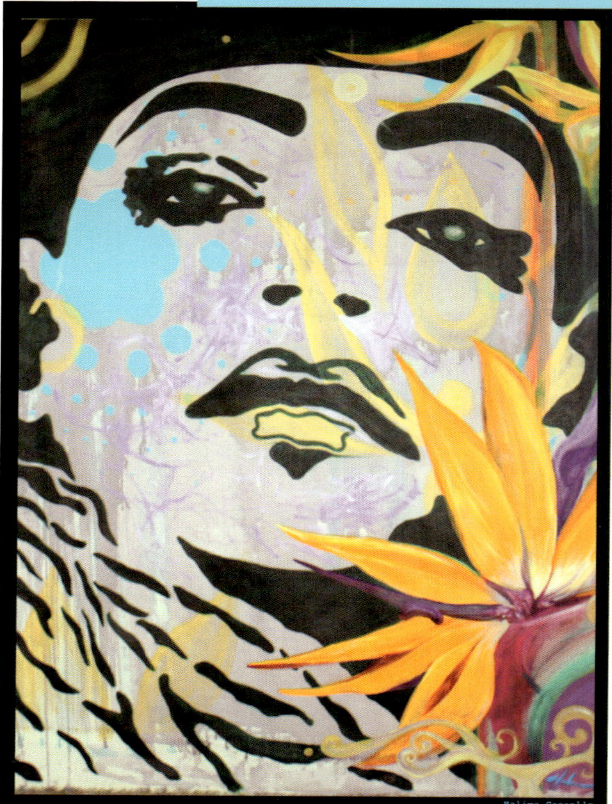

NORTH END
48202

JASMINE HARRIS

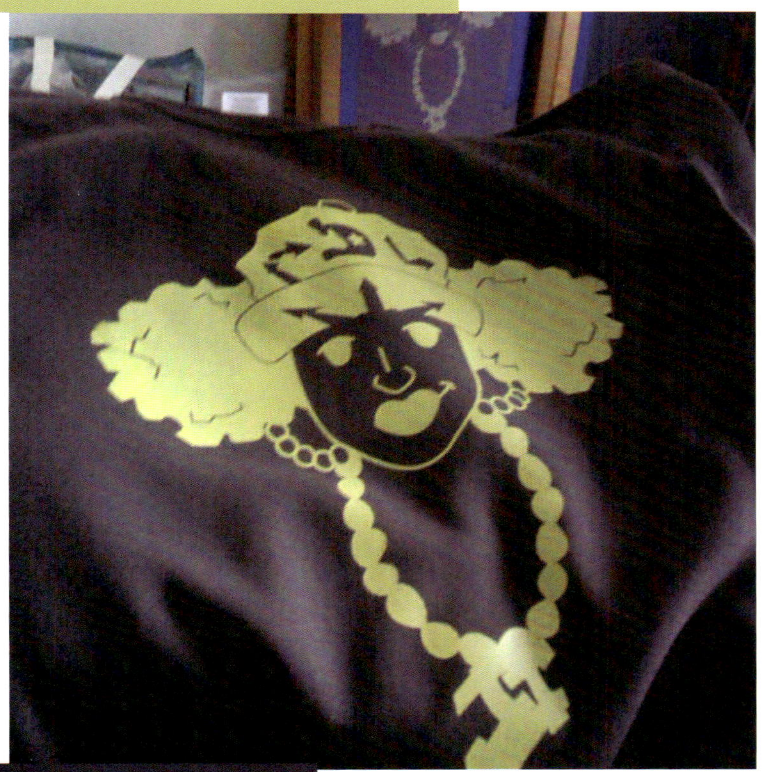

NORTH END
48202

What is it?

T-shirts and murals

I paint murals around the city, artwork in my house and make t-shirts in a room.

How did this start?

From looking at my uncle's sketchbooks

Recommendations?

Juan. You may have seen him riding down Woodward on one of his creations.

Meechii. He is a beast with his creations.

Chazz. He is Detroit Batman, his line work is really NICE.

CYNDY ANDERSON

What is it?

Apparel + Accesories: from deconstructed clothing

The Original Cyndy Bag is a line of bags that I make using deconstructed and repurposed materials. The bag pictured is a diaper bag featuring 16 pockets!

How did this start?

I always liked creating new things, and being different. And I always hated throwing stuff away, especially once-favorite jeans. So I began creating the Cyndy Bags from there.

Recommendations?

ifoma
Sabrina Nelson
Tre Marcel

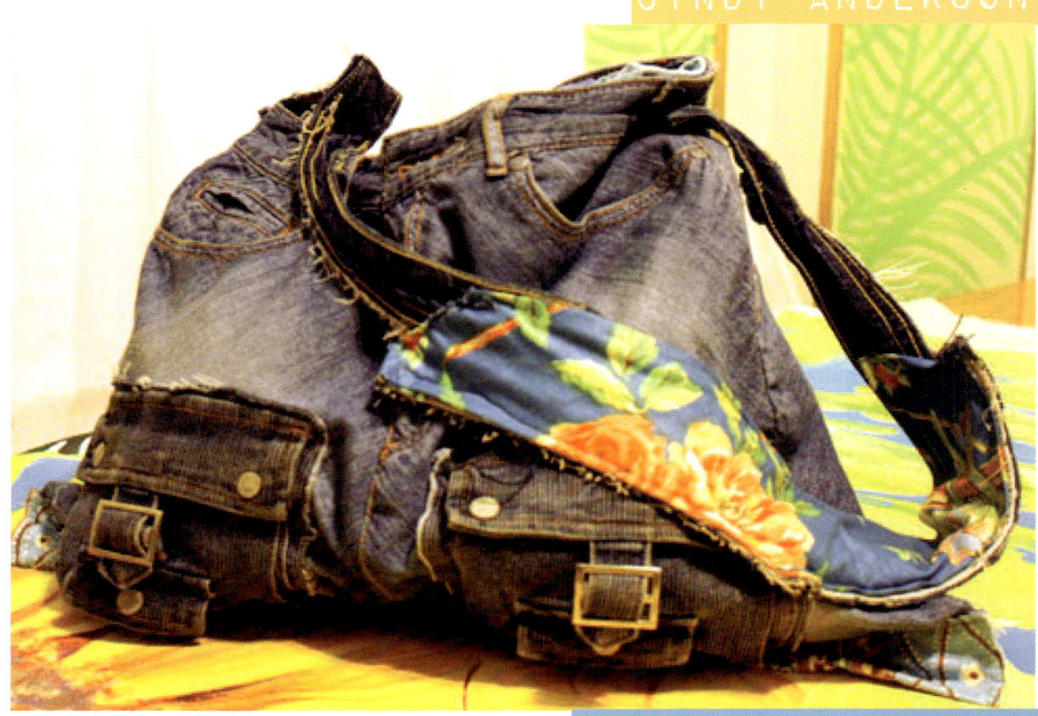

DOWNTOWN DETROIT
48207

136

WALT BUCHANAN

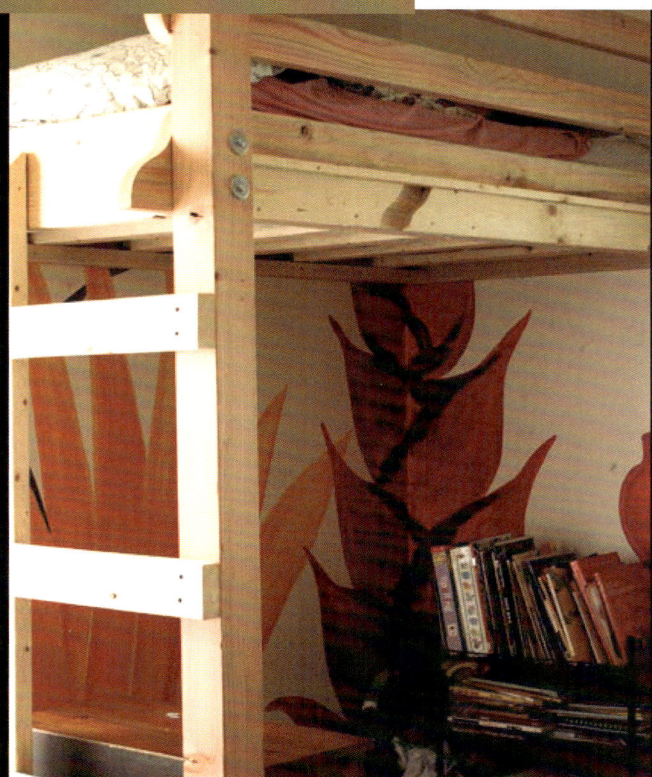

UNIVERSITY DISTRICT

48221

What is it?

Loft Beds + Elevated Platforms

Although I am a contractor, and can build a house (and everything in it), I most enjoy creating sturdy, one-of-a-kind interior space solutions for clients. Loft beds, elevated platforms, reading nooks with hidden storage, and solutions for artist/ recording studios are some favorite examples of my custom work.

How did this start?

I began offering built-in solutions for small spaces when I lived in Hawaii. There people have significantly less space in the home as compared with Detroit. After moving back, I realized that the need also exists here, as more people are living and working in lofts, and appreciate quality custom woodwork.

Recommendations?

Todd Stovall
Rob Henderson

What is it?

Bike trailers

Parts from local hardware stores and bikeshops, all within a two mile radius. The trailers are pared down, one containing a cooler-like removable container which can hold anything from a 36 pack to a small child. It supports about 150 pounds

How did this start?

I work at Brooks Lumber, Detroit's oldest business; seeing carpenters and construction workers all day who've been hit hard by the recession, along with a store that has seen better days. A car's gas and upkeep, on average, costs around seven grand a year.

I make stuff from local businesses, sell the product through those same businesses, to local consumers.

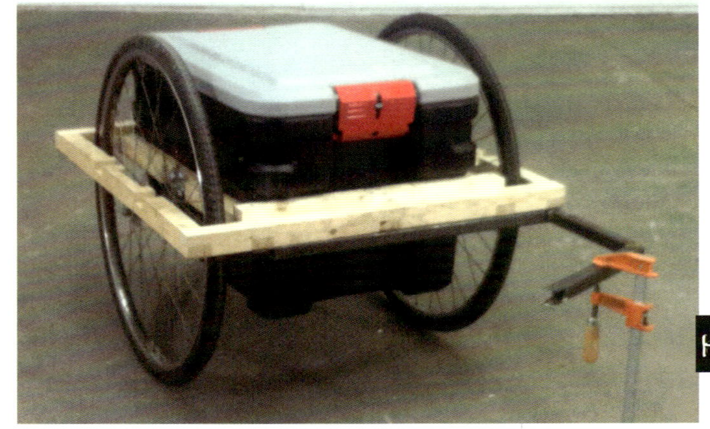

HAMILTON POE

NORTH END
48202

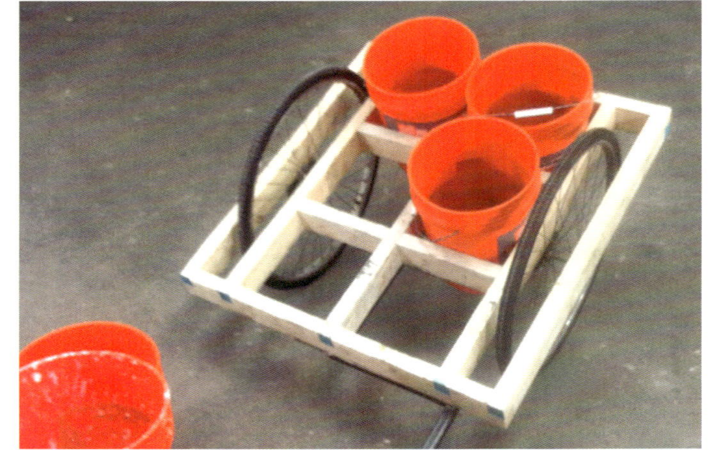

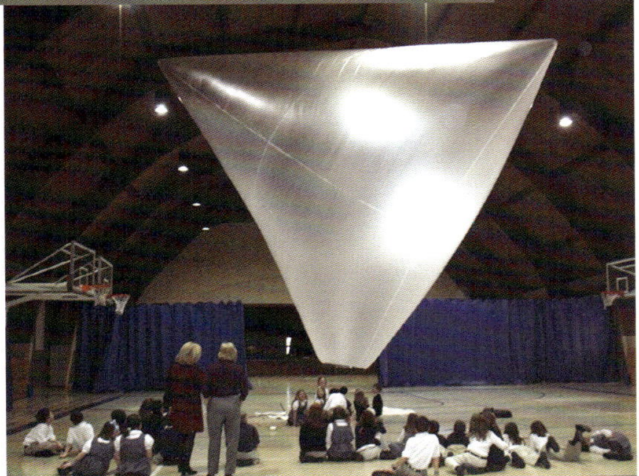

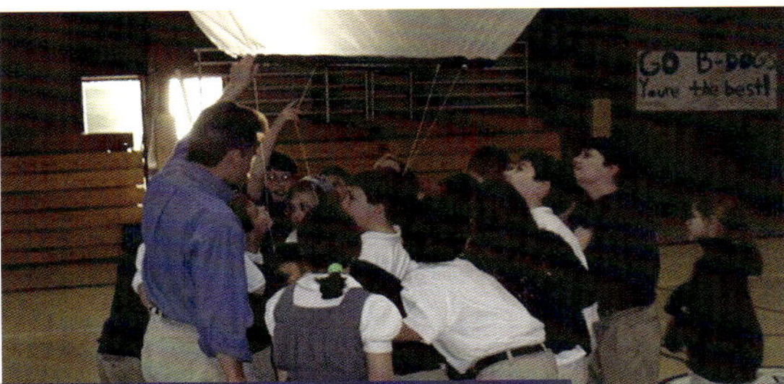

What is it?

I make balloons that fly to the stratosphere using only the power of the sun.

My tetrahedral-shaped, solar hot air balloons - or "solar tetroons" - are made from super thin plastic film and stand 35 feet tall when they are ready for launch. The plastic film is clear and absorbs little solar energy, so I pioneered the idea of using a black powder (dry tempera paint) clinging by static electricity to the inside of the balloon as a solar absorber. Underneath the solar tetroon I typically fly a GPS tracker that sends back position reports using an AM radio transmitter. My tetroons typically fly at about 65,000 feet for 12 hours or more (all day, plus a couple of hours for descent) and they have traveled as far as Nova Scotia.

How did this start?

It all started as a way to get students interested in science, technology and math. Back in the 90s whilst working in the corporate world, I dabbled in amateur rocketry and was a registered contestant for the original "Cheap Access to Space" award offered by the Space Frontier Foundation. In 2001, I started working at the Grosse Pointe Academy and began looking for safe and inexpensive ways to share my dreams about DIY spaceflight with students. The result of this quest (with much help from many who went before, especially Don Piccard, called by many the "father of modern hot air ballooning") was the creation of my solar tetroons. Since that time, I have built and flown over twenty solar tetroons.

Recommendations?

My brother - who also "fell out" of the corporate world some time ago - is an undiscovered artist who makes beautiful creations out of copper wire, pipe and solder. He is self–employed as a handyman of sorts and doesn't consider himself an artist - nor think especially highly of his creations - but his work is brilliant and inspired. His name is Rick Rochte.

What is it?

Underutilized auto + truck welding shop

The As-Built thesis group at Taubman College created a new storefront in North Corktown, Detroit, replacing the CMU wall that had sealed the original curved storefront with a new intervention that used steel and acrylic to create an innovative window focusing on the modulation of light, views, privacy, and security.

How did this start?

As-Built is a course collaboration between Maciej Kaczynski and Catie Newell which seeks to strategically interweave the efforts, time, and energy between the research-oriented methodology of thesis prep and the pragmatics of a fabrication seminar to coordinate, explore, and exploit the constraints and realities of actualizing.

Recommendations?

Joe Proper of Schmoe LLC

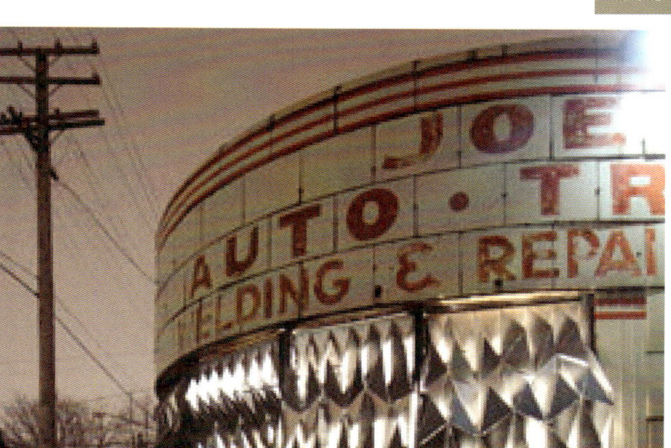

FACULTY INSTRUCTORS:
MACIEJ KACZYNSKI
CATIE NEWELL

STUDENTS:
ANAND AMIN
ANDREW AULERICH
LAUREN BEBRY
ASHLEY GOE
TARLTON LONG
JUSTIN MAST
ANDREW MCCARTHY
MATT NICKEL
KURT SCHLEICHER
ANDREW STERN
LAUREN VASEY
NING WANG
BRENNA WILLIAMS

NORTH CORKTOWN
48216

TODD STOVALL

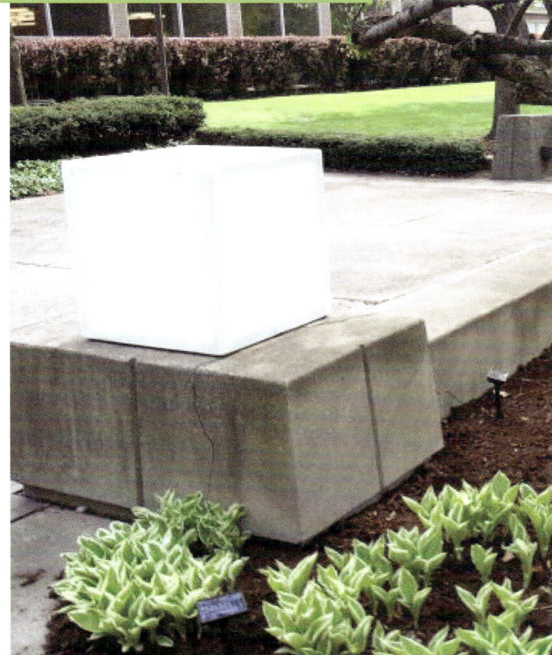

DETROIT
48202

What is it?

Minimalist art installations

My work is currently on view on Wayne State University's Reuther Mall. As an artist and electronic music composer, I combine principles of hip-hop, minimalist design and spiritual awareness into ambient but engaging beats, patterns and landscapes. General themes that are incorporated within the objects I construct are metal, wood materials and plexiglas. Areas of focus are furniture design, light fixtures and Avant-garde projects for exploration. Main influences for my projects are pop art, minimalism and music.

How did this start?

In 2004 I was a co-founder of the well-received underground art house Fi-nite Gallery. It was then that I began designing minimalist installations. Now as I pursue my BSEE at Lawrence Technological University, the infusion of engineering, design and artistic expression are my motivations to create.

Recommendations?

Maya Stovall is a dancer/musician/choreographer/conceptual artist who makes dance for the camera works and collaborates with me in an experimental music project, Flower Cabin. She blesses the streets of Detroit with contemporary ballet and uses art to amplify Detroit's unique voice.

**CATIE NEWELL
JOE PROPER**

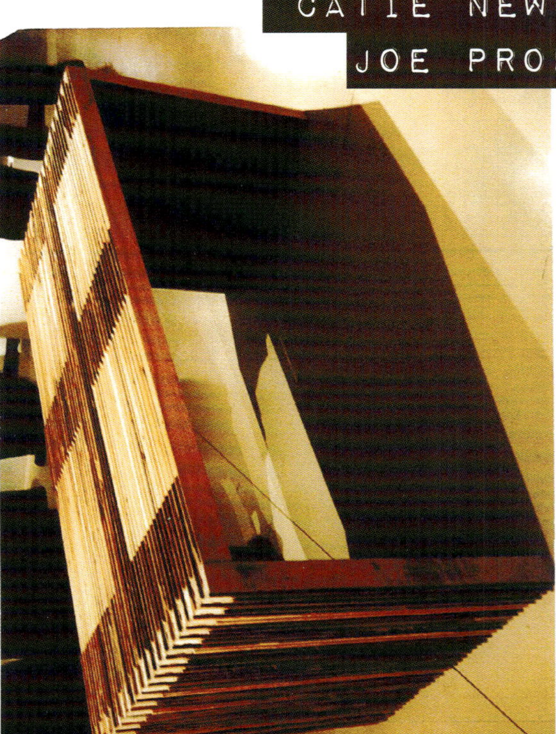

**B. WHAT DO YOU MAKE, MODIFY, IMPROVE OR REPAIR?
PLEASE DESCRIBE!**

Eating off the Floor!

A bench and table set that utilises rough and sanded salvaged wood floor boards to provide an elegant place for collective dining and dialogue. The accumulated wood is comprised through layers, stacking vertically.

C. HOW DID THIS START?

The wood was & collected from a deconstructed home in Hamtramck as part of the "Re-nailed" event

**HAMTRAMCK
EASTERN MARKET
48212**

IFOMA STUBBS

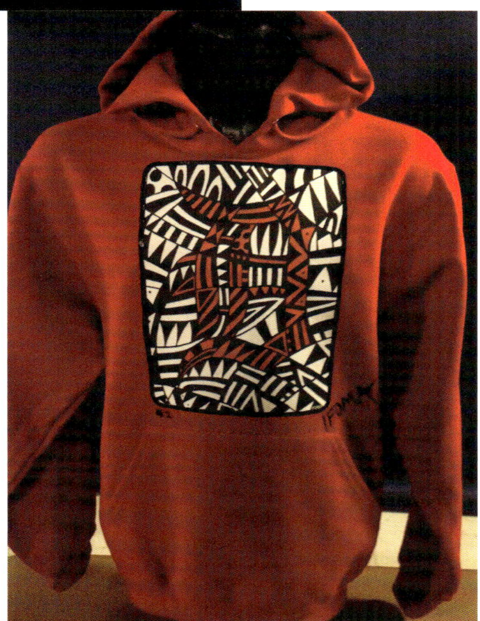

What is it?

I create art on canvas, baseball caps, shoes, clothing and other items.

I use different techiques to create art on clothing items paint, ink and burning tools.

How did this start?

I started with my own clothing and people asked me to create for them. Ifomascanvas started in 2008.

Recommendations?

Phil White

NORTH DETROIT

48221

AARON JONES

What is it?

chain link fence pipes

I buy interlocking pipes from Home Depot and bend them into a structural system which assembles into architecture.

How did this start?

This began with the realization that I could post-process this readily available material into something completely new.

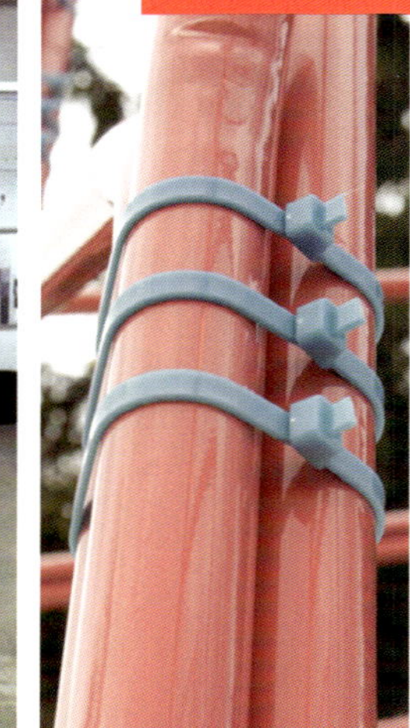

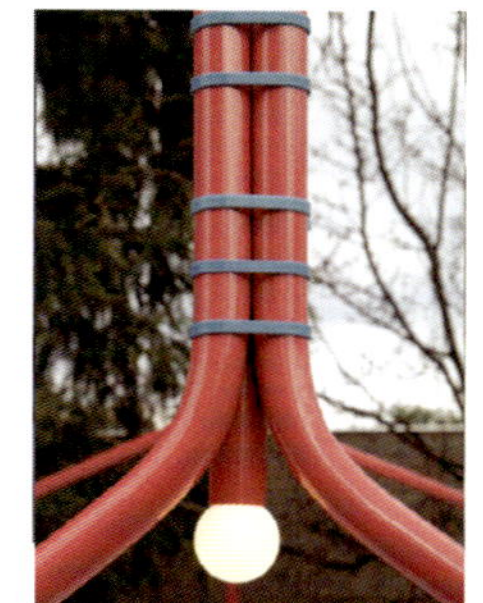

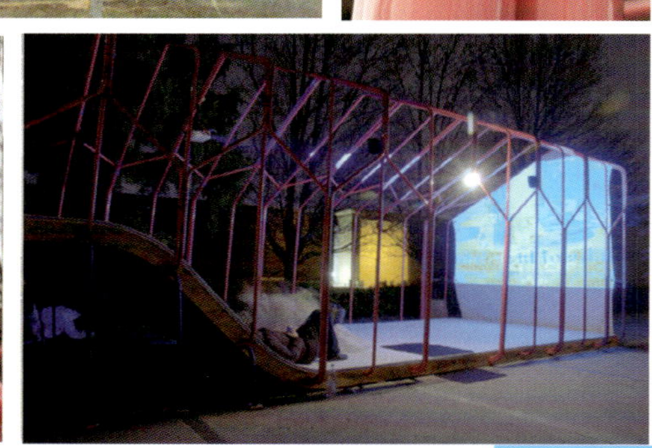

EAST SIDE
48234

ANSLEY PARKER

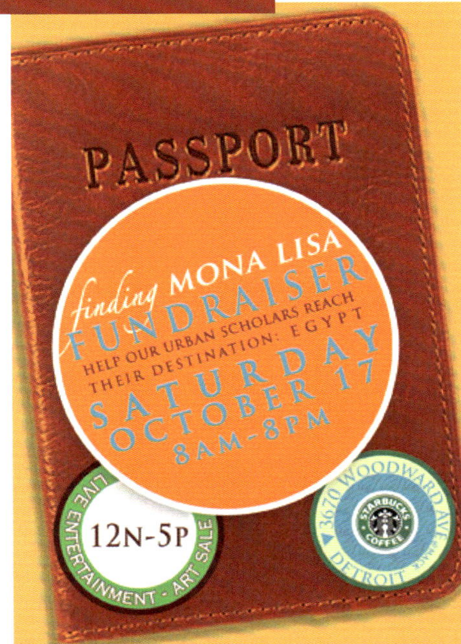

What is it?

We create visual communication tools for happy clients.

As a visual design agency, we create any form of visual communications that our clients need to share their message effectively with the world. We specialize in print, identity and web design.

How did this start?

Initially, I began doing graphic design work in support of a jewelry line I was producing, but discovered I enjoyed computer-aided design much more.

Recommendations?

Senghor Reid, Jocelyn Rainey, Gilda Snowden, Shirley Woodson, Be My Guest

OAKLAND COUNTY
48068

How did this start?

I guess it is fair to say that this all started as part of my education. I always wanted to be creating something that there was possibly not a market for, but the ideas were always what I was most passionate about. I graduated from College for Creative Studies in 2004 with a BFA in Interdisciplinary Studies Crafts /Industrial Design/Sculpture.

In 2006 I graduated from the 3-D Design department at Cranbrook Academy of Art with a focus in furniture. From 2006 on I worked with architect William Massie. Currently I am the Fabrications Coordinator at Cranbrook Academy of Art. These experiences have led me to make the objects and ideas that I dream up a reality.

Recommendations?

OmniCorpDetroit

What is it?

Products and furniture

The description below is of an object that was designed to protect against home invasion. Threat Manager 2 is a great accomplice to your favorite domestic bludgeoning device, golf club, bat or candle stick. TM2 is a hybrid device designed to disorient an intruder in a non-violent capacity. This single-handed object brings very bright light, a laser beam and voice amplification/modulation in one package.

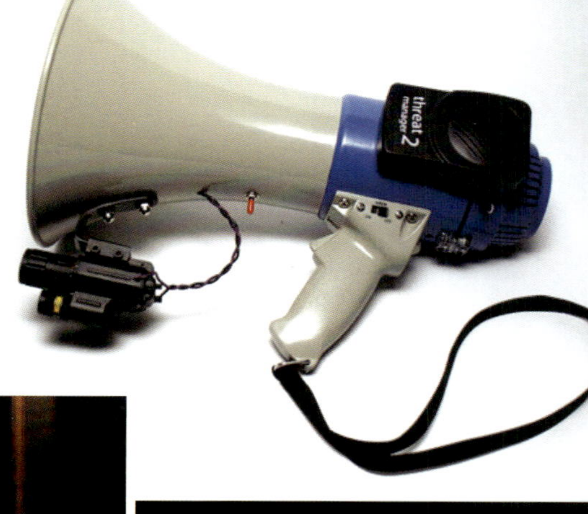

RACHEL HARKAI

WOODBRIDGE
48208

How did this start?

My poetry writing began in the American west. As a college student I spent a lone summer following a team of geologists around Wyoming, Utah, Nevada, Idaho and Montana as they documented and discovered the most bizarre land formations I could have imagined. I spent many nights sleeping uncovered beneath the stars. As we traveled from town to ghost town, I narrated experiences and catalogued them geographically – Gold Hill, Utah; Thermopolis, Wyoming; Angel Lake, Nevada.

What is it?

Poetry and nonfiction essays from
WHAT WE THOUGHT WE KNEW

Recommendations?

other great Detroit writers: Vince Carducci, Matthew Olzmann, Vievee Francis, Peter Markus

---

*

There is always something else to wonder at.
I mean it.

You only get to have a thing until you don't anymore;
part of the having is the not having. To start, this is
everything I want to remember:
the city spread below us like a fan,

the importance being the texture of air like that –
still as a glass of water.

Find thunderclouds. Find power outages.
Find the full green meaning of summer.
A sound, a color, a vision of nothing in particular:
prairie grass on a day in August.

I used to understand geometry.
Now here I am, all spread out

with a beer can between my knees like a picnic.
What are we going to do?
Plant little scraps of yellow paper all around the
desk again?
A garden of words to harvest?

*

How many things do you want to return to?
Cities, apartments, loves?
For a long time I wanted every place I had lived
to disappear,

too many memories
re-folded into someone else's like paper.

We saw a whole building pulled skyward one
night,
waves of phosphorescence pulsing.

Flames are just versions of falling water sucked
backwards,
versions of light.

I had never seen a house on fire.
The kids who did it hadn't either.

But they wanted to.

*

You can make anything disappear that you want.
You just can't make it come back.

I thought I knew a lot about leaving.
Dawn light, disembodied light,

daylight bending backwards.
It all comes down to angles, anyway.

Dogs were cutting holes in the air with their
mouths
when you said:

I want to show you something.
That was what you said. A secret.

What is supposed to be here?
The raised red lines I made and then followed?

Memories you can move through and between,
back and forth in the mind like a finger on a line.

For a long time after I went to all the same places.
It was the difference between pretending to sleep
and sleeping.

But the funny thing about time is that there is no
going back.
Nights we made imperfect circles in the grass.

Or a first snow:
the alleys like perfect chambers of moonlight,

haloes of breath rising.
I want them to be secrets.

But they are just forgotten avenues to nothing.
Reminders of something beautiful

that doesn't exist
anymore.

B. WHAT DO YOU MAKE, MODIFY, IMPROVE OR REPAIR?
PLEASE DESCRIBE!

To Improve the ART
world in Detroit

C. HOW DID THIS START?

At 5 Years of Age
From my Mother teachings

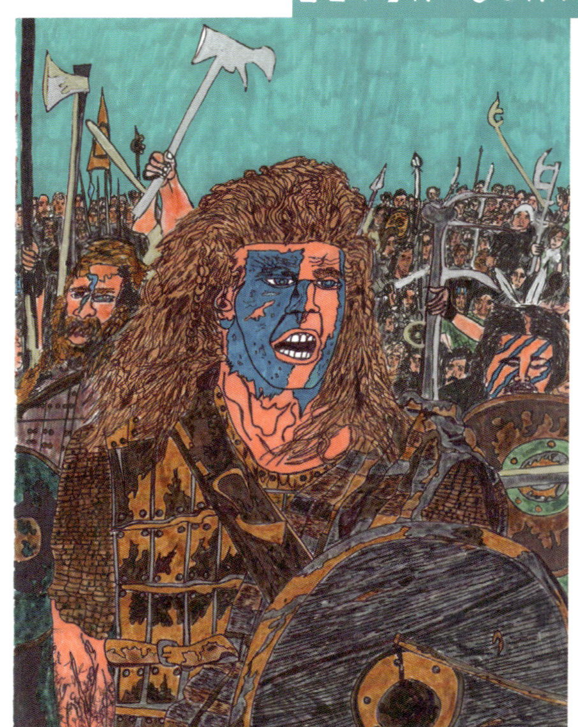

BRYCE

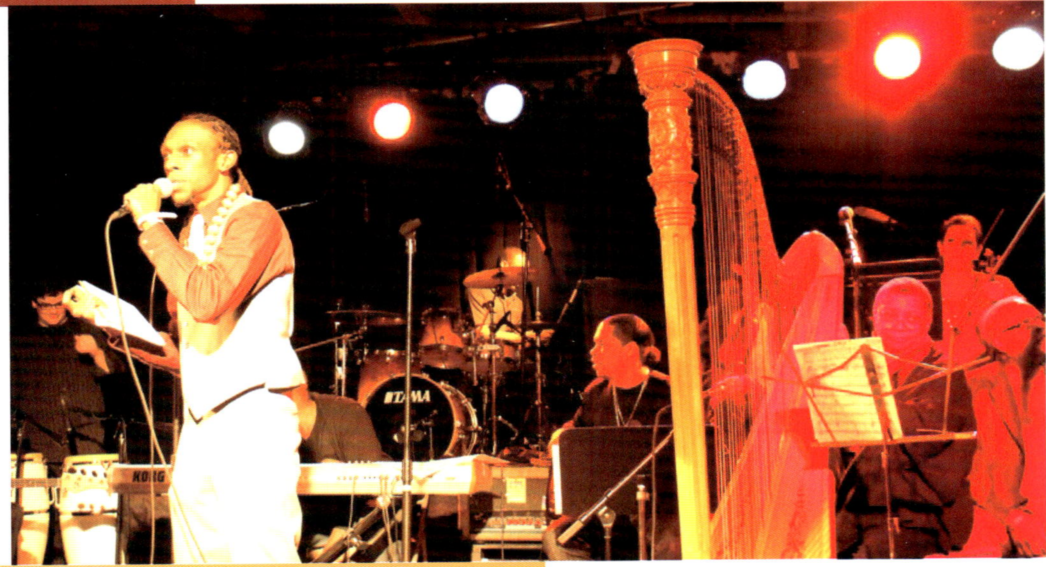

Recommendations?

Kadiri Sennefer
Piper Carter
DJ Sicari Ware
Halima Cassells

What is it?

21st century Detroit music for world distribution

As a label owner, record producer and performing artist, 21st century Detroit Music symbolizes the new, progressive, urban sound (from Detroit) that masterfully fuses imagery of environmental awareness, community, self-valuation, spirituality, and self–determination, into the most highly accessible and viable music products the world has yet to see and hear.

How did this start?

My path began in 2001 and was born out of the burning desire to create a multinational media company with the capacity to introduce and expose our products/ messages into any and all major and tertiary world markets that espouse positive and productive spiritual, moral, and personal values, as opposed to the standard fare of urban records that promote criminality and gross-consumerism, to our urban youth.

What is it?

I make one-of-a-kind jewelry pieces.

I purchase materials from Metro Detroit stores and create necklaces, earrings, rings, and bracelets. The styles can range from a classic charm necklace to an entirely outrageous piece consisting of multiple chains, baubles, and other random objects. Creating jewelry has been a passion for me for about ten years.

How did this start?

My favorite game growing up was called "Pretty Pretty Princess" and ever since then, I've known that making funky jewelry was for me. I took my first jewelry-making class at about 10 years old and I've been in love ever since.

Recommendations?

Angela Kiel! She's an amazing artist with her own unique flair.

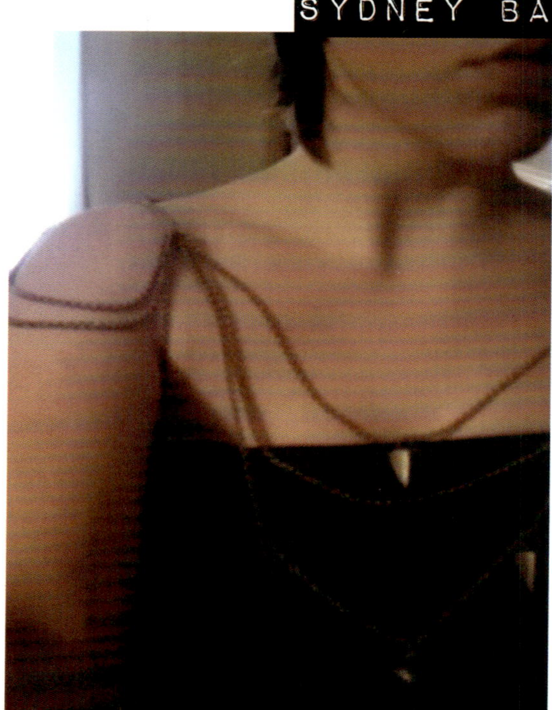

TANNISHA L. REID

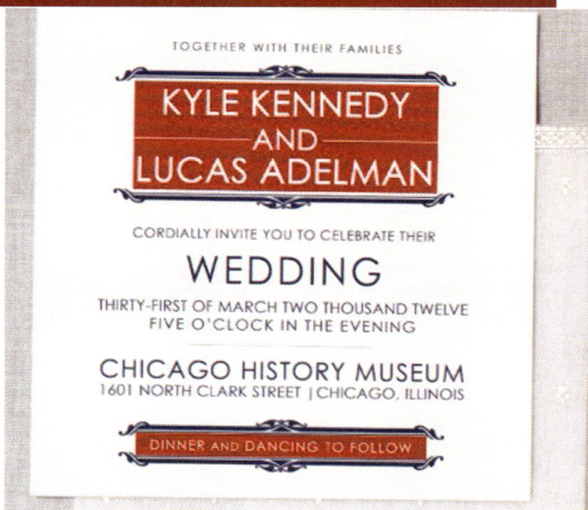

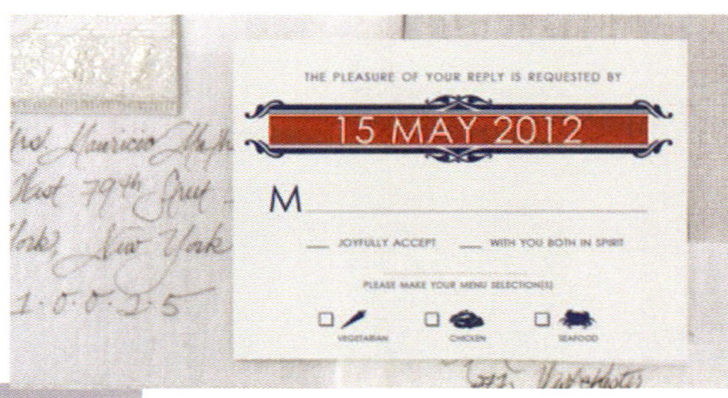

What is it?

I create bespoke special event + wedding invitations

The invitations I create marry handmade papers with foil details and beautiful embellishments with modern design and typography. Every event, organization and couple is unique, so it's wonderful to provide them with print design services that helps them communicate beautifully.

How did this start?

This work actually started when I designed my own wedding invitations almost 8 years ago. I work as a graphic designer, but I've become very interested in the wedding and special event industry as well. Recently I decided to create an independent invitation studio that allows me to fully explore both of my interests and launched Be My Guest Design.

Recommendations?

Ralph Jones {photographer}, Jozeph Alberti {engineer, pioneering the fuel cell work to improve lives in developing countries}, Halima Cassells {muralist + community gardner}, Senghor Reid {painter, filmmaker + arts educator}, Sydney James {painter, clothing designer + community art garden cultivator}, Jocelyn Rainey {artist, educator + community leader}

DEMETRUIS GREEN

What is it?

The profection comes from the abstract ideal being brought to life

A mixture of my grandma's collages and my artwork... I work with oil and canvas... my first series was named Leaving America... the latest is an ethereal version of Jesus. I love origami... I want to put it in my everyday living so this is a crane lamp.

How did this start?

3rd grade just by reading.

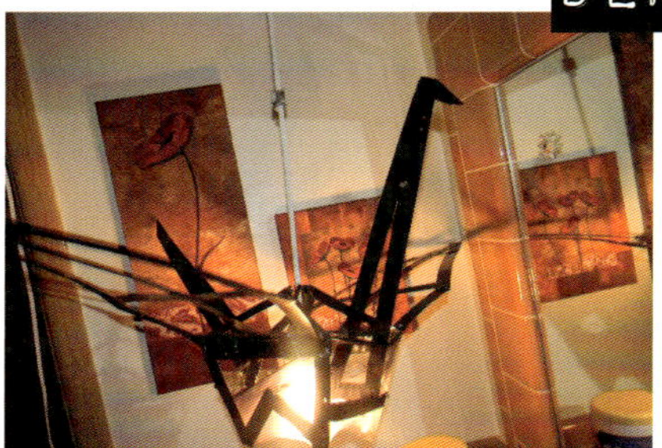

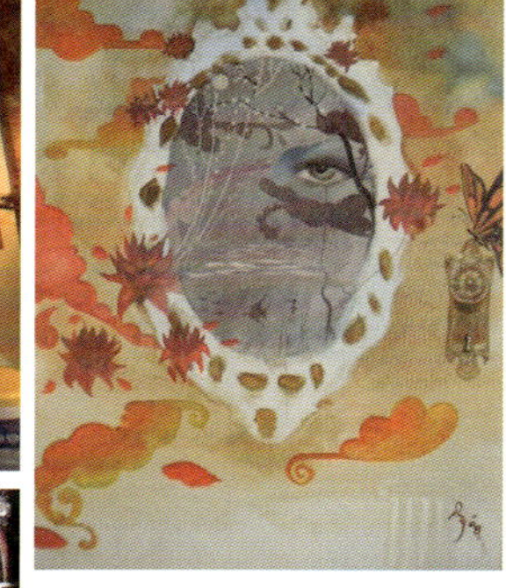

CHENE AND JEFFERSON
48207

TRACEY MARCEL BOZEMAN

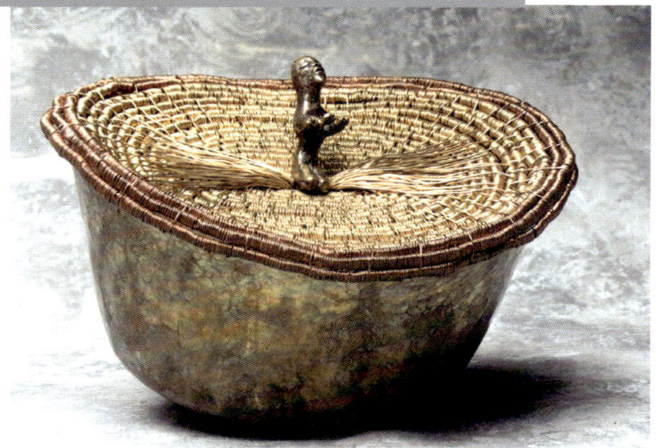

4 MILE RADIUS OF DOWNTOWN DETROIT 48207

What is it?

I modify metal by raising hammering, braising, cutting, and weaving.

Majority of my work centers on the vessel, a container of the material matter, the conveyer of thoughts, and the holder of history.

How did this start?

A fourteen year old with a bent piece of wire in one hand and a torch in the other.

B. WHAT DO YOU MAKE, MODIFY, IMPROVE OR REPAIR?
PLEASE DESCRIBE! SWEET GRASS BASKETS
DREAM CATCHERS + MEDICINE WHEELS
NECKLACES MADE FROM STONES + BEADS

JAMES AQUASH

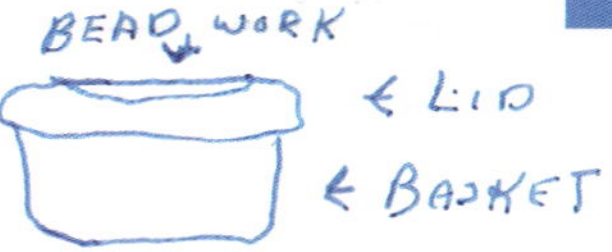

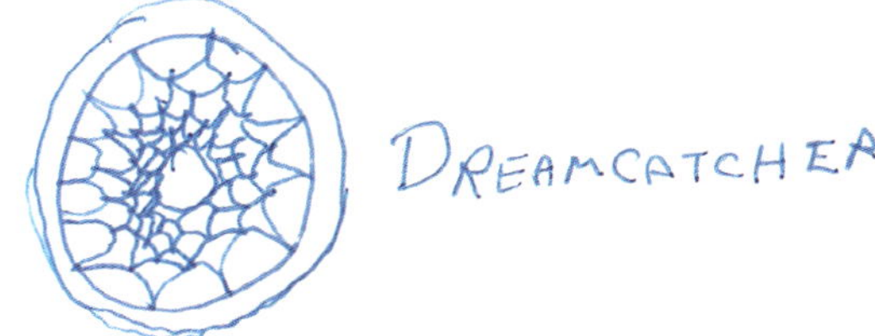

C. HOW DID THIS START?
WATCHED MY MOM

MELVINDALE
48122

MIKE GOULD

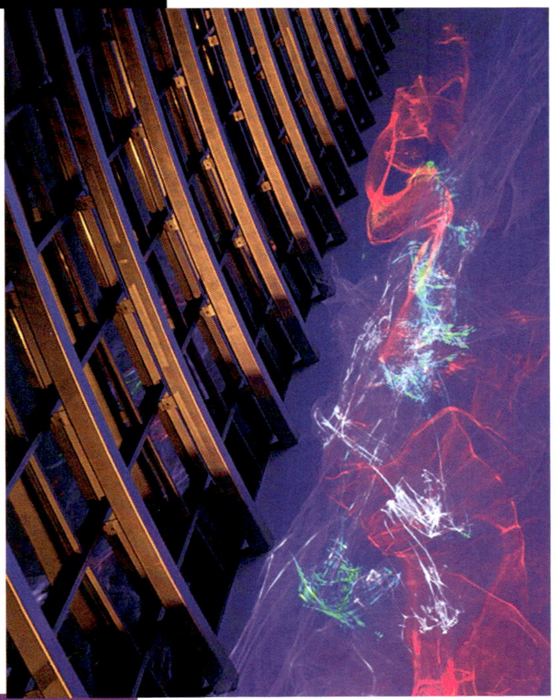

What is it?

Laser lightshows

We buy antique stage lights and projectors, gut them, and build laser lightshow devices into them.

How did this start?

Part of the Illuminatus Lightshow. As seen at Maker Faire 2010.

ANN ARBOR
48197

THOMAS CARRIER

What is it?

Ability, from scraps

I find the most attractive and durable objects that are then manufactured, are discarded once their purpose is gone. I collect this resource, and build things of purpose and beauty.

How did this start?

I once made a bar from the cockpit of a small airplane. I just couldn't see some stuff left in the trash. It accumulated quickly. Now whenever I need something, a table or lamp, or chair... or a friend needs something, I just make it. I cut, weld, shape, paint, and polish. Once you have these processes, the media is suprisingly trivial.

Recommendations?

I am the weirdo in my bunch, not big enough to have creational relationships yet...

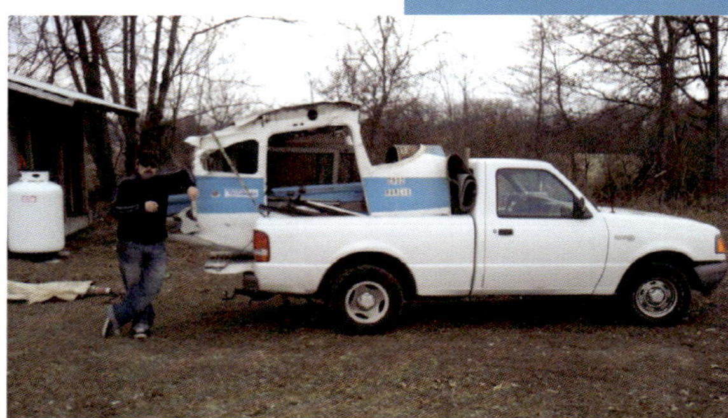

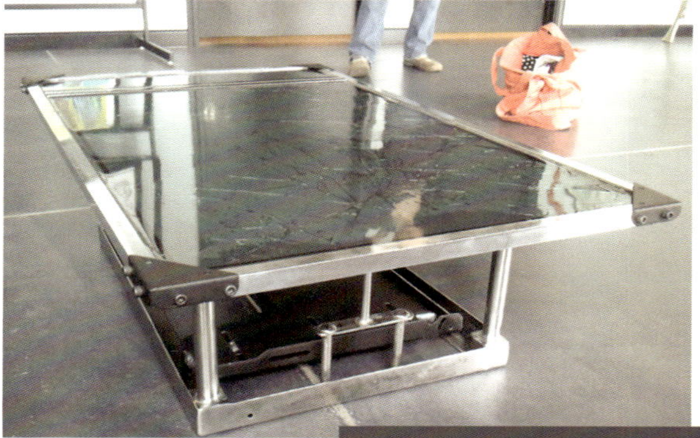

MADISON HEIGHTS
48071

DENNIS & CHRISTINA JACOBS

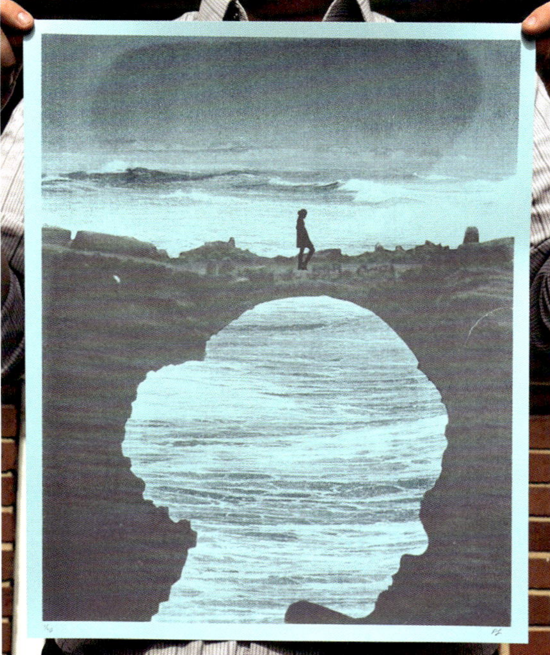

What is it?

Art prints and posters

We are designers and printmakers with a small studio space in Corktown. We make hand–pulled, screenprinted gig posters, art prints and paper goods. We started printing out of Dennis's parents' garage in 2008.

How did this start?

The first thing we made was our wedding invitations. We slowly grew as we started doing craft shows, gallery shows and custom commissioned work.

Recommendations?

Yes! We've been blogging about Michigan artists for several years now. Take a look at past posts and you will find tons of local creators.

perfectlaughter.com

CORKTOWN
48216

KAREN SNOW

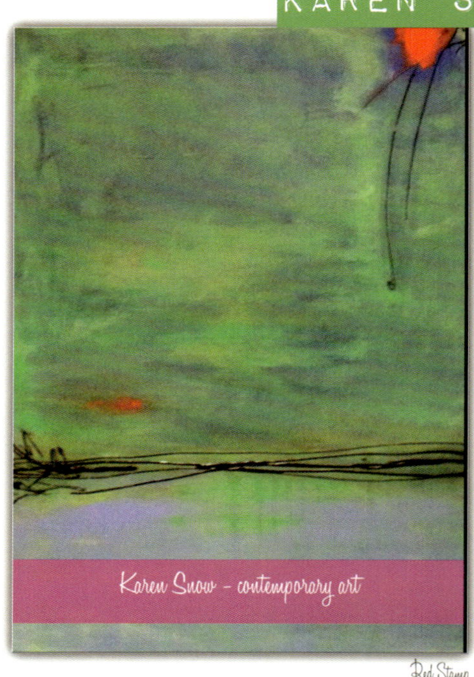

What is it?

I remove stress from my body.

I learned that painting removed all the stress from my body that accumulates during my day job. Contemporary abstract painting uses a totally different part of my brain. My mind wanders and I begin to create something that only I can control and make real. It takes me to a place that I enjoy.

How did this start?

I started painting in December. I had always wanted to paint but never found the time. In December, I lost my job and decided that it was now time to do what I wanted to do. Don't worry about finding a job. Just do something that has been on your list forever.

Recommendations?

My entire family. We all need to 'make' something to feel good.

BLOOMFIELD HILLS
48304

CLARE FOX

EASTERN MARKET
48207

What is it?

I make multi-media art.

My practice includes prints, photographs, textiles, video, and installations. I often use recycled, reclaimed, and found objects and materials.

I employ traditional printmaking techniques such as lithography, serigraphy, intaglio, letterpress and relief, often on handmade paper. I make books, sculptures, videos, and large-scale installations. I use digital cameras, scanners, laser and inkjet printers on occasion. Much of my work contains layers of collage or chine–colle and includes darkroom and antique photographic methods such as cyanotype and gum bichromate. (brief excerpt from my artist statement) My curiosity in collected objects is driven by the myth of personal history - the imagined experience, or skewed reality to which memories constantly refer. Many of my collected objects have become souvenirs and relics. They spell out a strange constellation of romantic preoccupations intertwined with a slight obsession in material culture.

I attempt to expose the cusp of reality and fantasy by examining my own mythical history. While I employ many methods and mediums, techniques both contemporary and archaic, most of my work begins with deconstructed photographs, clothing, linens, and other personal objects. With a finite focus on the inanimate objects that bear witness to emotional events, the work resides in a blurry realm bordering fact and fiction. Truth is certainly stranger than fiction and my created narratives are steeped in both. The work offers a glimpse of autobiographical truth, while simultaneously fulfilling a fetish for myth and nostalgia.

How did this start?

Creating my work within the realm of printmaking began to make the most sense after my first experience with traditional block printing. Although most of my finished work resides on paper, I get to experiment with wood, metal, acid, machines, hand tools, power tools, inks, solvents, and various materials.

What is it?

Ceramics Works fabricated by Pewabic Pottery can be seen throughout the United States in such places as the National Shrine of the Immaculate Conception in Washington, D.C., the Nebraska State Capitol, the Science Building at Rice University in Houston, and the Herald Square installation commissioned by the New York Metro Transit Authority.

In Michigan, Pewabic installations can be found in countless churches (including Christ Church at Cranbrook, Holy Redeemer Church and St. Paul Cathedral in Detroit), schools, commercial buildings and public facilities (such as Detroit's Guardian Building, Northwest Terminal, Shedd Aquarium in Chicago, the Detroit Public Library, and the new Comerica Ballpark,) public spaces (Detroit People Mover Stations) and private residences (particularly in Detroit's Indian Village and nearby Bloomfield Hills and Grosse Pointe.) Pewabic art pottery can also be found in many private and public collections including the Detroit Institute of Arts and

the Freer Gallery at the Smithsonian Institution in Washington, D.C. Today, Pewabic Pottery is a multifaceted institution with active and growing education, exhibition, museum and design and fabrication programs.

How did this start?

Pewabic Pottery was founded in 1903 by Mary Chase Perry (later Mary Chase Perry Stratton) and her partner, Horace Caulkins (developer of the Revelation Kiln), at the height of the Arts & Crafts movement in America. Pewabic's first home was a stable on Alfred Street in Detroit. Four years later, Pewabic Pottery moved to a new facility on East Jefferson designed by architect William Buck Stratton in the Tudor Revival style. In 1991, the building (which still houses the Pottery) and its contents were designated a National Historic Landmark and today is Michigan's only historic pottery.

PEWABIC POTTERY

INDIAN VILLAGE

48214

A. WILL YOU DRAW WHAT YOU MAKE?
OR ATTACH A PHOTO?

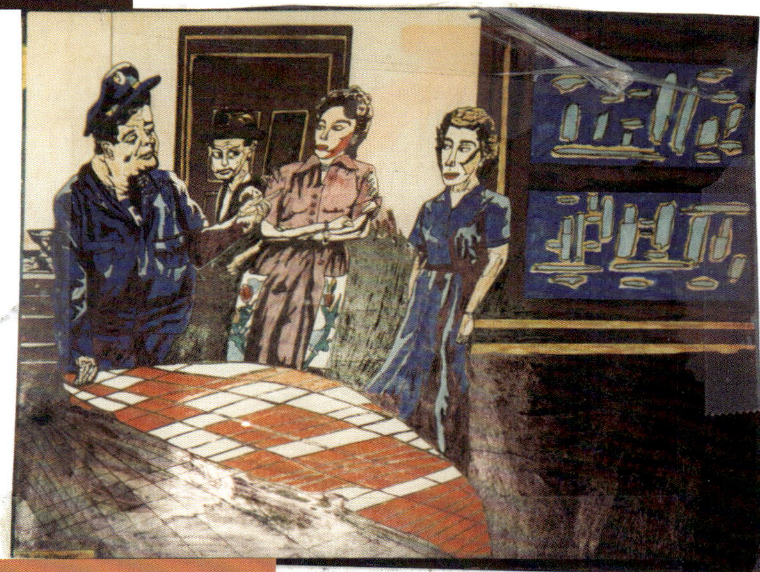

B. WHAT DO YOU MAKE, MODIFY, IMPROVE OR REPAIR?
PLEASE DESCRIBE!

TO BRING , Religion
threw ART

C. HOW DID THIS START?

iN High school
ARt class

B. WHAT DO YOU MAKE, MODIFY, IMPROVE OR REPAIR?
PLEASE DESCRIBE!

I CREATE DETROIT CENTRIC PSYCHEDELIC ROCK'N'ROLL POSTERS PAST PRESENT and FUTURE...

C. HOW DID THIS START?

I GOT A POSTER JOB WORKING FOR THE GRANDE BALLROOM in 1967

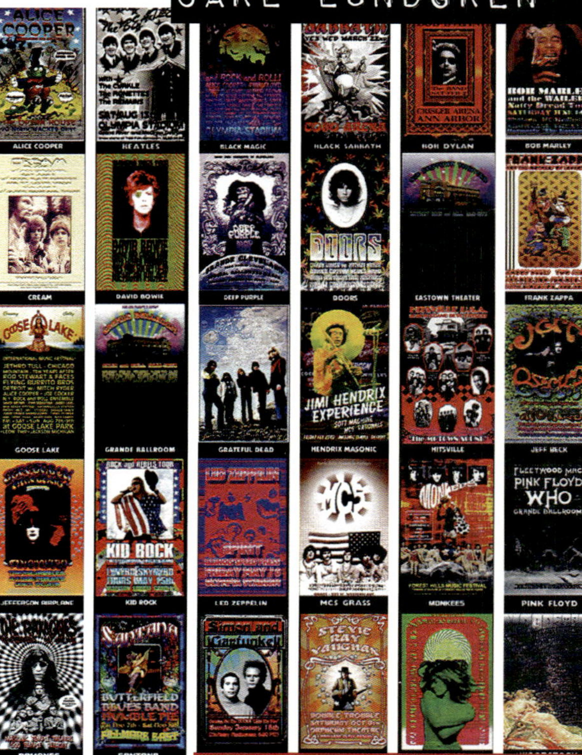

NICOLE MACDONALD

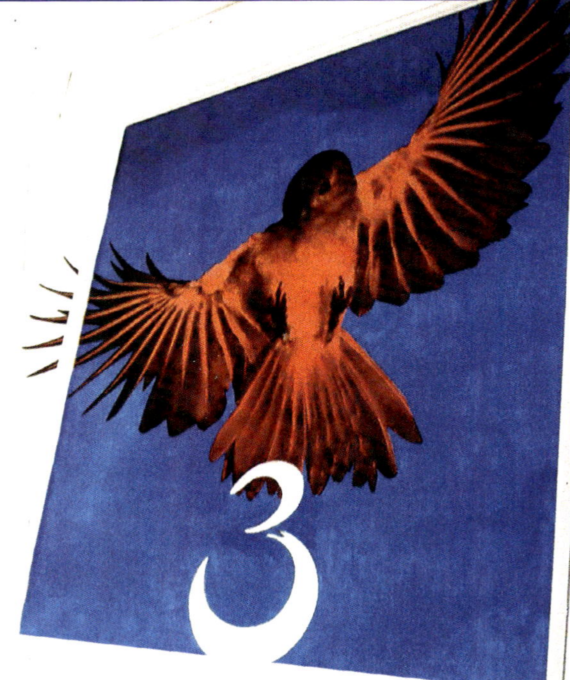

CASS CORRIDOR
48201

B. WHAT DO YOU MAKE, MODIFY, IMPROVE OR REPAIR? PLEASE DESCRIBE!

I make collages installed permanently or temporarily throughout Detroit, on walls in Eastern Market warehouses, doors in Woodbridge rentals, and in non-traditional larger spaces like the Bankle Building and Burton Theatre, Team Detroit and the downtown YMCA.
I have also put work outside for the weather to change and/or for the public to view and sometimes remove. My visual themes are Detroit-specific, attempting to explore the surreal side of the city through images that seem to run counter to one another. Often I focus on nature and the environment and the influence it has on the city today.

C. HOW DID THIS START?

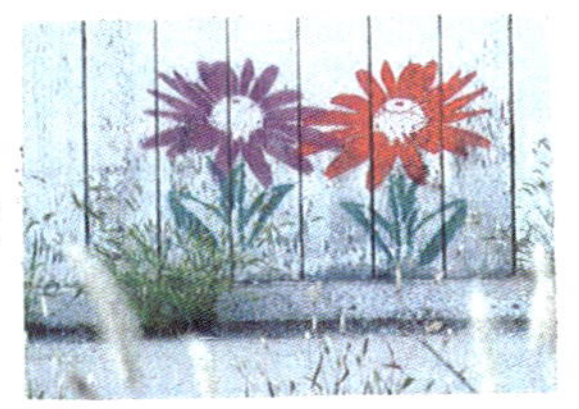

I started by making stencils to put outside, but wanted to make more detailed outdoor art that took longer to execute. This led to the idea of making wheat pastes that were collaged indoors, before mounting them outside. Some of the collages I started keeping, or just keeping inside -- to install various places on a semi-permanent basis. These collages evolved into differently-sized collages for different purposes.

RICK GOODRICH

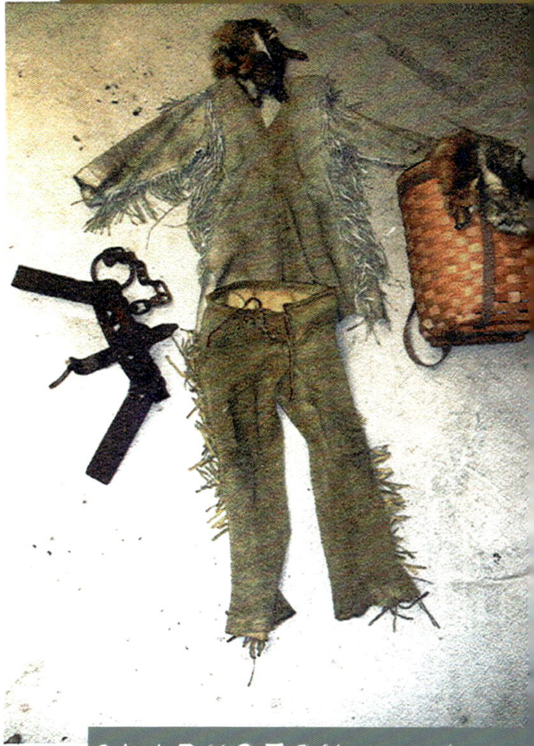

CLARKSTON, MI
48346

B. WHAT DO YOU MAKE, MODIFY, IMPROVE OR REPAIR?
PLEASE DESCRIBE!

Buckskin outfit I made from:
Mule deer, whitetail, red fox

C. HOW DID THIS START? I joined the
National Muzzle Loading
Rifle Association in
Friendship, Indiana in 1972.
Became fasinated with the
fur trade era.

LAURA BEYER

A. WILL YOU DRAW WHAT YOU MAKE?
OR ATTACH A PHOTO?

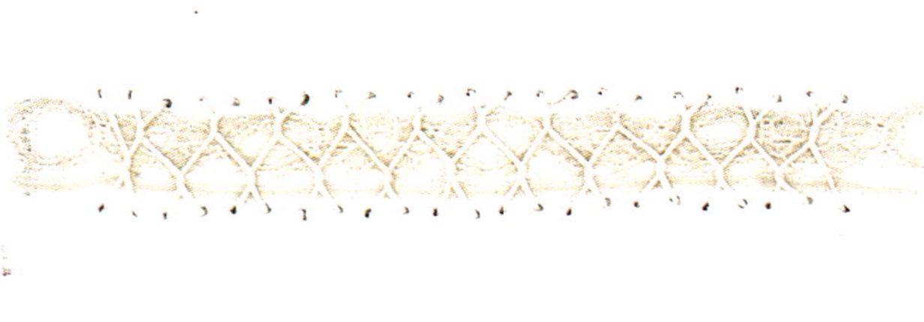

Model of a Link Stitch Binding.
sewn through tapes

B. WHAT DO YOU MAKE, MODIFY, IMPROVE OR REPAIR?
PLEASE DESCRIBE!

I'm a fiction writer and a
printmaker, I fit prints and
words together and bind them
into books.

I also make zines, paper, and
sculpture.

C. HOW DID THIS START?
When I was a kid I made a book
about a red ball that took a trip
around the neighborhood then
returned for dinner.

I never stopped making stories.

What is it?

Robotic Creature Sculptures

I take apart old toys and appliances with motors and reassemble them to make new "creatures". I then re-fur or dress the new creatures accordingly. I carve the heads from flower potting material and attach them to the motors so they move independently.

How did this start?

I started making the creatures as an extension of a photo series I was working on in order to have something physical to display with the photos. They took on a life of their own and soon I had a small little creature army.

Recommendations?

Jeremy Daly - He takes apart TVs and VCRs and reconnects them in multiples to make patterned TV loops and recordings.

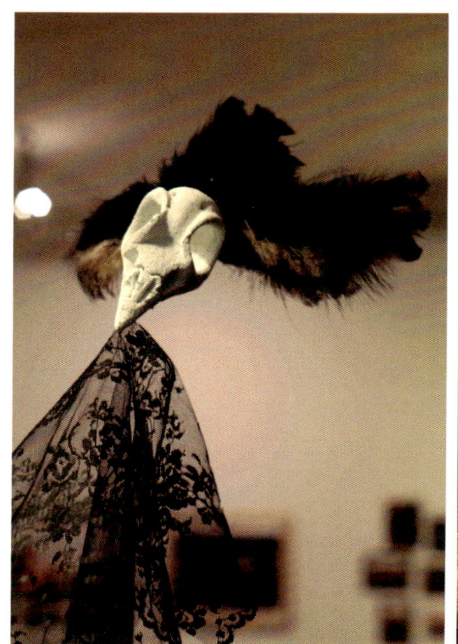

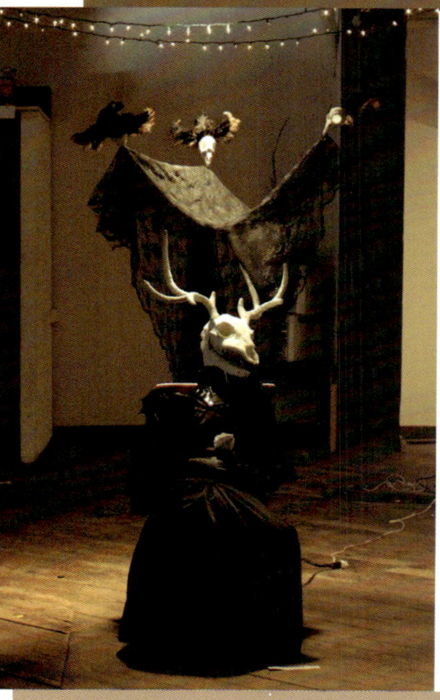

CRAIG L. WILKINS PH.D. / AIA

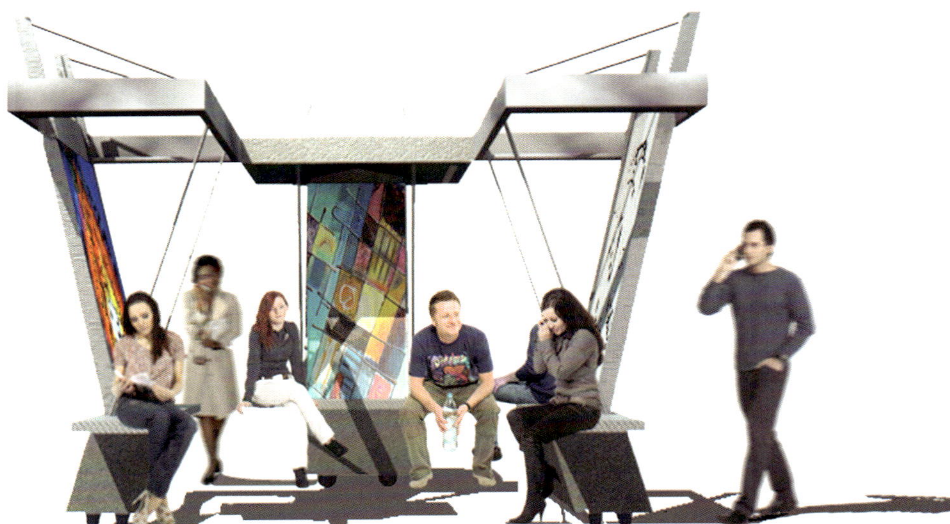

What is it?

transit seating

The poor performance of the public transportation system makes waiting on the bus a less than pleasurable experience. We have designed seating to make that experience a little more humane

How did this start?

I was watching a woman in her 70s with groceries wait for 3 hours on her feet for a bus ride home.

MIDTOWN 48202

B. WHAT DO YOU MAKE, MODIFY, IMPROVE OR REPAIR? PLEASE DESCRIBE!

Sprayed black paint on canvas for paintings.

For "Tragedy of Privilege" I broke an American Flag dish, broke a wall clock, glued an old gasoline container, cleaning gloves, wine bottle & ruler to a 5' x 3' wooden plank.

For "Can you shine this, boy?" I glued a spray painted black sneaker & a dollar bill on on ex's face.

C. HOW DID THIS START?

I grew up privileged in Grosse-Pointe and after getting my ass kicked by my dad, by white people, by black people, by women, & by gay people, I just decided to stop giving a fuck.

ROBERT P. YOUNG

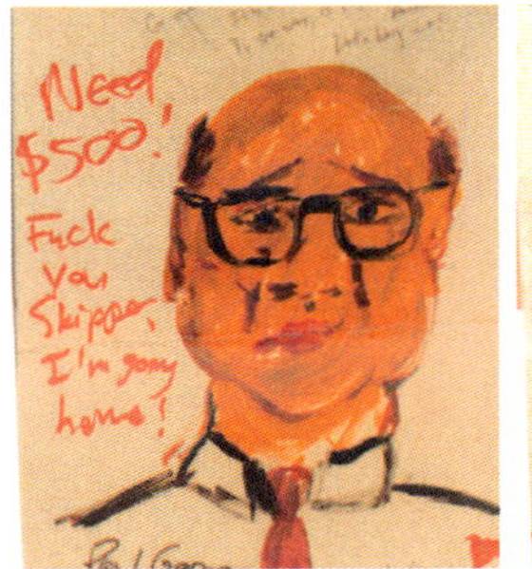

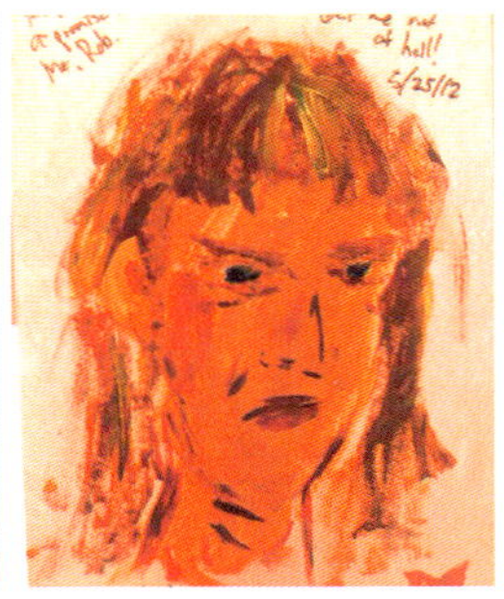

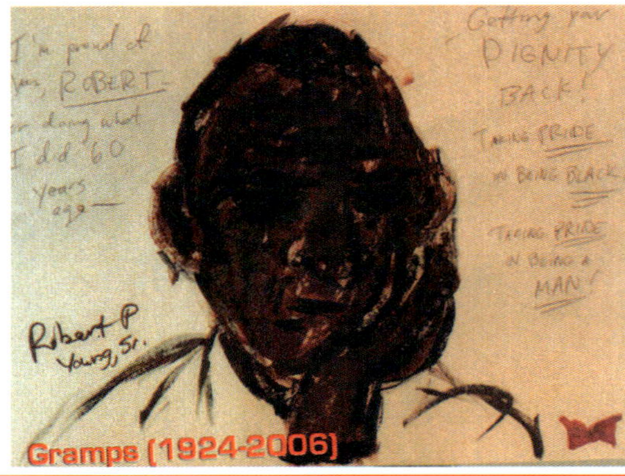

GROSSE POINTE PARK
MI. 48230

MICHAEL ZAKAR

METRO DETROIT
48085

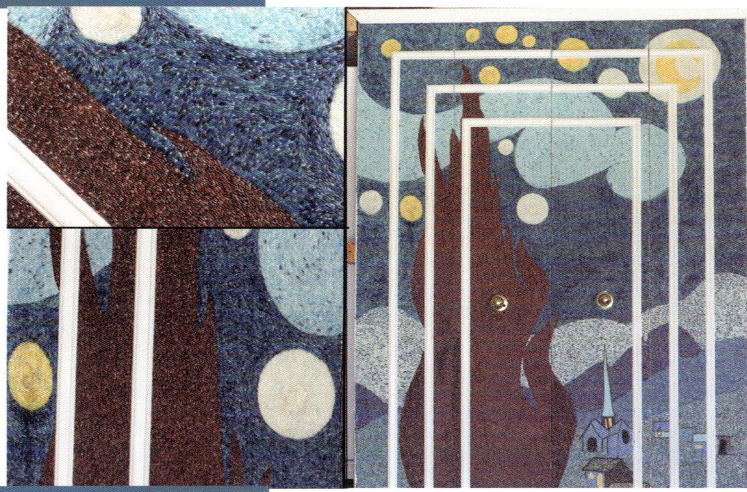

What is it?

Mural

My recreation of Van Gogh's Starry Night completely out of grains of rice on my closet

Riverside Railing

You can usually see glitter on the city towers from this side of the river –it's usually there, though on this soupy night, No, no glitter. The glass is dull, and black soot surrounds every pane all the way up the columns refracting sun from the river water and making surfaces look like end of day market scales. From left to right, the rest of the city does not refract light. It is ashy, fired out, and feral animals weave in and out of concrete basements. The window-holes are soft black, velvety and absorbing, so that shiny foreheads and teeth catch the light.

You are in a crisp white button down with blue lips and teeth, looking very moral and peach faced staring on from this riverside railing. You wish to be there in those buildings. The Ferris Wheel behind you has put on its lights and metal: Safety calls. It is almost dark now, and you can hear your

*Mom's voice shouting from beyond. Shouting: Fin-chey! Wear a jacket! I'll pack you some soup in your thermos but there's no way in hell! I'm letting you out without a jacket, Do you hear me!" All the stores have closed; the holiday display at the Hudson's Department Store is smashed and looted, and the building is balled down.
Tomorrow. Tomorrow you will go.*

What is it?
Short Stories

Writing very short stories usually from the view of a character, I enjoy constructing a narrative by inhabiting a distant perspective or idea.

OLIVIA LORI

ACROSS THE
DETROIT RIVER
48226

How did this start?

I wanted to make something publicly readable from my personal notebooks, as well as enjoying the game or riddle of putting a story together coming directly from the jumble and fragment of sight, running discourse, and sound.

Recommendations?

There are many, I'm sure…
Prof. Michael Farrell for repairing/restoring and then living in a home on Alfonse.

arthousetours.com comes to mind.

ESTEBAN CASTRO

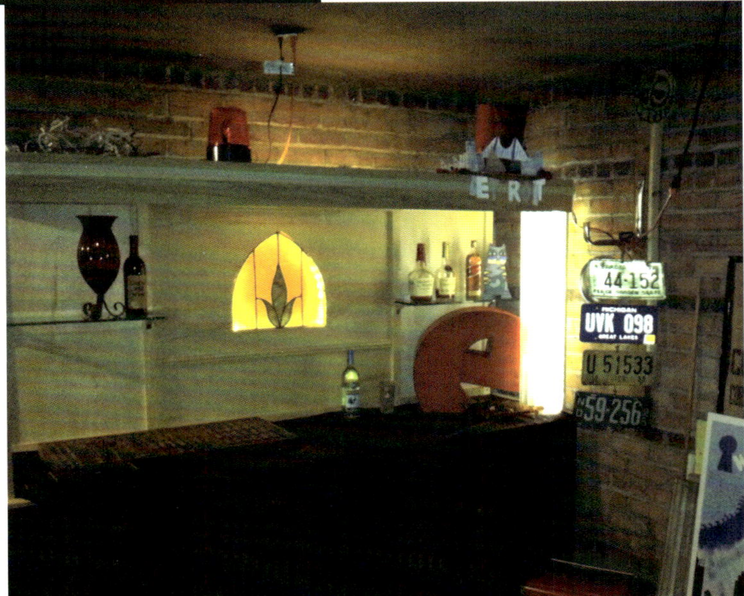

SPRINGWELLS (SOUTHWEST DETROIT) 48209

What is it?

I make bookshelves, cabinets and bar service stations. Home improvement and historic restoration of home and furniture.

I have a beautiful home built in 1927. I spend time on restoration and preservation of this house and the antique furniture pieces that I have acquired over the past 6 years. My latest project is a bar space in my garage to assist in events and dinner parties. The purpose is to build the city through people.

How did this start?

I was already working in the house using the skills with woodworking that I learned at an old job. Then a friend (Kate Daughdrill) convinced me to activate my attached garage during a series of projects based on Detroit communities.

KATHY TOTH

What is it?

Photographs

I've spent a fair amount of time photographing the vanishing elements of community, such as small stores and businesses in the Detroit area as a reaction against all the industrial ruin porn I have seen. Many of the small shops and businesses have not been looted and scrapped and have potential for reuse.

How did this start?

First visit to Detroit

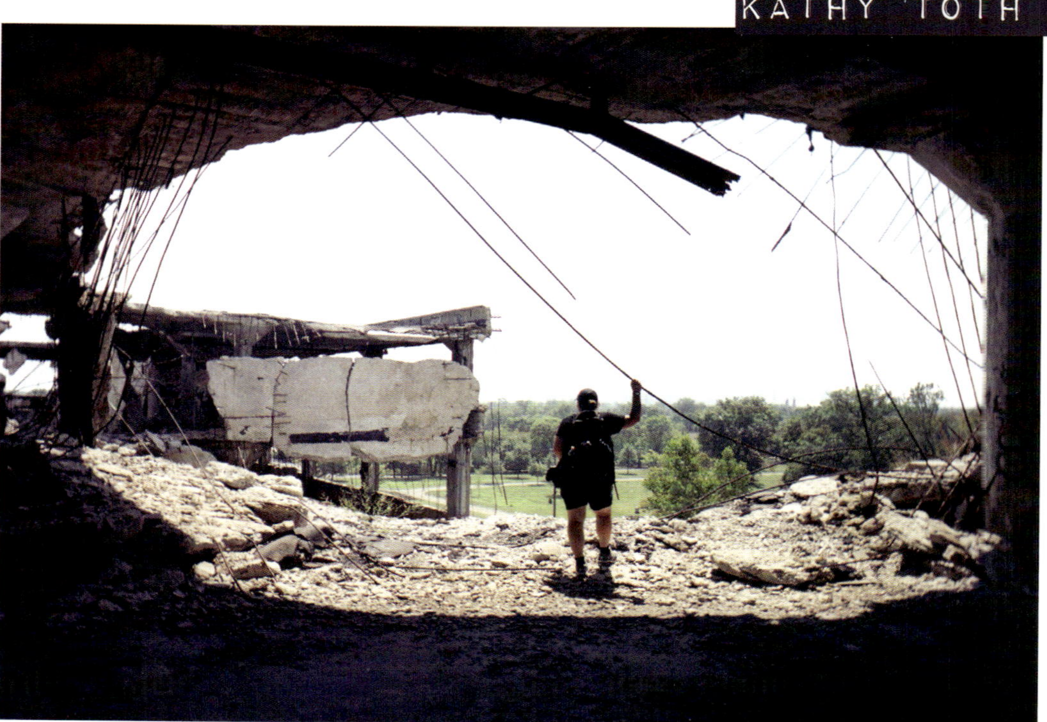

ONTARIO
M4V2.9

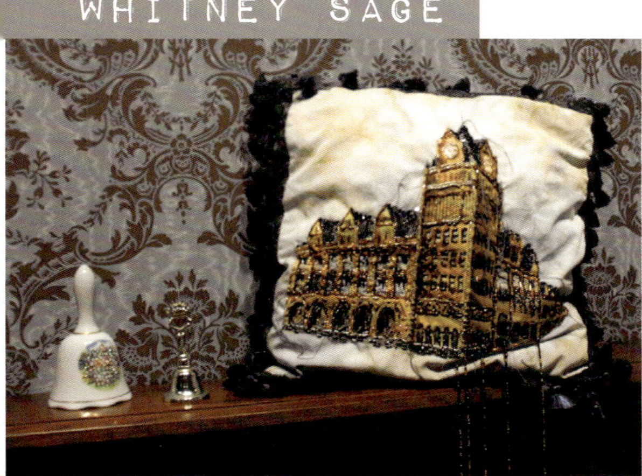

What is it?

Handmade Detroit Souvenirs

Hand painted pillows featuring images of Detroit buildings no longer standing. The images are painted and embellished with glass beads.

How did this start?

This work started in response to an interest in World's Fair collectors items and the heroic image of the building within these items. I was interested in the nostalgic longings we have towards a place that no longer exists. In conversations about Detroit there is often talk about its gilded age - the days of the auto's reign, a place so distant in the contemporary rearview mirror that it is no longer relevant to the current conversation of Detroit's identity and struggles. The souvenir itself is frozen in time and it remains an object suitable for display only. These idealized visions of Detroit function much the same: delicate, nostalgic and antiquated.

My installation of these handmade objects spoke to the almost religious reverence for a history no longer practical in post-industrial Detroit, while stressing the seamless, everpresent integration of this sort of idealism into our lives.

Recommendations?

John Glick

What is it?

I strive to improve the spirit of the downhearted. Using life experience, I try to give hope to the faint of heart. I try and give a voice to those that have an unclean history. I try and teach scruples through the unscrupulous and vow to give spirit to the spiritless.

How did this start?

This started a few years ago when I realized that things can fall apart, but can always be built back up fresh and new. Life can take hold of people for the worst and a good story, a good true story and the willingness to tell your own story and see light with every crazy, foolish thing that you might've done or said has meaning and builds character.

So now, me, being a recovering addict/ alcoholic, want to give hope to others that have found out the hard way that parties always come to an end, and God may not be there all the time to pick you back up. I'm living proof that you don't have to be an AA fanatic to survive addiction. You just have to forgive yourself and with YOUR past experience and guiding light, you can breed hope in others.

Recommendations?

Jeremy Mathew-
Quite Scientific Records - Ann Arbor, MI

Newcombe Clarke-
Ghostly International - Ann Arbor

ALEXANDER LESNER

WEST VILLAGE

48214

GWEN JOY

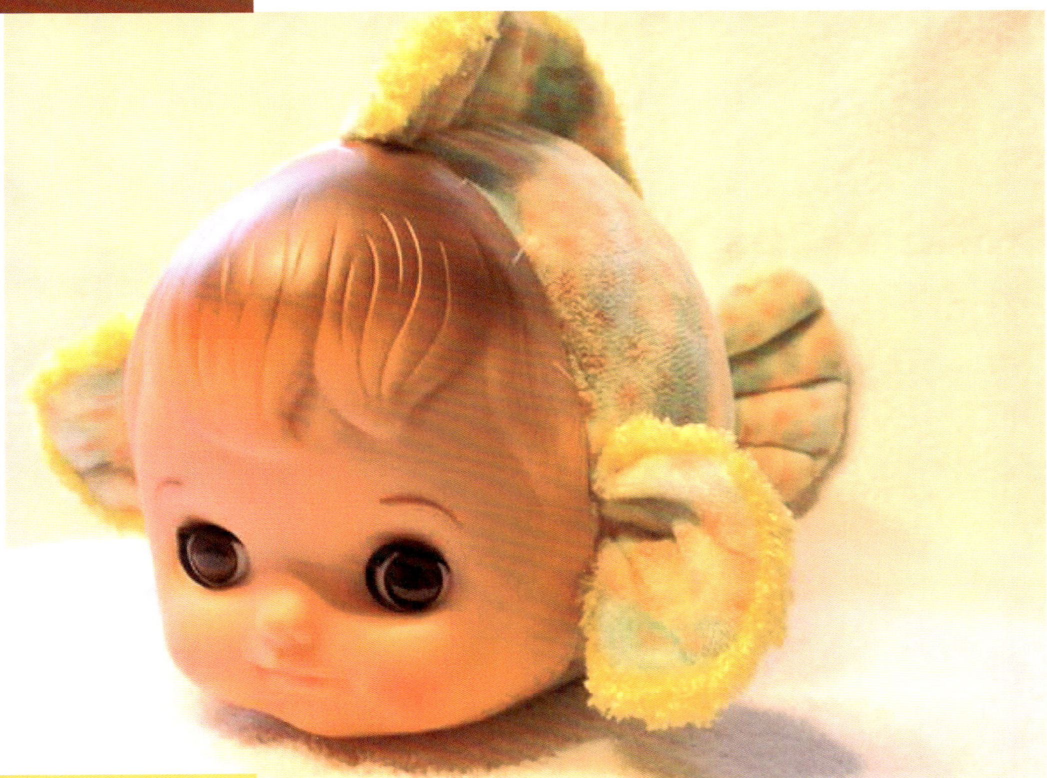

What is it?

toys, jewelry and folk art

I make one of a kind toys, bold vintage found object jewelry, and folk art paintings. I modify toys and transform them into something new, using two differing parts. For instance a duck head on a pig's body. I use that same mode when making my jewelry and also use this thinking when coming up with subject matter for my painting.

How did this start?

I have been painting since a young teen, doing the necklaces since age 21 and the toys since I was 26.

gwenjoy.com
.

REDFORD
48240

What is it?

LED Billboard in Detroit

Through the Billboard Art Project in Detroit, Michigan I submitted several images that used common advertising phrases and displayed them against a calming cloud background, appropriated commercial language and transforming the commonly used words into free reflective messages.

How did this start?

I wanted to reinterpret corporate promotional spaces, transforming the notion of "advertising" into something more about contemplation than acquiring.

Recommendations?

There was an open call for submissions for this particular billboard in Detroit, Michigan

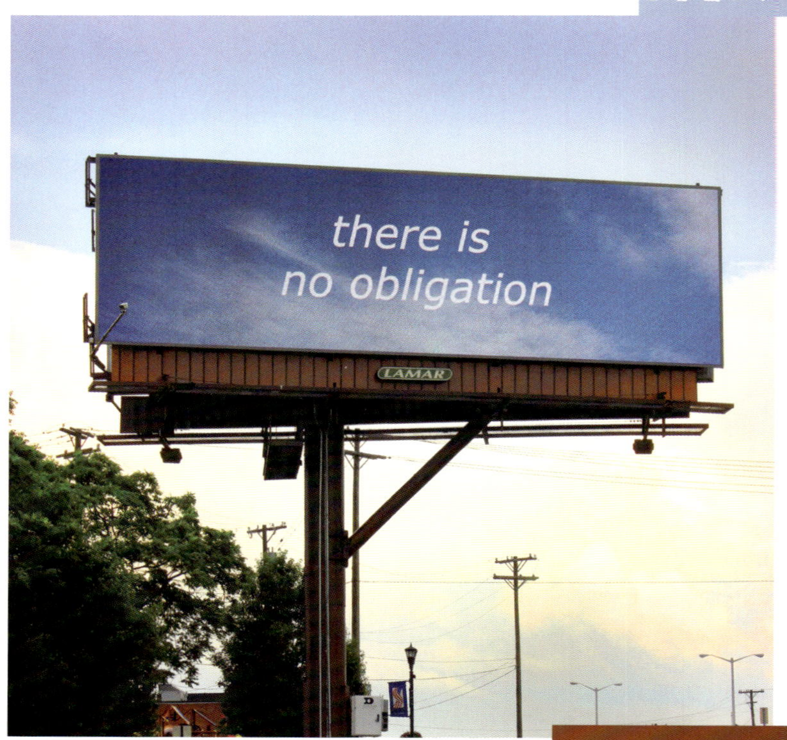

ANN ARBOR

23507

PETER CHRISTENSON

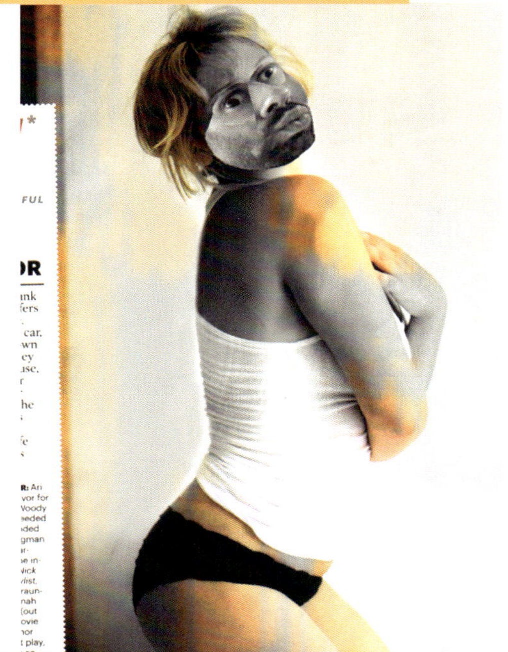

ROCHESTER HILLS
48307

What is it?

Objects and Non-Objects

I make things that concurrently do and don't do stuff

How did this start?

These processes began as a tyke with my older brother when we first attempted to develop a protoype for a bunk-bed mounted, hands free light switch and back scratchers.

Recommendations?

my big brother :)

ERIC SWIATOWY

B. WHAT DO YOU MAKE, MODIFY, IMPROVE OR REPAIR?
PLEASE DESCRIBE! I make many things, mostly of metal. I make everything from candle holders to large statues to cars/dune buggies. I tell my family + friends that if its metal/mechanical and it can be made or fixed, I can fix it, I do some inventing as well. I am a problem solver, designer, inventor, mechanic (machinery) + most of all an artist

C. HOW DID THIS START? I've always been a tinkerer and an artist so I combined that with my thirty years of machining + fabricating skilled trades experience + started doing metal art. A lot of my work has been with the human shape but has expanded and now is using recycled materials as well as new. My work is sometimes functional as well as interesting.

I have a page on Facebook although it, by no means, has a very good sample of my work. I haven't updated in a while.

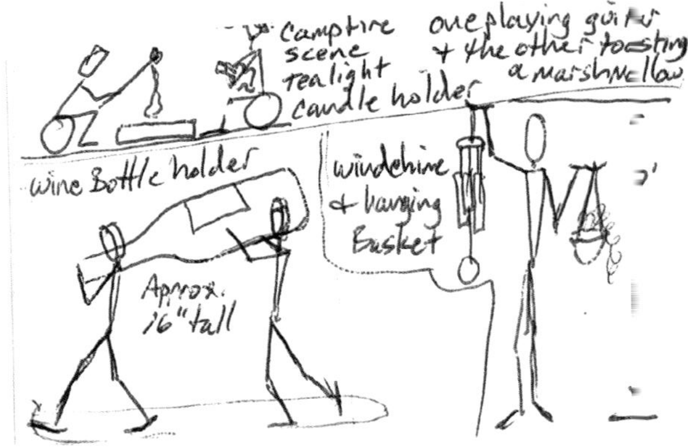

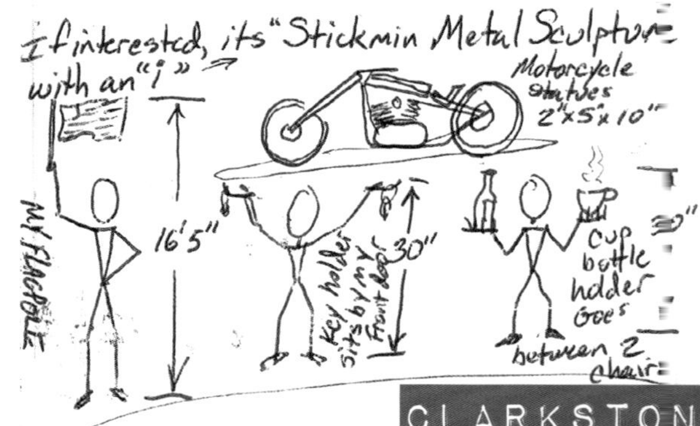

CLARKSTON
48346

HENRY BOGLE

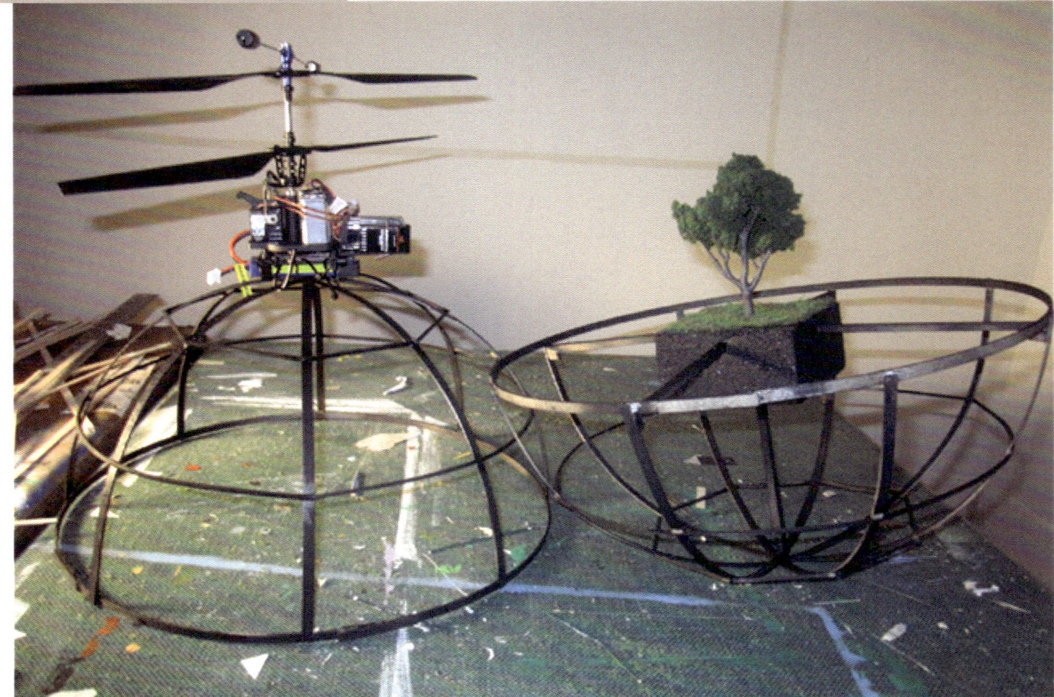

What is it?

Flying Sphere Sculptures

Flying spherical environments that contain dioramas of trees, houses, etc. I want to include them in the current urban dialogue about Detroit.

How did this start?

Idea I've been thinking about for years but only recently started building them, contacting model makers to assist me. Influences from sci-fi movies like Silent Running to visionary architecture.

Recommendations?

Andy Krieger makes great 3 dimensional paintings with a Detroit spin.

DETROIT AREA
48198

SARAH LAPINSKI

B. WHAT DO YOU MAKE, MODIFY, IMPROVE OR REPAIR?
PLEASE DESCRIBE!

I generally sew things for fun, money + utility. It is engineering, architecture, sculpture + art. Clothes, structures, environments, Displays, costumes, inflatables — I've sewn them all.

C. HOW DID THIS START?

Observing beautiful "stacks of naked undressed cardboard tubes at my fabric go-to-spot, a seed was planted. There's is too much waste in the garment/sewn product industry to let go to waste.

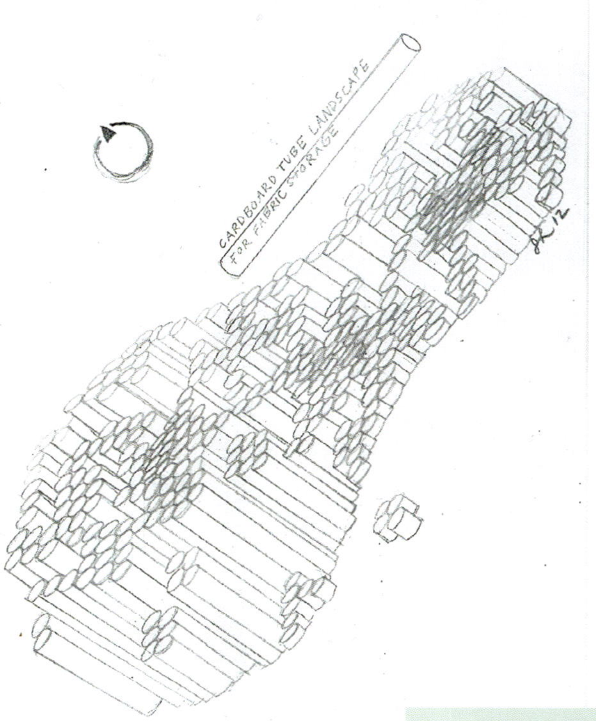

CORKTOWN
48226

RANDY LEBAR

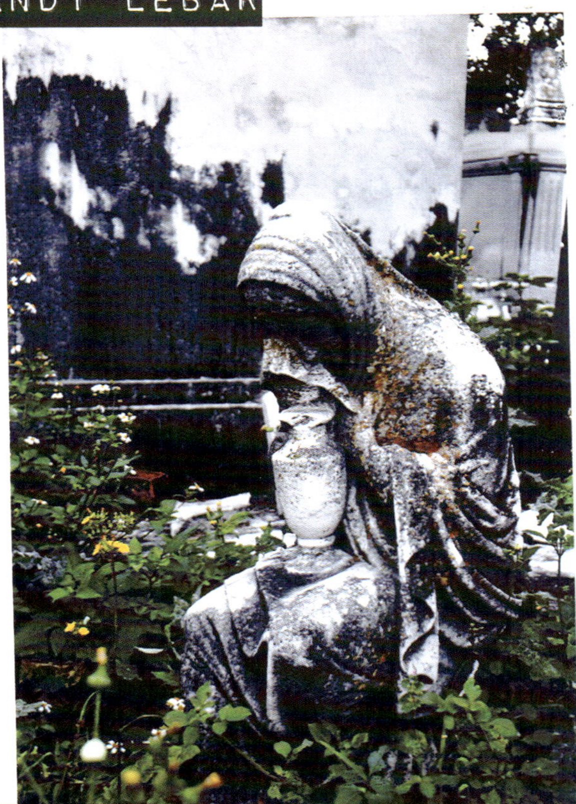

TRENTON
48183

B. WHAT DO YOU MAKE, MODIFY, IMPROVE OR REPAIR?
PLEASE DESCRIBE!

a lot do photography. I take pictures
of things that I see out of the
normal, any thing different.
This is my favorite photo from New Orleans

C. HOW DID THIS START?

I started to do photography because I
wanted a hobby.

A. WILL YOU DRAW WHAT YOU MAKE?
OR ATTACH A PHOTO?

B. WHAT DO YOU MAKE, MODIFY, IMPROVE OR REPAIR?
PLEASE DESCRIBE!

Beaded dreamcatchers
Beaded boxes
     "   earrings

C. HOW DID THIS START?

began with earrings. +
had a teacher come in
several times a week
to assist with beaded
boxes + then went into
dreamcatchers

DORIS GIASSON

DETROIT
48209

ROBERT MIREK

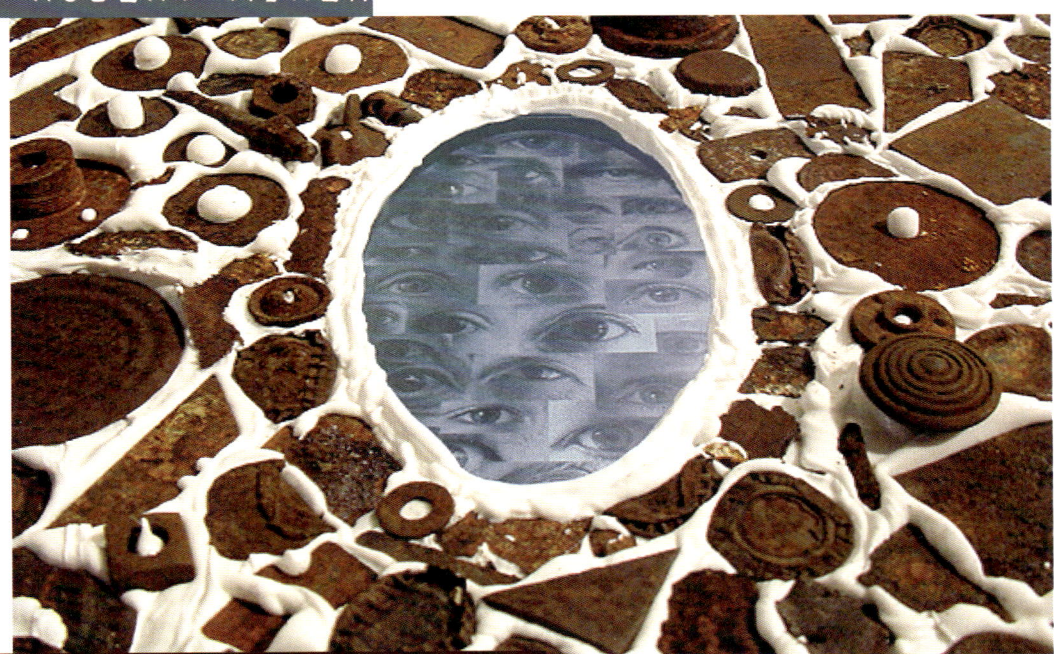

What is it?

Recycled street detritus and old laptop

Found rusted metal fragments found on the street and coupled with a working animation from an outdated Mac black and white computer depicting a sequence of eyes opening and closing to emphasize the notion of seeing, looking, caring about one's place in the world.

How did this start?

Throughout the years of street fragment collecting and the notion of paying attention to what most would see as trash can be used within another context and given yet another "life".

Recommendations?

Dick Cruger, Detroit Michigan

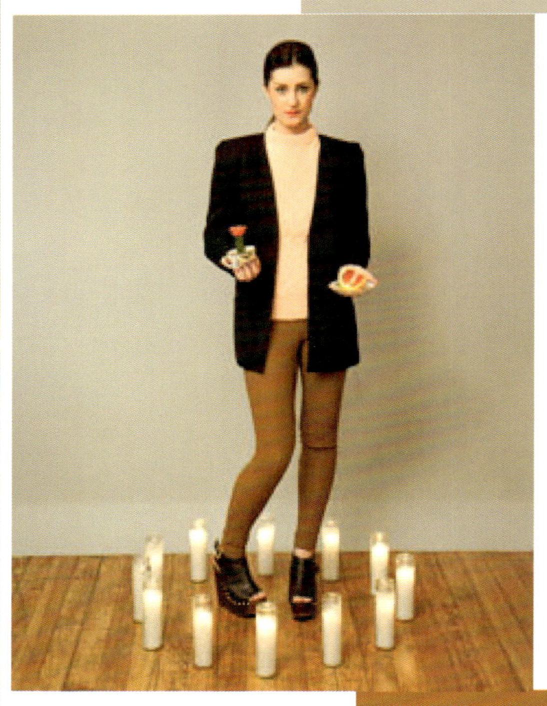

What is it?

Outfits

I create narratives through modifying the look of clothing on certain persons in certain photographs.

How did this start?

I decided clothing was important as what you have to say on a daily basis.

Recommendations?

Matthew Bustamonte

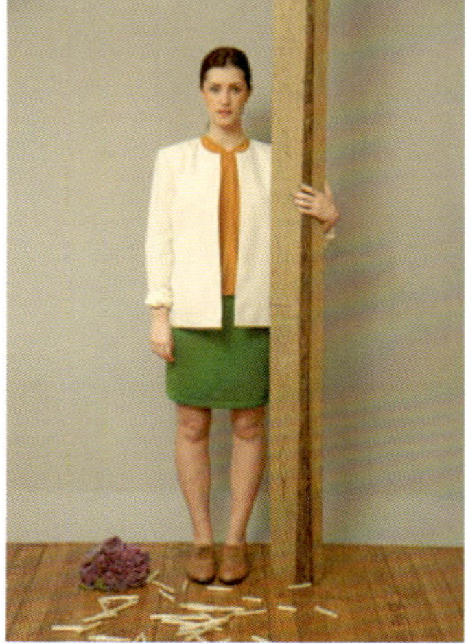

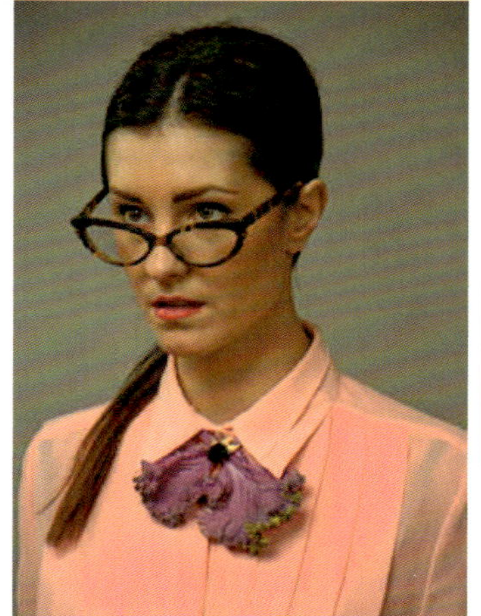

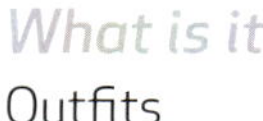

ALEXANDER PORBE

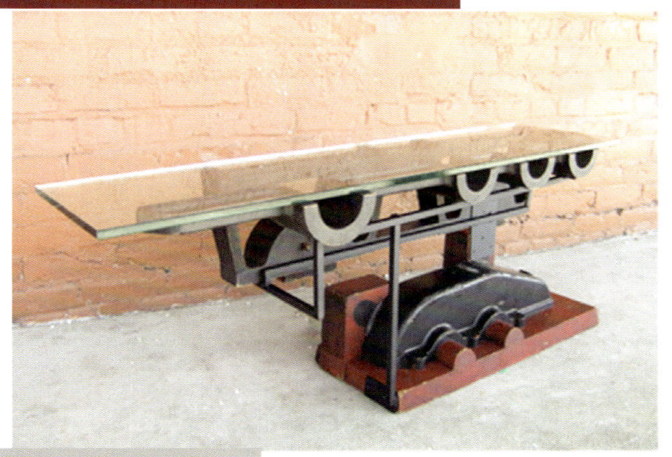

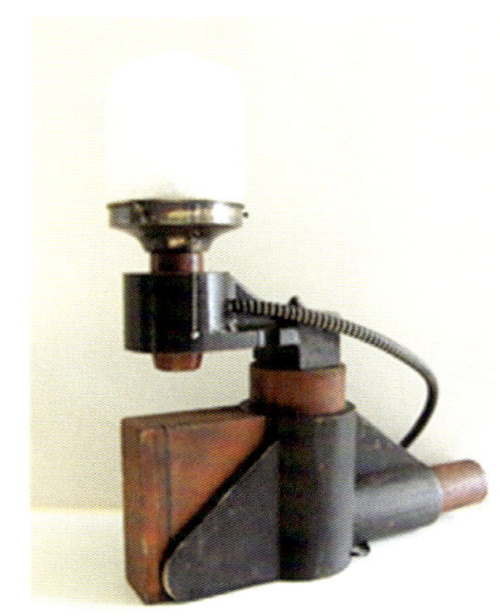

What is it?

My work is mostly fabricated from a variety of metals. Found industrial objects are incorporated on occasion, but I also build my own designs from scratch. One facet of my functional art incorporates the use of antique wooden casting patterns from a defunct Detroit Crane factory.

How did this start?

I graduated from The Center For Creative Studies with a BFA in Industrial Design in 1991. I started my own business, Incite Design, LLC shortly thereafter, designing and building a variety of projects such as restaurant interiors, custom lighting, and hand rails. I have always used an industrial aesthetic in my work which culminated in my early days of rummaging around in Detroit's numerous scrapyards for raw materials. Though I currently work out of a barn in Tecumseh, MI, I spent from 1991-2004 in Detroit. I had shops in Corktown, Rivertown, and the near East Side of Mack and Mt. Elliot.

CHRIS RIDDELL

B. WHAT DO YOU MAKE, MODIFY, IMPROVE OR REPAIR?
PLEASE DESCRIBE!

I collect magazines
and make collages.
I explore Detroit
and collect material.

C. HOW DID THIS START?

a hybrid of
hoarding and art
school at Wayne State.

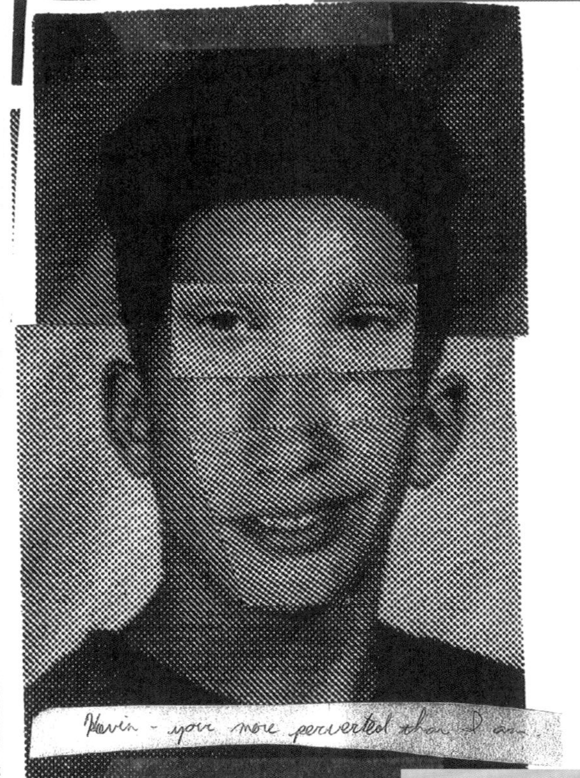

HAMTRAMCK
48212

DAVID SMITH

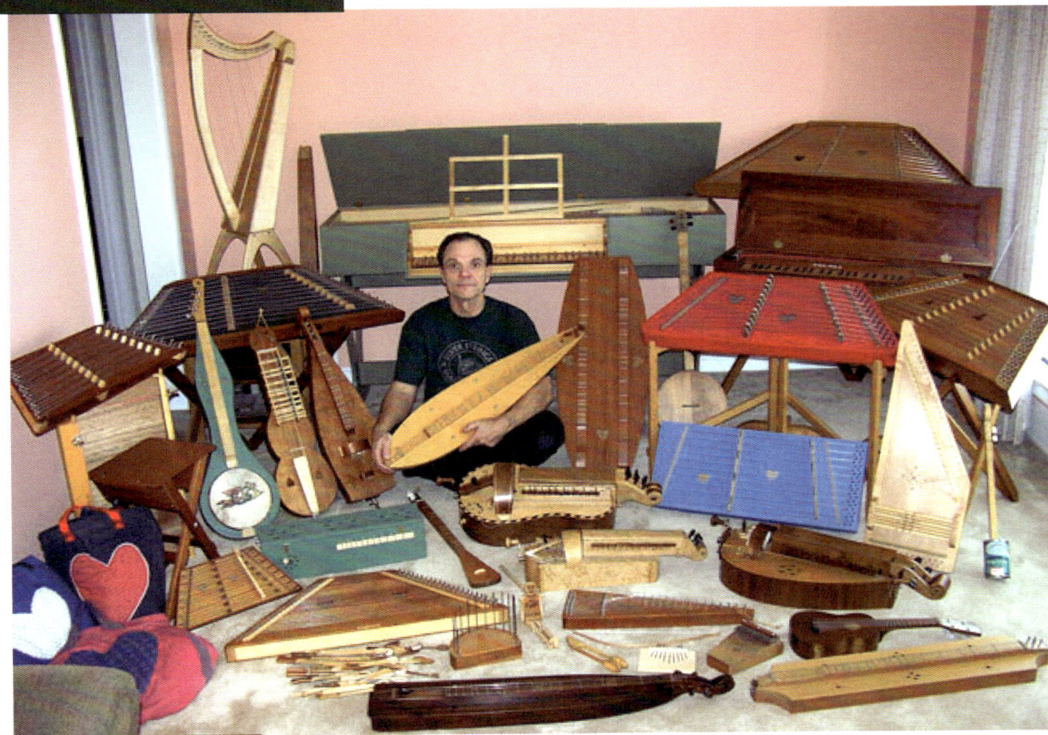

DEARBORN
48214

What is it?

Folk music instruments

For the past 35 years I have constructed approximately 40 Folk Music Instruments, 9 Hammered Dulcimers, 7 Mountain Dulcimers, 2 Harpsichords, Clavichord, 3 Hurdy Gurdies, Dulcigurdy, Bowed and Plucked Psalteries, Nail Violin, Tin Can Violin, Hungarian Citera, Swedish Nyckelharpa, Folk Harp, Thumb Piano as well as collecting and refurbishing various novelty musical instruments. A very few instruments were built from kits but most were built using designs and plans that I created. Creating instruments has led me into playing them too and I belong to a Dulcimer Club and Ukulele Group as well as perform occasionally at open mic nights.

How did this start?

Since I was very young I have enjoyed working with my hands and tinkering with anything mechanical as well as working with wood (furniture, clock cases, model airplanes and boat building).

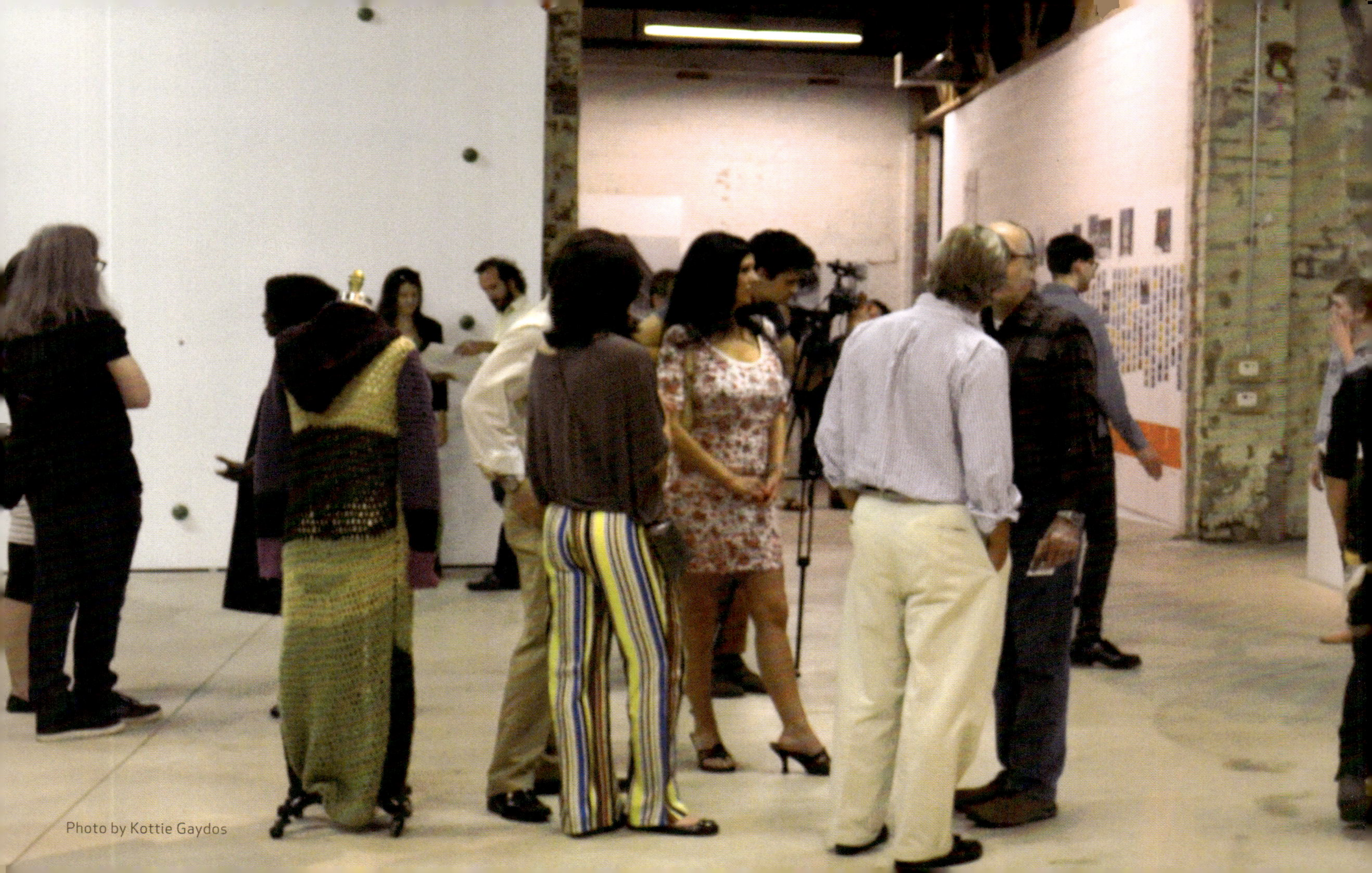

Photo by Kottie Gaydos

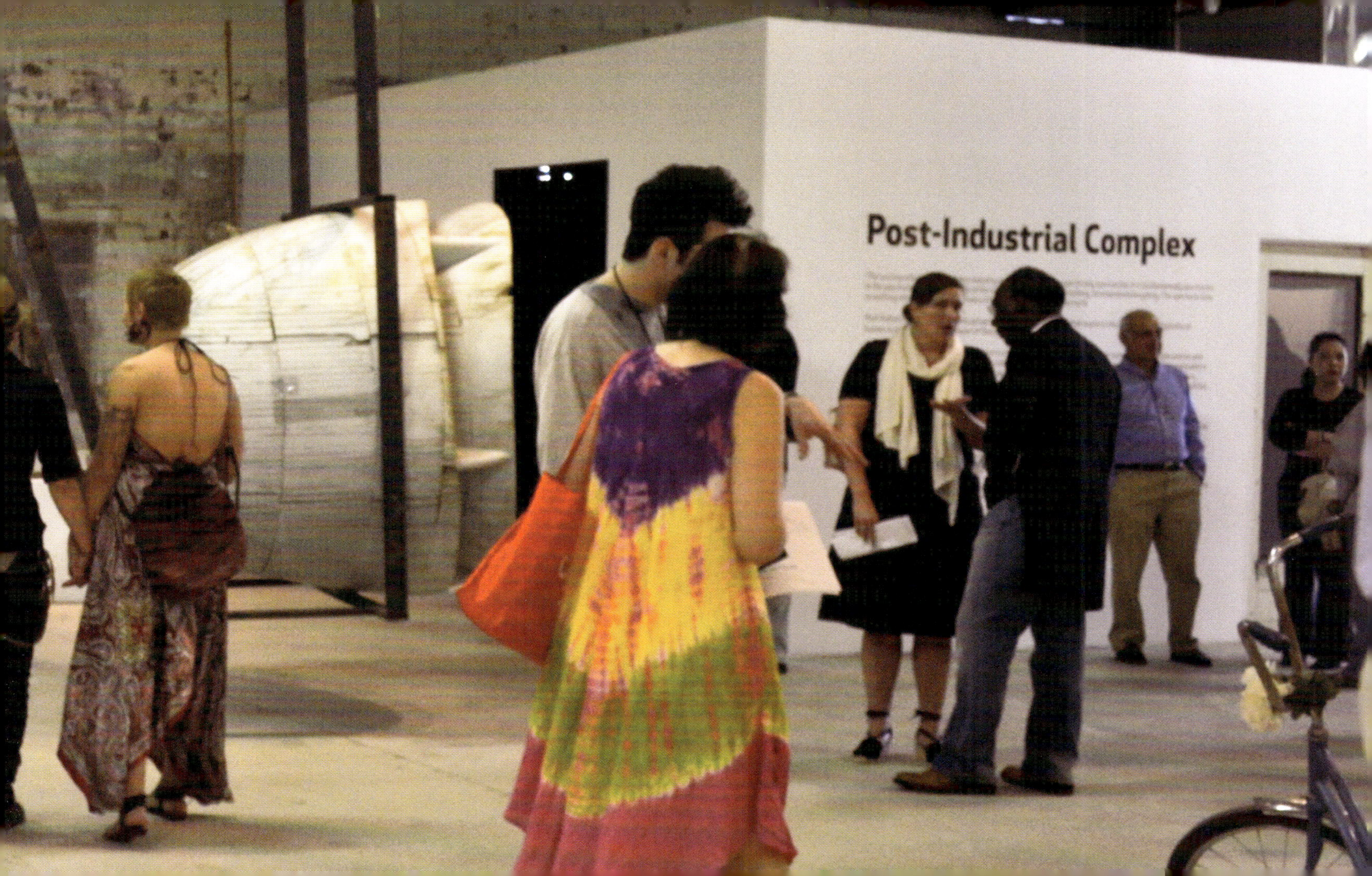

Post-Industrial Complex

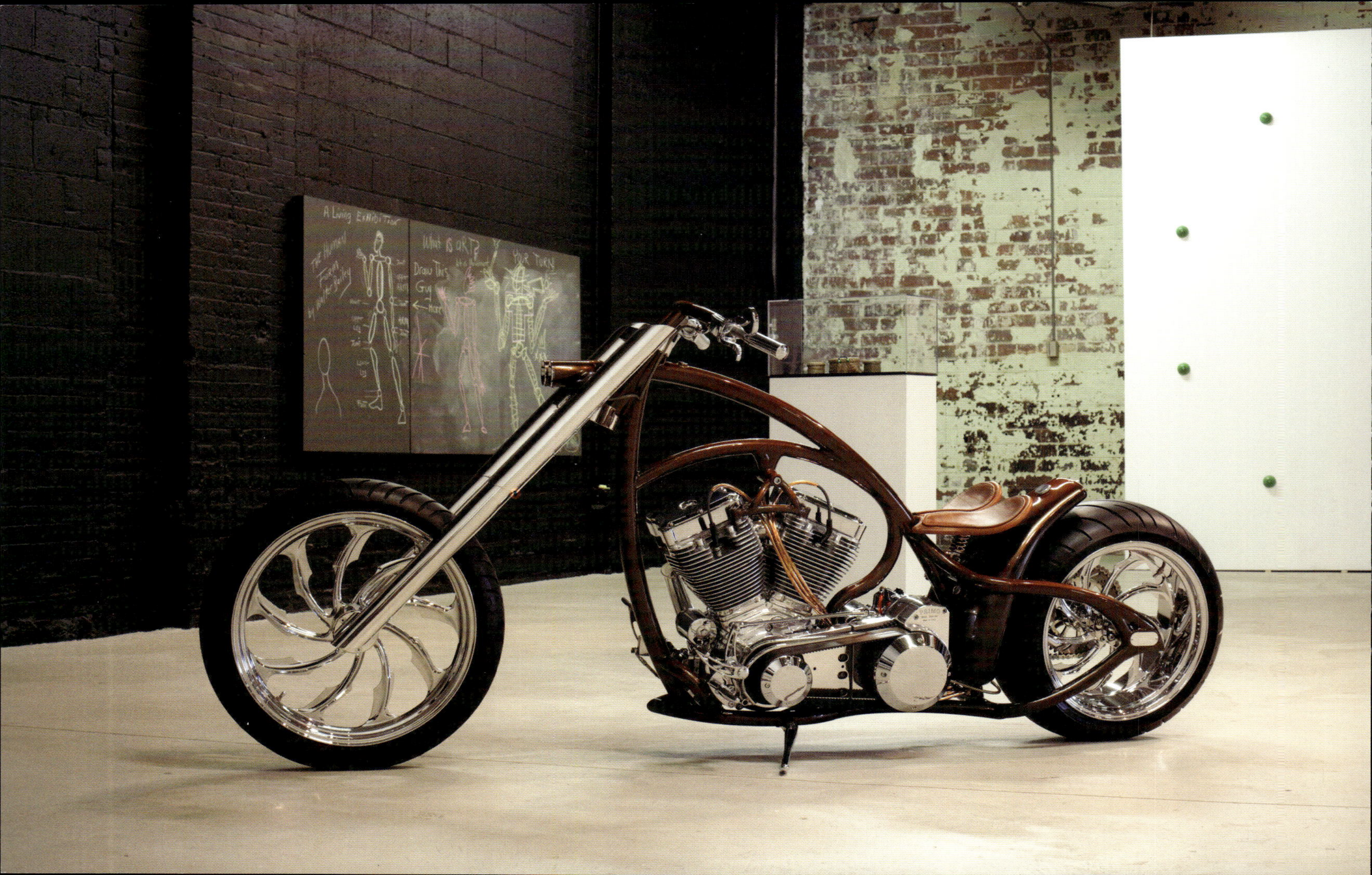

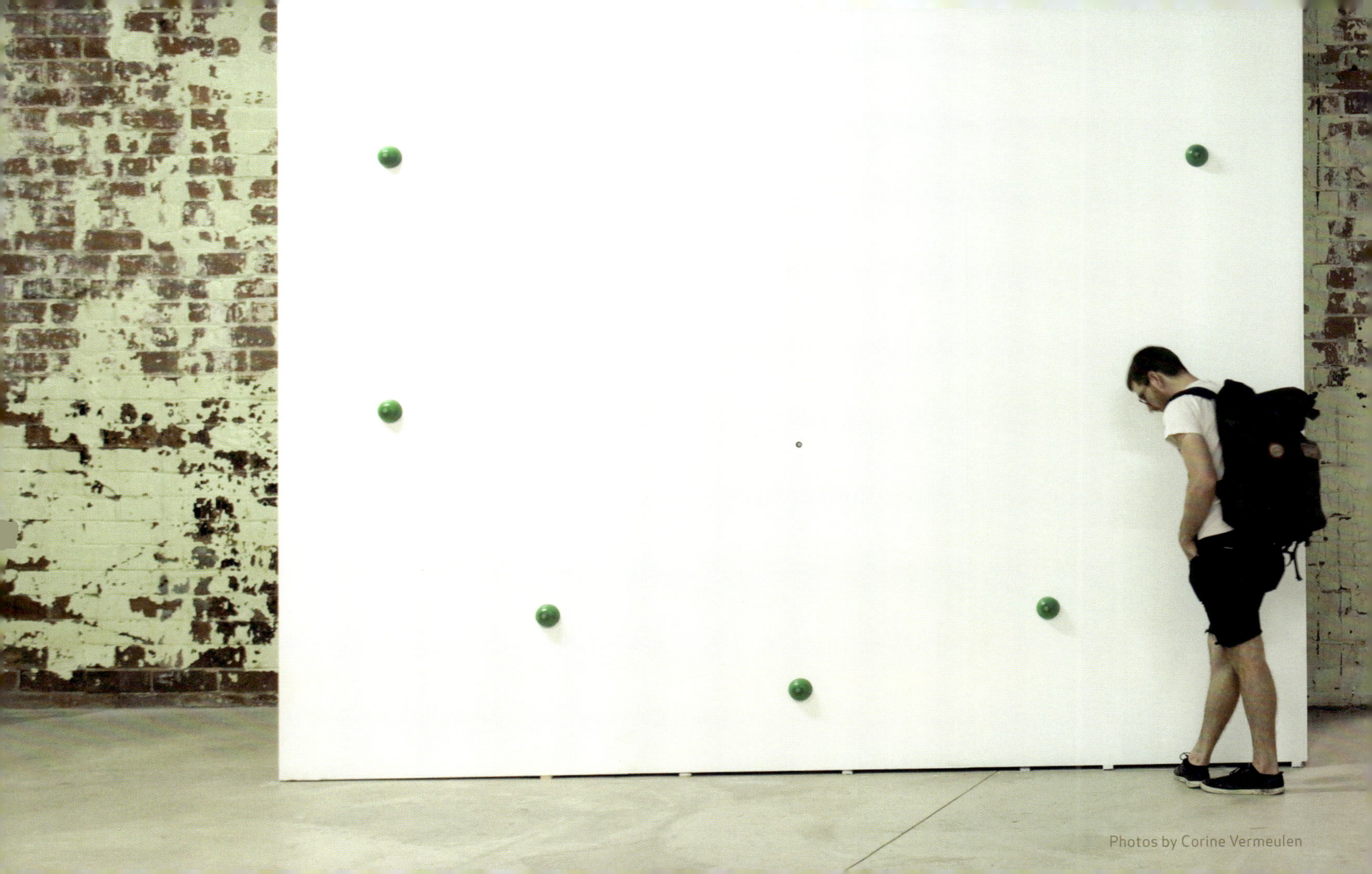
Photos by Corine Vermeulen

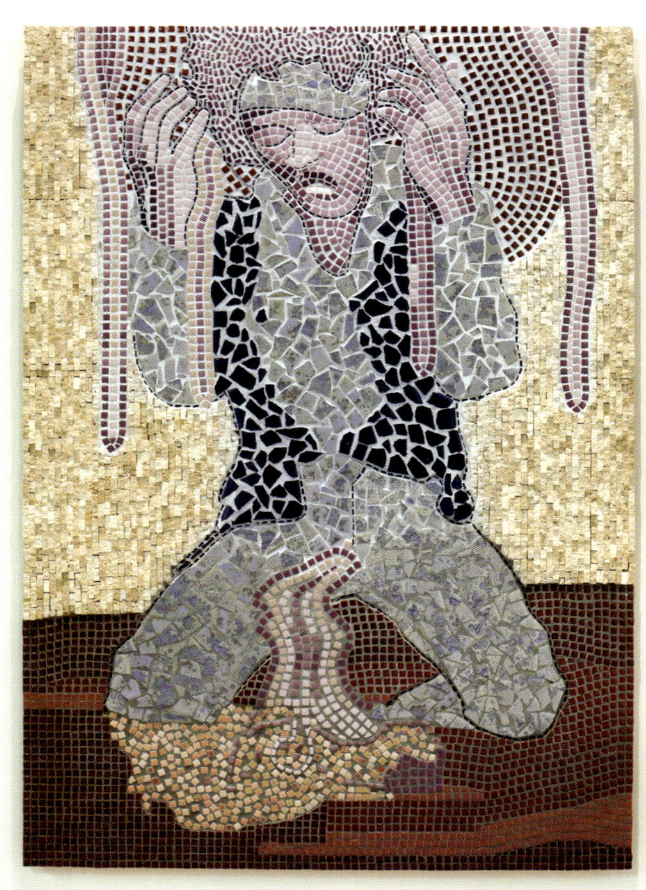

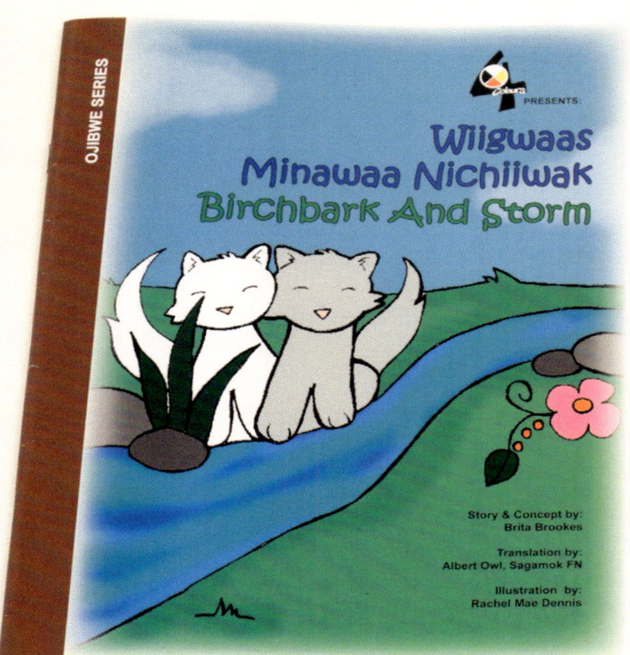

OJIBWE SERIES
PRESENTS:
Wiigwaas
Minawaa Nichiiwak
Birchbark And Storm
Story & Concept by:
Brita Brookes
Translation by:
Albert Owl, Sagamok FN
Illustration by:
Rachel Mae Dennis

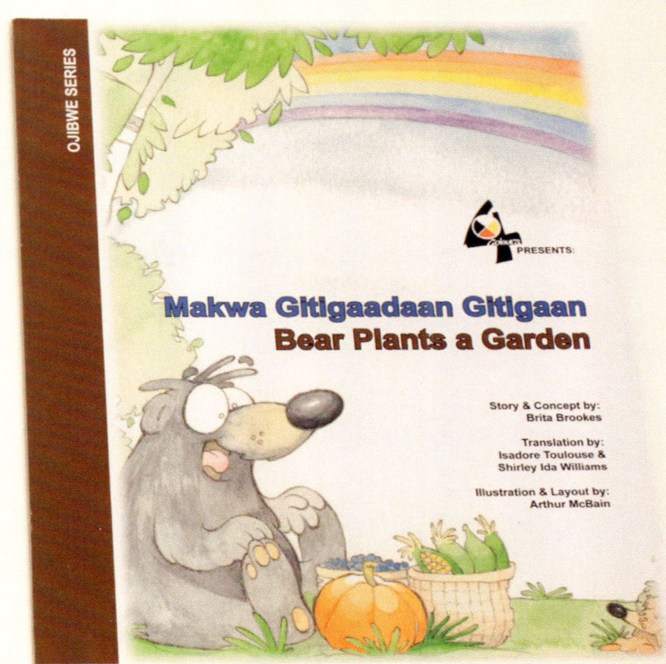

OJIBWE SERIES
PRESENTS:
Makwa Gitigaadaan Gitigaan
Bear Plants a Garden
Story & Concept by:
Brita Brookes
Translation by:
Isadore Toulouse &
Shirley Ida Williams
Illustration & Layout by:
Arthur McBain

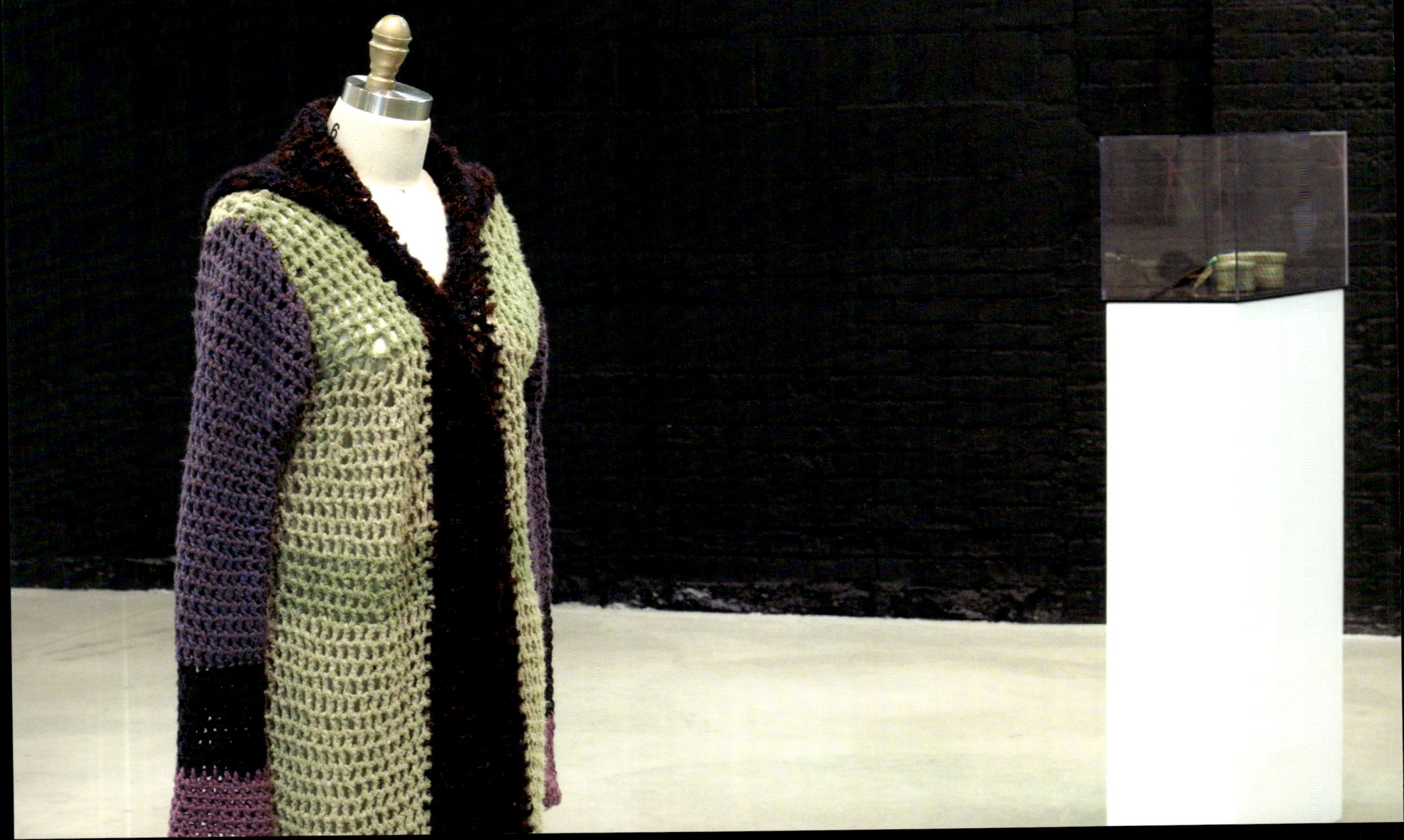

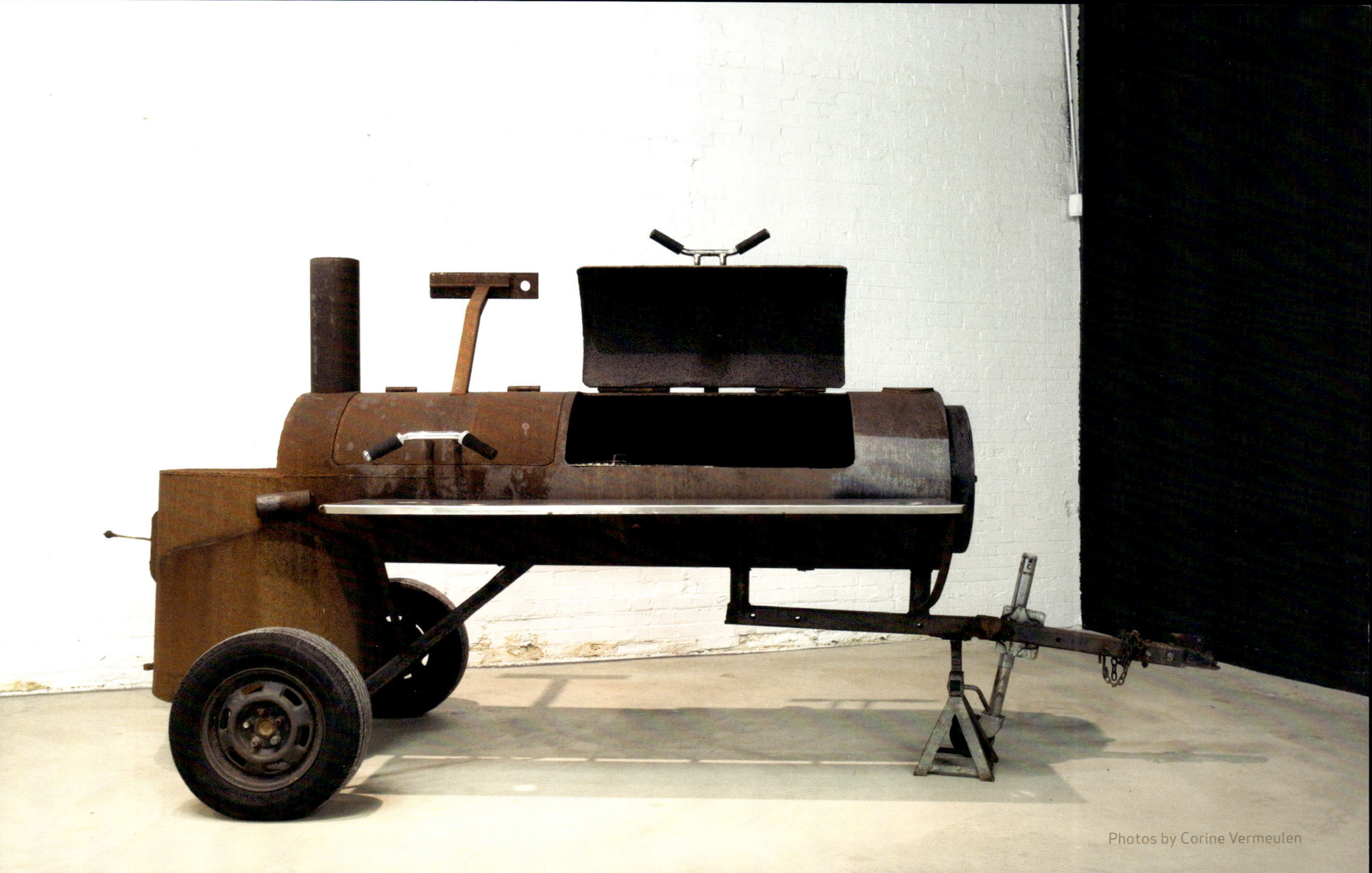
Photos by Corine Vermeulen

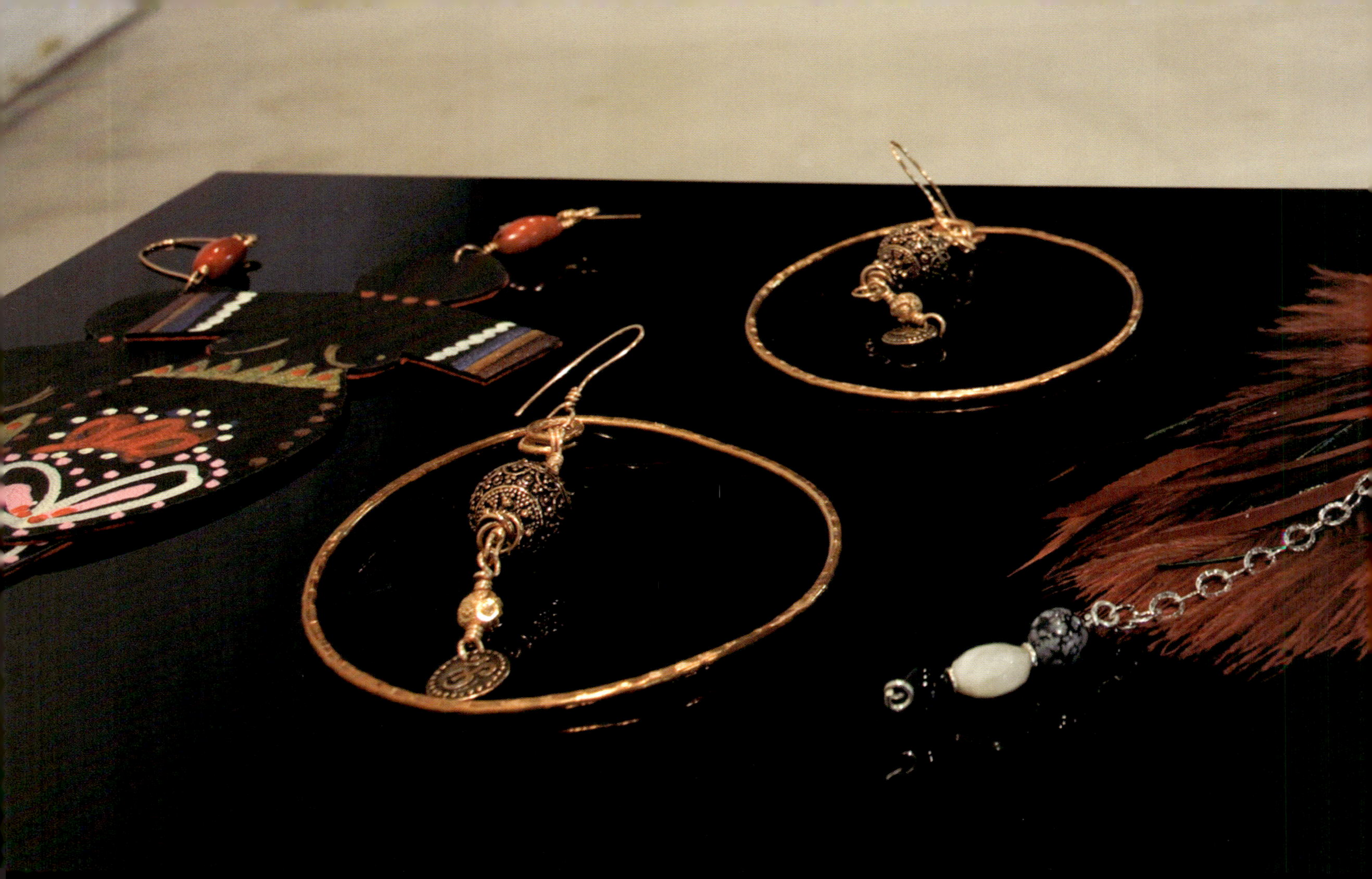

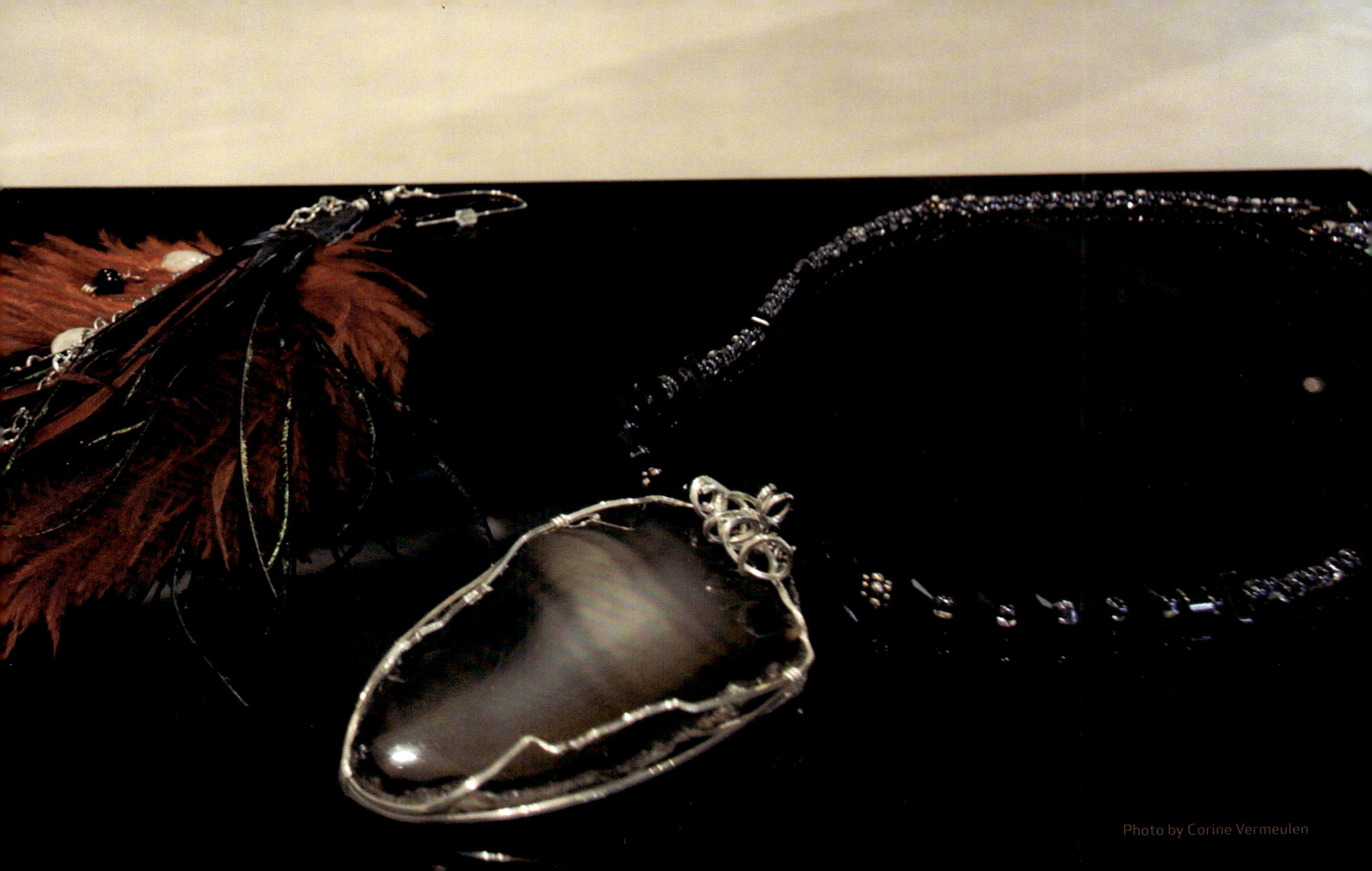
Photo by Corine Vermeulen

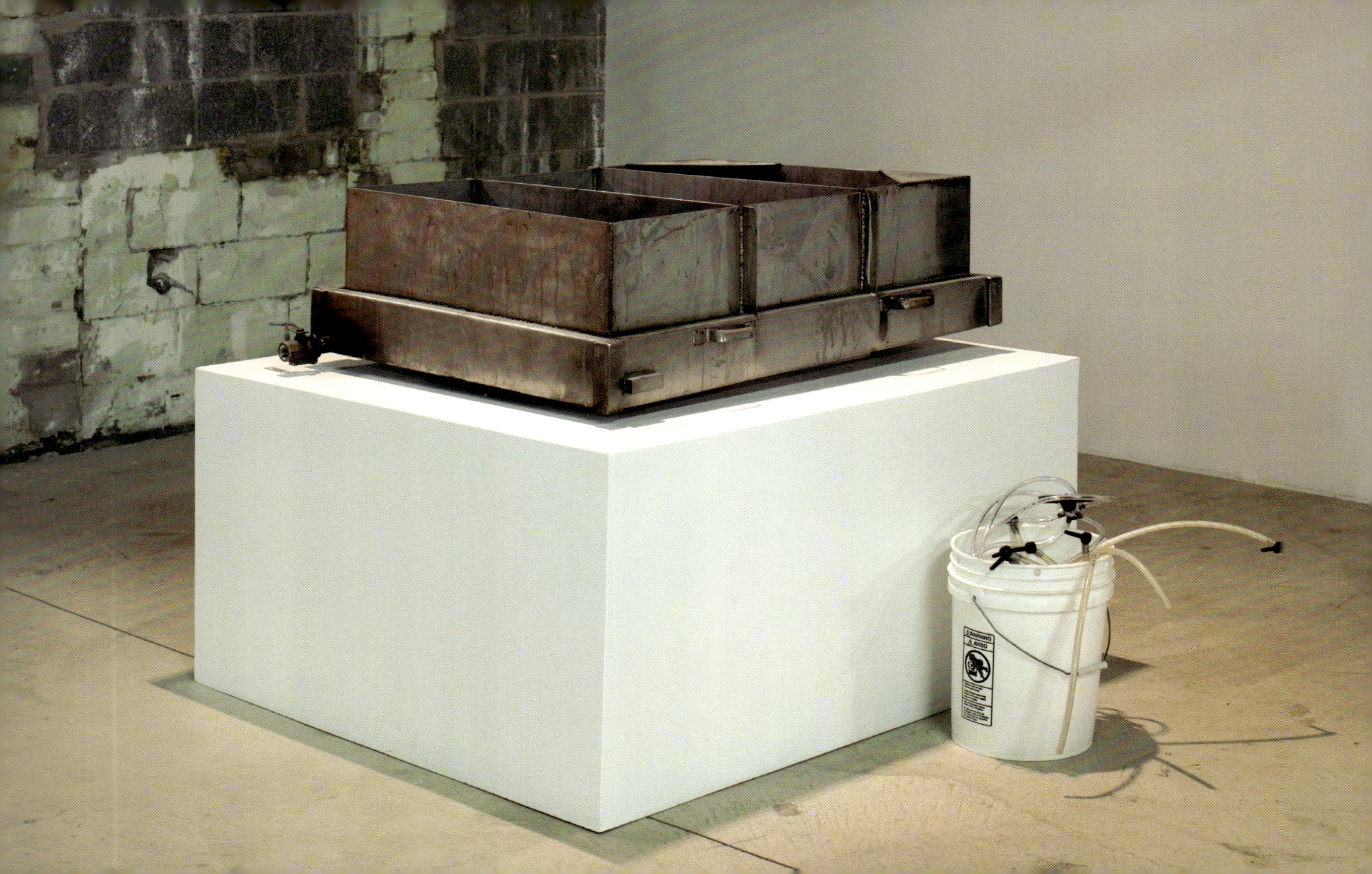

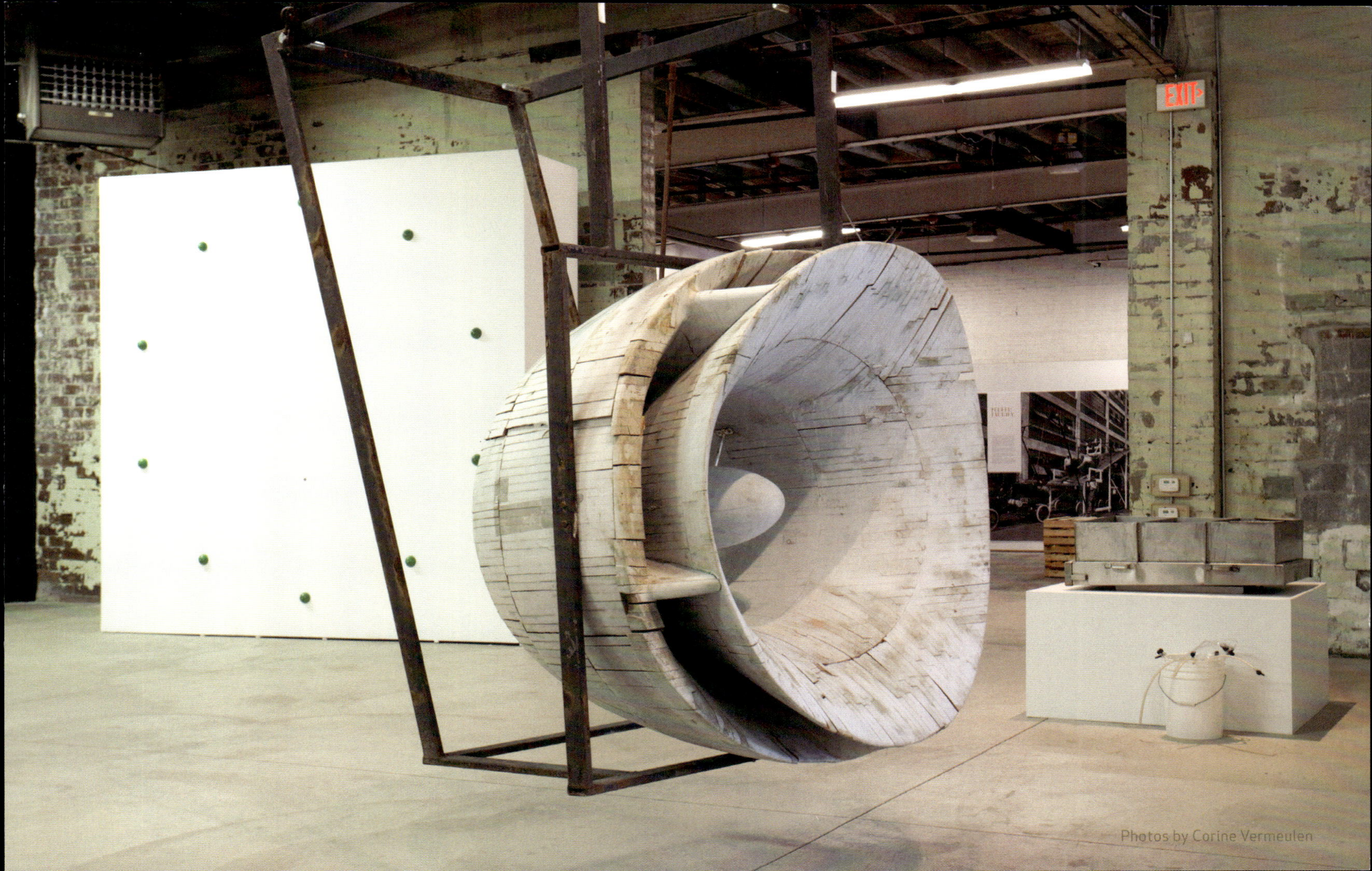
Photos by Corine Vermeulen

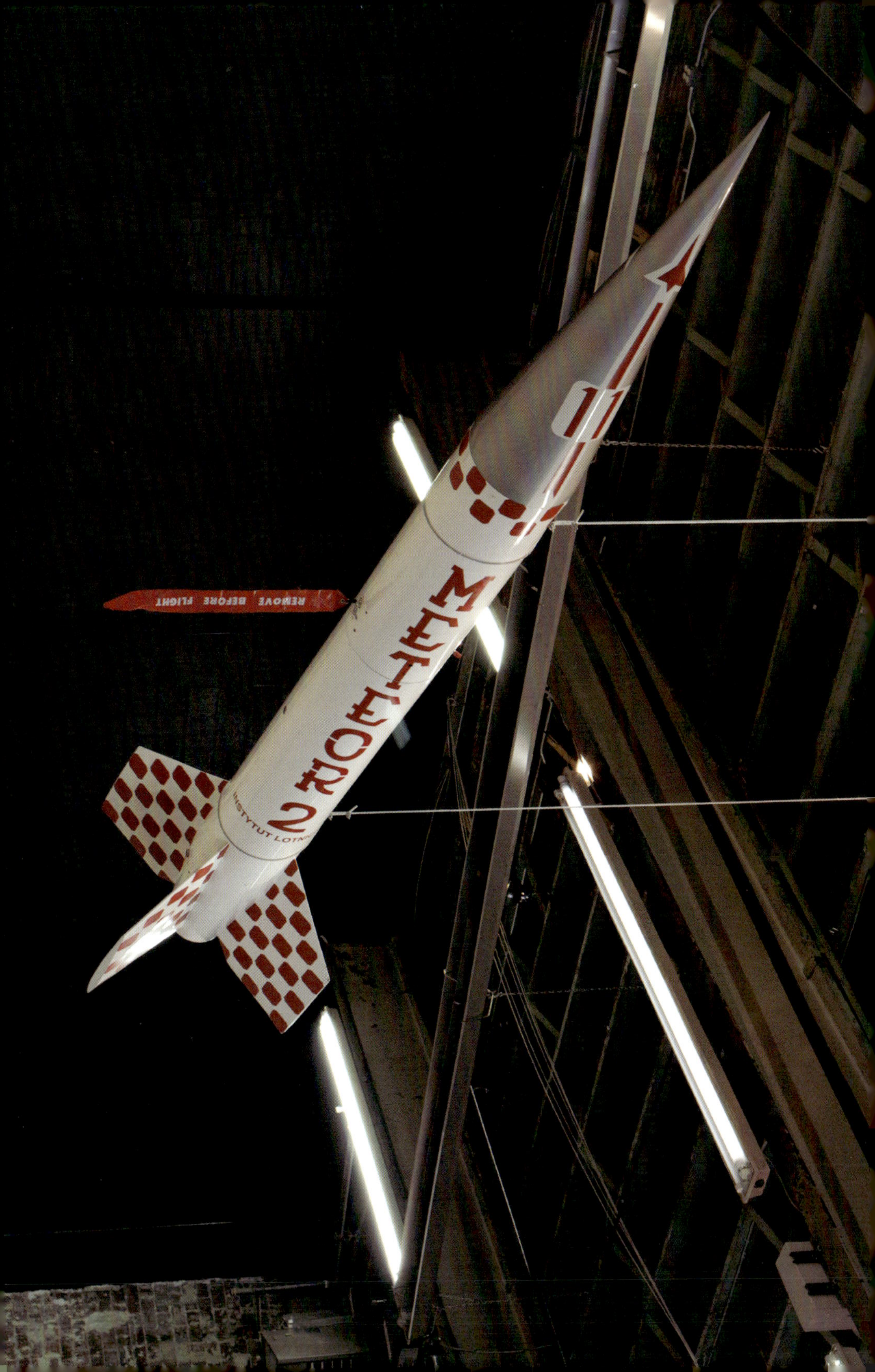
11
METEOR 2
INSTYTUT LOTN
REMOVE BEFORE FLIGHT

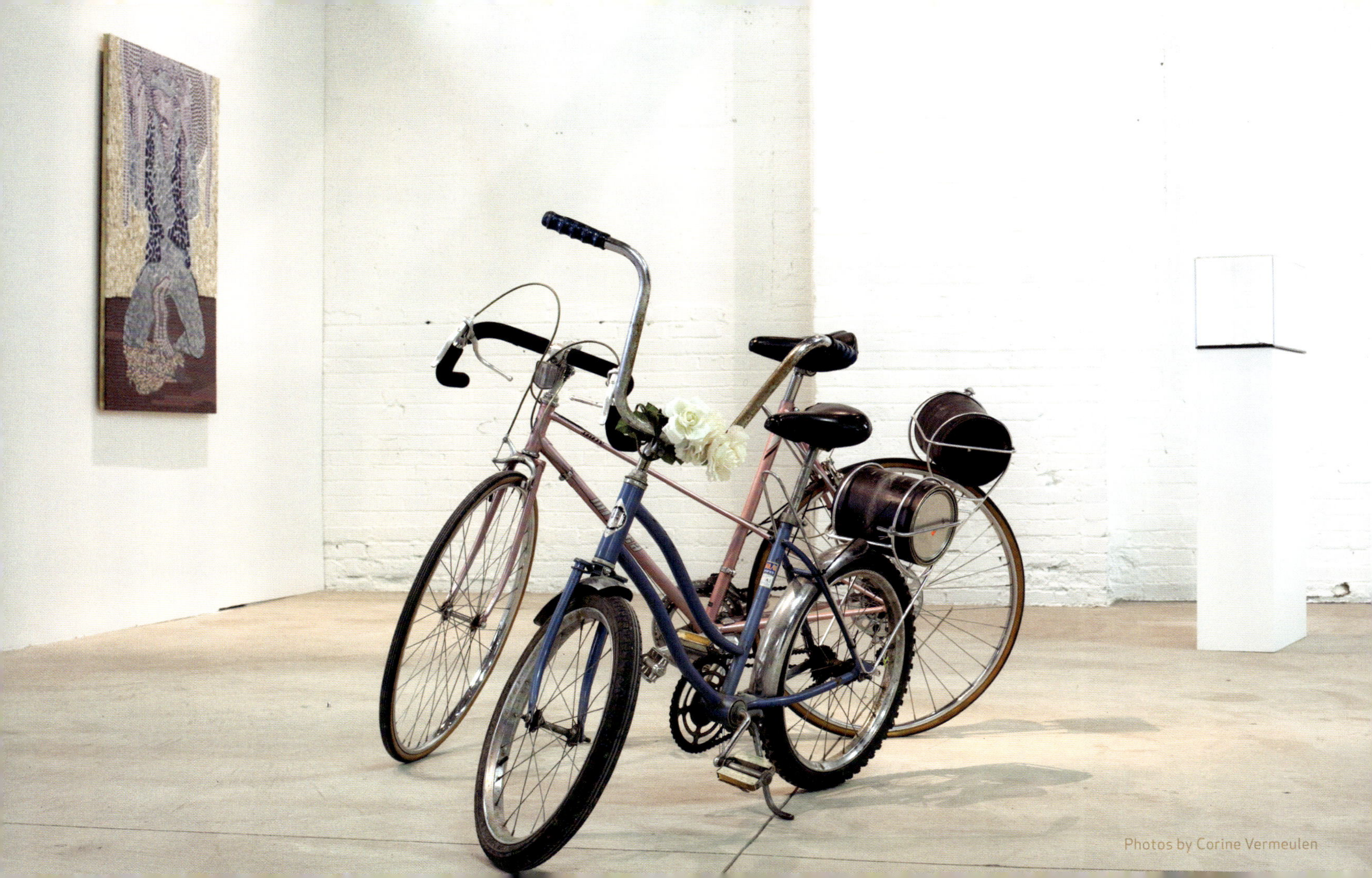
Photos by Corine Vermeulen

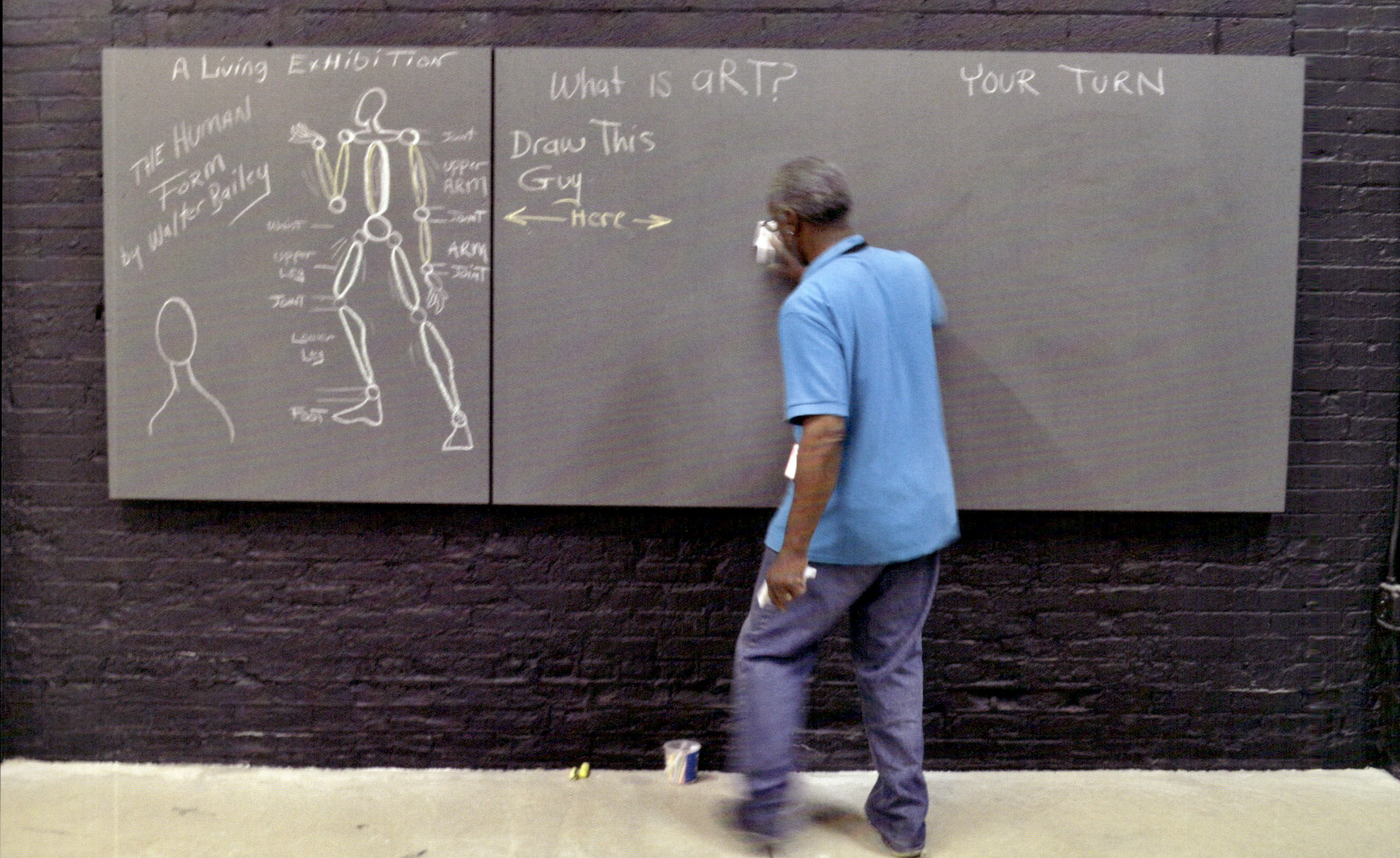
A Living Exhibition
THE Human
Form
by Walter Bailey
What is aRT?
YOUR TURN
Draw This
Guy
← Here →
Joint
Upper
ARM
Joint
ARM
Joint
Waist
Upper
Leg
Joint
Lower
Leg
Foot

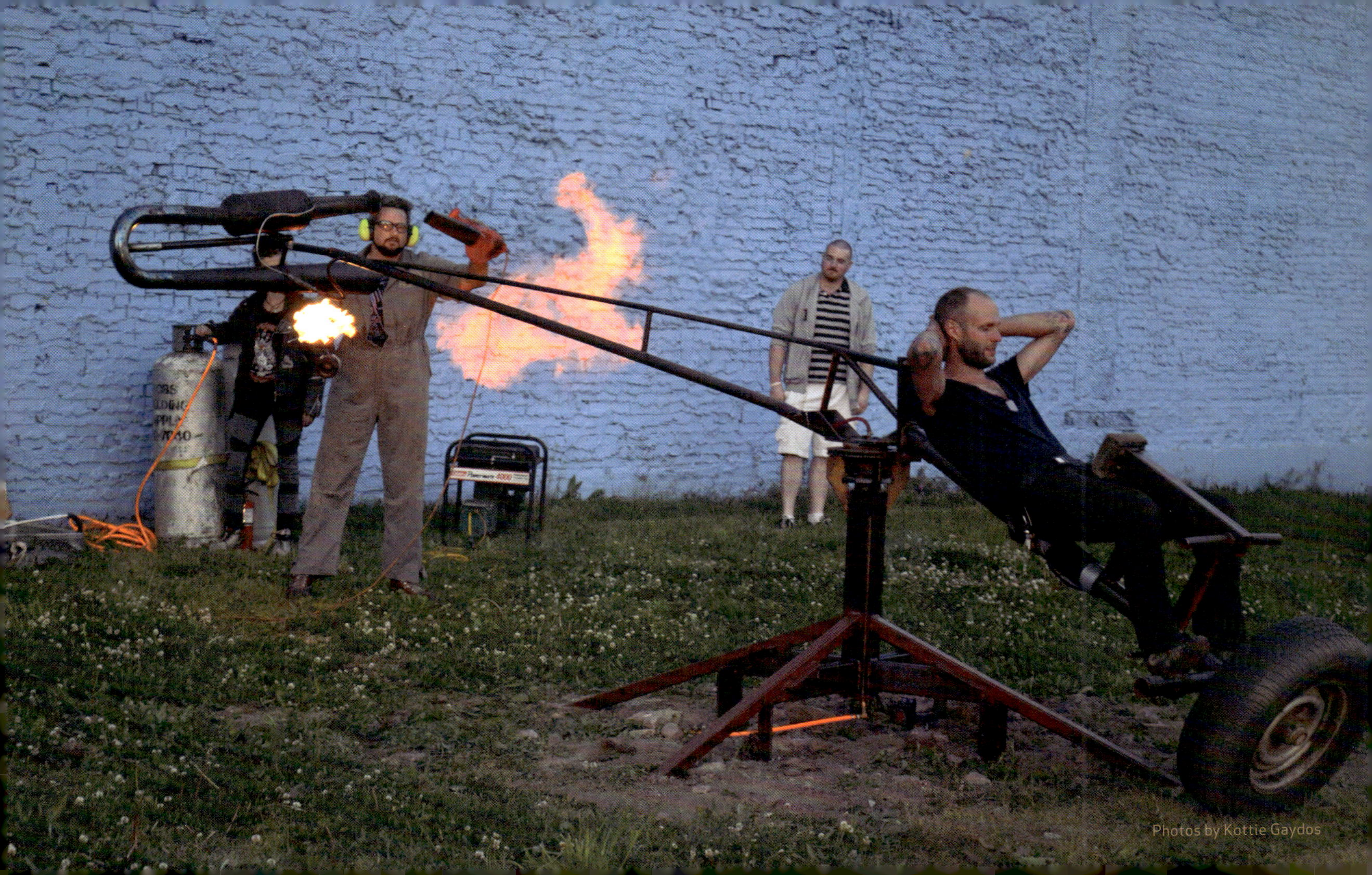
Photos by Kottie Gaydos

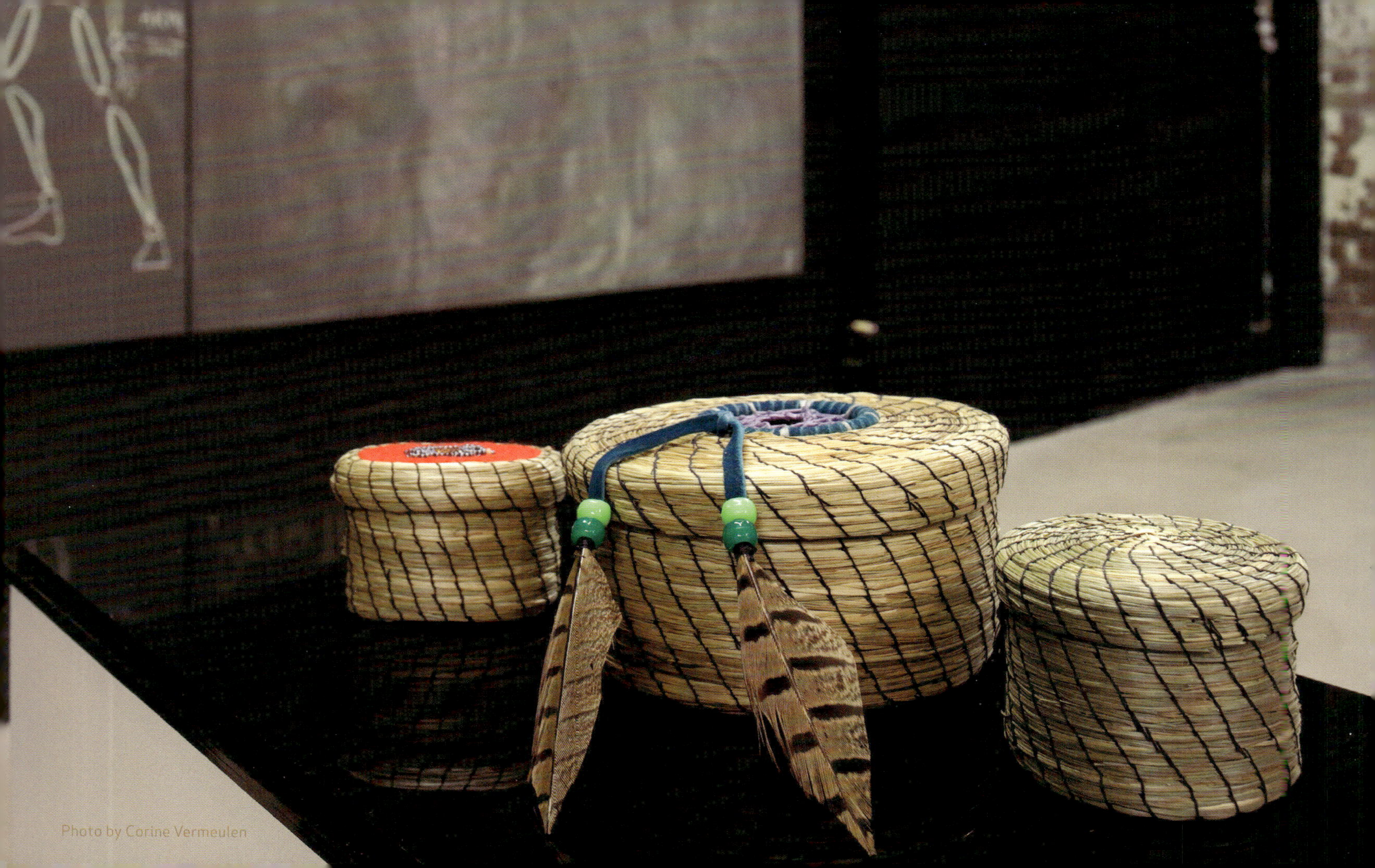
Photo by Corine Vermeulen

Post-Industrial Complex was the Museum of Contemporary Art Detroit's summer 2012 exhibition, May 11-July 29, 2012. The project was conceived as a group exhibition and educational source book to explore the ingenuity and adaptivity of human-scale production in the Detroit area.

Submissions are presented here as they were submitted to MOCAD.

Post-Industrial Complex was curated by Jon Brumit and Katie Grace McGowan.

Artists featured in the *Post-Industrial Complex* exhibition:

Fred Ellison: mosaic
James Aquash: sweet grass baskets
Anthony Reale: water turbine prototype
Angela Kiel: *Ten-Year Sweater*
Evelyn Pinkard-Phenomenal Woman: handmade jewelry
Dozer-Dozer Cycle: *Muse*, custom motorcycle and pipe-bending barbeque
Cezanne Charles and **John Marshall:** *ba-b&l (11111011100)*, sound installation
Mr. Motin: maple syrup collection system
Walter Bailey: drawing workshops
Bill Kozy: *Meteor II*, scale model of Polish rocket
Aisling Arrington and **Jill Bersche:** bicycle-powered cement mixer
Ryan C. Doyle: *The Regurgitator*, pulse jet powered spinning ride
FOUR Colours Productions: Ojibwe language children's books
    Brita Vija Brookes - founder, writer, artist
    Isadore Toulouse - translator
    Shirley Ida Williams - editor, cultural advisor
    Rachel Mae Butzin - artist
    Albert Owl - translator
    Arthur McBain - artist